WOMAN'S FICTION

A Guide to Novels by and about
Women in America, 1820–1870

WOMAN'S FICTION
A Guide to Novels by and about
Women in America, 1820-1870

NINA BAYM

Cornell University Press
Ithaca and London

First published 1978 by Cornell University Press.
Published in the United Kingdom by Cornell University Press Ltd., 2-4 Brook Street, London W1Y 1AA.

International Standard Book Number 0-8014-1128-9
Library of Congress Catalog Card Number 77-90897
Printed in the United States of America by York Composition Co., Inc.
Library of Congress Cataloging in Publication Data
(For library cataloging purposes only)

Baym, Nina.
   Woman's fiction.

   Bibliography: p.
   Includes index.
   1. American fiction—Women authors—History and criticism. 2. American fiction—19th century—History and criticism. 3. Women in literature. I. Title.
PS149.B38   813'.03   77-90897
ISBN 0-8014-1128-9

Contents

Acknowledgments

I am deeply grateful to the John Simon Guggenheim Memorial Foundation for a fellowship, and to the University of Illinois for a concomitant research leave so that I could write this book. I thank the affable personnel at the reference desk of the University of Illinois Library for unfailing help with interlibrary loans. I am grateful to my colleague and husband, Jack Stillinger, who read a close-to-final draft of the manuscript and helped improve its argument and prose. Finally, I thank the growing number of historians and literary scholars—they are cited individually in the Bibliographical Note on Secondary Material—whose work provided climate and context for my own investigations.

NINA BAYM

Urbana, Illinois

WOMAN'S FICTION

A Guide to Novels by and about
Women in America, 1820–1870

1

Introduction and Conclusions

This book reports on a large body of once popular but now neglected American fiction, the many novels by American women authors about women, written between 1820 and 1870. This fiction was by far the most popular literature of its time, and on the strength of that popularity, authorship in America was established as a woman's profession, and reading as a woman's avocation. Today we hear of this literature, if at all, chiefly through detractors who deplore the feminizing—and hence degradation—of the noble art of letters. A segment of literary history is thus lost to us, a segment that may be of special interest today as we seek to recover and understand the experiences of women.

Through this fiction, as I say, American women became authors and readers. In content, too, it is profoundly oriented toward women, and in this content one probably finds the secret of its success. The many novels all tell, with variations, a single tale. In essence, it is the story of a young girl who is deprived of the supports she had rightly or wrongly depended on to sustain her throughout life and is faced with the necessity of winning her own way in the world. This young girl is fittingly called a heroine because her role is precisely analogous to the unrecognized or undervalued youths of fairy tales who perform dazzling exploits and win a place for themselves in the land of happy endings. She

also fits the pattern of comic hero, whose displacement indicates
social corruption and whose triumph ensures the reconstruction
of a beneficent social order. In Jungian perspective, her story
exemplifies the difficult but successful negotiation of the undif-
ferentiated child through the trials of adolescence into the indi-
viduation of sound adulthood. The happy marriages with which
most—though not all—of this fiction concludes are symbols of
successful accomplishment of the required task and resolutions of
the basic problems raised in the story, which is in most primitive
terms the story of the formation and assertion of a feminine ego.

In the chapters that follow I concentrate on plot analysis for
three reasons: because the first step in familiarizing oneself with a
type of fiction is to learn its story; because all these fictions are
linked by their participation in one overplot; and because individual authors are distinguishable from one another largely by
the plot elements they select from the common repertory and by
the varieties of setting and incident with which they embellish the
basic tale. In Chapter 2, I set out the overplot and draw out some
of its relations and general thematic implications. In Chapter 3,
I discuss Catharine Sedgwick, whose novels are the earliest in
America to embody the tale, and several other women whose
novels in the 1820s, 1830s, and 1840s approximated the form.
Chapters 4 through 7 take up the most popular writers in the
genre—Maria McIntosh, E. D. E. N. Southworth, Caroline Lee
Hentz, Susan Warner, Anna Warner, Maria Cummins, Ann
Stephens, Mary Jane Holmes, and Marion Harland, all active in
the 1850s—attempting to show by close plot study and discussion
how each achieved an individual thematic and temperamental
emphasis by her variations within formulaic constraints. Chapter
8 studies Caroline Chesebro', whose work was not popular but
nevertheless represents some original and complicated handlings
of the genre. Chapter 9 looks at a selection of novels by less
popular or less prolific women writers. Chapter 10 surveys the
work of Augusta Evans, whose *St. Elmo* is a kind of culmination
because it was both the most popular novel in the form and one

of the last to be written completely within its terms. The chapter concludes by suggesting some of the changes in woman's fiction in the late 1860s and 1870s that signify the fact that the genre had run its course. Where biographical information exists, I briefly discuss the authors' lives with particular emphasis on the circumstances that influenced them to choose careers as professional writers.

Although abstractly speaking the story told in this woman's fiction—as I shall henceforth call it—might have been told by men as well as women, in fact during this period only women did so, and it absorbed the full energies of almost all the women novelists in America for fifty years. That men did not compose in this genre was surely not accidental. Most of them assumed an audience of men as a matter of course, and reacted with distress and dismay as they discovered that to make a living by writing they would have to please female readers. Only three men before the Civil War enjoyed widespread success with women—Timothy Shay Arthur, Nathaniel P. Willis, and George Mitchell (his *Reveries of a Bachelor,* by "Ik Marvel," was the young Emily Dickinson's favorite book). But none of these was a novelist. Arthur was basically a tract writer (we remember him now for his sensational *Ten Nights in a Barroom*), while Willis and Mitchell worked exclusively in shorter, impressionistic forms. Their specialty was in anatomizing the male psyche for female readers, as the title *Reveries of a Bachelor* implies, not in demonstrating the reaches of female heroism.

After the Civil War, the domination of the reading public by women became a fact that writers could ignore no longer. Some men sought to engage with women—with general success, one might note—by writing stories of social or religious consciousness that would presumably speak to their widely assumed humanitarian interests. Others—notably Henry James and William Dean Howells—tried to tell women's stories; interestingly enough, their good women were far more passive than the female protagonists created by women themselves. Still others tried to attract women readers by insulting or shocking them. Mark Twain is the most obvious example. Overall, it would appear that to represent experience from a woman's point of view lay outside either the capabilities or interest of most of the male writers. If they feared that in writing for women they would have to feminize themselves they would have found it particularly difficult to write tales about the triumph of the feminine will.

Women's experience also seems to be outside the interests and sympathies of the male critics whose judgments have largely determined the canon of classic American literature. Of the many clearly major American women writers—Emily Dickinson, Harriet Beecher Stowe, Edith Wharton, Willa Cather, Ellen Glasgow, Kate Chopin, Gertrude Stein—until recently only Dickinson was universally acknowledged to be of classic stature. The tremendous vogue of woman's fiction in the middle years of the nineteenth century is cited simply as evidence of the deplorable feminine taste in literature. By extension it is used to characterize the horrible situation facing any would-be serious writer in America.

A reexamination of this fiction may well show it to lack the esthetic, intellectual, and moral complexity and artistry that we demand of great literature. I confess frankly that although I found much to interest me in these books, I have not unearthed a forgotten Jane Austen or George Eliot, or hit upon even one novel that I would propose to set alongside *The Scarlet Letter*. Yet I cannot avoid the belief that "purely" literary criteria, as they have been employed to identify the best American works, have inevitably had a bias in favor of things male—in favor, say, of whaling ships rather than the sewing circle as a symbol of the human community; in favor of satires on domineering mothers, shrewish wives, or betraying mistresses rather than tyrannical fathers, abusive husbands, or philandering suitors; displaying an exquisite compassion for the crises of the adolescent male, but altogether impatient with the parallel crises of the female. While not claiming literary greatness for any of the novels introduced in this study, I would like at least to begin to correct such a bias by taking their content seriously. And it is time, perhaps—though this task lies outside my scope here—to reexamine the grounds upon which certain hallowed American classics have been called great.

It is not at all strange that American men forebore to write or to praise woman's fiction, but it seems odd that the most important woman author in the era of its preeminence, Harriet Beecher Stowe, did not write any works in the genre. Over the course of her career, Stowe had three major preoccupations: slavery, Calvinism and the problem of belief, and New England life in the early republic. Since her regional depictions were controlled by her sense that faith was the chief preoccupation of the New England mind, Stowe's local-color writing can be subsumed within her religious concerns. Her novels about slavery and about Christian belief propose a maternal, loving ethic in opposition to prevailing patriarchal values, but the actual distribution of events and qualities among her characters did not follow sexual lines. She perceived both slavery and religion as issues transcending gender, and treated them accordingly. A writer cannot command her interests, and Stowe's set her apart from the other American women writing fiction in her day.

Nevertheless it is mainly from this writer, who was not fundamentally concerned with "woman's place," that we have derived our present day idea of what Stowe's age thought women should be. And we have based our idea on a portrait not of a woman, but of a child—Little Eva—who is repeatedly and elaborately labeled as one whose destiny prevents her ever becoming a woman. In Stowe's time, when the Calvinist idea of natural depravity was losing ground to the romantic idea of natural innocence, the image of the divine child was put to special use. In fiction, poetry, and consolatory literature we often find a child marked out from other children by a precocious spirituality and unusual goodness and known by these special signs to be designed for early death. The notion that there were, among ordinary children, extraordinary ones not meant to reach adulthood clearly had immense reconciling power in an era when many children did in fact die young. Such deaths became more bearable when these children were conceived to have been set apart from the first and consecrated to a special mission. Little Eva is so clearly identified as one of this tribe by Stowe that the equation of her with an ideal of womanhood by several critics seems almost perverse in its disregard of the author's intention.

At the same time *Uncle Tom's Cabin* contains a gallery of other female characters, many of them admirable without being either angelic or childlike. Mrs. Sherburn, Mrs. Bird, and Rachel are all exponents of various degrees of active idealism who subvert or break the law. Eliza is a true heroine in every sense. And finally there is Topsy (her character most resembles a heroine of conventional woman's fiction), who grows from deprivation through trials and by example into a noble woman. Ultimately, however, we cannot strictly compare any female character from *Uncle Tom's Cabin* or any other Stowe novel with a heroine of woman's fiction, because the novel does not participate in the essential overplot and hence feminine roles are differently related to the structure.

One wishes that Stowe had tried her hand at the genre, partly because her gifts were substantial enough to have produced the truly major work that no writer in the genre achieved. Was this failure a defect in them, or the type? Could these talented women who failed to produce literature of the first rank have done better? If so, why didn't they? One explanation lies in their self-conception; they saw themselves not as "artists" but as professional writers with work to do and a living to be made from satisfactory fulfillment of an obligation to their audience.

What was this obligation? Evidently, since these were writers for a mass audience, it had to be entertainment; but entertainment is not a simple concept since there are such divergences in what different groups find entertaining. The authors' rhetoric makes clear that they expected their effect to be more than ephemeral, that they meant readers to take away something from their reading that would help them in their lives. There is, hence, a didactic intention, a lesson conveyed and assented to if the work succeeds. Instruction is not at cross-purposes with entertainment in this fiction, nor is entertainment the sweet coating on a didactic pill. The lesson itself is an entertainment in that the heroine's triumph over so much adversity and so many obstacles is profoundly pleasurable to those readers who identify with her.

Since all woman's fiction shares the same story of "trials and triumph" it is reasonable to assume that the obligation of which I speak is contained in that story. And I assume that the story succeeded in its purposes, if it did, by engaging and channeling the emotions of readers through identification with the heroine. To the extent that readers saw the heroine's dilemma as their own, they had an outlet for their angers and frustrations in detesting her enemies; and to this same extent they could rejoice in her triumph and—here is where the lesson comes in—accept the author's solution to her difficulties as pertinent to their own lives. Her dilemma, simply, was mistreatment, unfairness, disadvantage, and powerlessness, recurrent injustices occasioned by her status as female and child. The authors' solutions are different from case to case and somewhat less simple than the dilemma, but all involve the heroine's accepting herself as female while rejecting the equation of female with permanent child. Thus, while commiserating with the heroine in difficulties not of her own making, the stories hold her entirely responsible for overcoming them.

It is difficult to speak of stories like these and their "message" without having one's discourse biased by ideology. In the past, almost every critic who approached this fiction did so in a prefeminist or antifeminist frame of mind; recent scanning of it is invariably a feminist activity. The earlier critics castigated this literature for certain allegedly female qualities, as the product of a timid, sentimental, narrow, trivializing sensibility, and some recent feminists, agreeing with this depiction, have seen the authors as hacks and traitors to their sex. Others, however, have claimed a covert feminism for these works, discerning beneath their sugary texture a poisonous brew. My own view is that these novels represent (what some might consider a contradiction in terms) a moderate, or limited, or pragmatic feminism, which is not in the least covert but quite obvious, needing only to be assessed in mid-nineteenth-century terms rather than those of a later century to be recognized for what it is. That is, it was feminism constrained by certain other types of beliefs that are less operative today. For example, these authors interpreted experience within models of personal relations, rather than classes, castes, or other institutional structures. The shape of human life was perceived not as determined by various memberships, but by various private interactions. Again, the authors, both as Christians and as Victorians, were disinclined to acknowledge the body and physical sexuality as elements of self either inherently spiritual or capable of being spiritualized. Especially where sexual politics was concerned (this point will recur in later chapters), they saw themselves as disadvantaged compared to men. Hence rather than integrating physical sexuality into their adult personalities they tried to transcend it.

They had a nonandrogynous certainty that men and women were essentially different. Though the difference might eventually come down only to a radical disparity in physical strength, they saw this distinction as significant enough to warrant a stratified society based on it, with appropriately different behavior and occupations for the two sexes. They were profoundly Victorian in that they had an oppressive sense of reality and its habit of disappointing expectations, and they believed that duty, discipline, self-control, and sacrifice (within limits) were not only moral but actually useful strategies for getting through a hard world. They were not cultural or historical relativists and consequently failed to see that many aspects of their situation might be functions of time and place rather than the will of God.

At the time these women wrote, many thinkers were in the process of finding some or all of these assumptions to be mental constructs rather than natural facts, and hence working their way free of them. I must admit that woman's fiction does not partake of the more obviously advanced thought of its day. Nevertheless, there is much in it that is progressive and feminist in a less obtrusive way—not a hidden feminism, again, but an unspectacular feminism.

The thrust of all this fiction has to do ultimately, and obsessively (with variations from author to author that will be detailed below), with how the heroine perceives herself. At the outset she takes herself very lightly—has no ego, or a damaged one, and looks to the world to coddle and protect her. She makes demands on others as a function of not making demands on herself. She expects nothing from herself because she recognizes no inner capacities. To some extent, her expectations are reasonable—she thinks that her guardians will nurture her, for example. To some extent, her demands are unreasonable. But the failure of the world to satisfy either reasonable or unreasonable expectations awakens the heroine to inner possibilities. By the novel's end she has developed a strong conviction of her own worth as a result of which she does ask much from herself. She can meet her own demands and, inevitably, the change in herself has changed the world's attitude toward her, so that much that was formerly denied her now comes to her unsought.

In other words, these books are about the psychology of women. They say that the way women perceive themselves is a libel on their own sex, and that this false self-perception more than any other factor accounts for woman's degraded and dependent position in society. Although they identify her treatment and training by society in the shape of powerful others as responsible for her damaged self-esteem and consequent impoverished personality, they separate cause from effect and insist that in nineteenth-century America women have the opportunity and responsibility to change their situation by changing their personalities. Hence these authors do blame women who make no effort, no matter how wronged such women may actually be. They are especially severe on those who cling to a degrading image of themselves out of laziness. The rare woman who manages to be coddled and pampered all her life is at once an object of envy and commiseration, but above all she is a dangerous model for the rest of the sex, since her good fortune is so exceptional. Far better to adopt a philosophy of the fortunate fall, showing that the woman cast out of childhood's garden of Eden has the opportunity to develop a truly noble moral and intellectual nature.

Once a woman takes herself seriously, she enters the real world (alternatively, once she is thrown into the real world she must take herself seriously) and discovers how deplorably she has been fitted by education or upbringing to deal with it. Hence she has much to do by way of self-development. She must fight the recurrent temptation to give up and excuse herself by the fact of her gender. A sense of self-worth is fragile, and it is not the end but the beginning of change. Happily, every new achievement intensifies one's self-respect and provides the motivation for further effort. The end of change, finally, is a new woman and, by extension, the reformation of the world immediately around her as this new person calls out different relations and responses from her environment.

Since this reformed world is primarily affectional and domestic it may appear to have much the same shape, to a twentieth-century reader, as the old. But, as I will argue at some length, most of these novels see their old world as neither affectional nor domestic and they hope to impose these values on a society that seems to them governed purely by mercenary and exploitive considerations. They espouse a so-called "cult of domesticity" but not as that cult is generally analyzed, as a conservative or traditional ethos.

Did these novels perform their intended function? If they did not change the world, did they at least begin the change of individual women readers? Or at the very least were they supportive of such changes that received their initial stimulus from some other source? Unfortunately, neither our methodology nor our evidence is adequate to answer this question. We are interested in the answer as it applies to millions of obscure women who left no evidence. Besides, what sort or quantity of evidence would be sufficient to demonstrate a conclusive relation between the reading of novels and a change in women's self-concepts and behavior? We have no models for uncovering this sort of information even in contemporary audiences and in an age of sociological investigation. We can scarcely hope to retrieve it for a past century, at least not in the near future.

There is, clearly, general evidence of all sorts that women's lives were in ferment during the nineteenth century and that women were increasingly aware of their situations as gender determined and increasingly demanding of themselves and the world. But clearly too this phenomenon had multiple causes, and to assign a specific percentage of the cause to the novels they read is impossible. The novels might as much be evidence of a change as cause of it; or, like so many other things, the novels may have been both a sign of change and a contribution to it.

The most we can say is that these novels were read in unprecedented numbers, that their intent is clear, and that if they succeeded they would have inspired a moral revolution in many young readers. The least we can say is that, beyond all doubt, the story of young women discovering and asserting their powers, thereby wresting respect and recognition from a hostile and indifferent world, was immensely pleasurable to a huge number of American women. These many novels told them something that was most satisfying to hear. On the strength of that telling, women novelists dominated American reading habits for most of the nineteenth century.

2

The Form and Ideology
of Woman's Fiction

Works of the genre that I am calling woman's fiction meet
three conditions. They are written by women, are addressed to
women, and tell one particular story about women. They chronicle the "trials and triumph" (as the subtitle of one example
reads) of a heroine who, beset with hardships, finds within herself
the qualities of intelligence, will, resourcefulness, and courage
sufficient to overcome them. The genre began in America with
Catharine Sedgwick's *New-England Tale* (1822), manifested
itself as the favorite reading matter of the American public in the
unprecedented sales of Susan Warner's *Wide, Wide World*
(published late in 1850), and remained a dominant fictional type
until after 1870.

The critical, as opposed to popular, reception of these novels in
their own time was mixed. Theoretical opposition to the novel
was by no means dead in mid-nineteenth-century America, and
popular successes naturally bore a significant percentage of the
attack. The moralistic tone of much woman's fiction did not
placate antagonists; on the contrary many clerical opponents of
the novel thought that women were trying to take over their
functions and hence attacked all the more fiercely. Similarly, some

male authors felt threatened by the apparently sudden emergence of great numbers of women writers. Their distress showed itself in expressions of manly contempt for the genre, its authors, and its readers.

On the other hand, the women had a powerful ally—their publishers, who not only put these works into print but advertised them widely and enthusiastically. Many reviewers approached these works as serious entrants in the race for literary reputation, and wrote about them with attention and respect. They distinguished between the works of the different authors, identified individual strengths and weaknesses, and gave no sign that they considered woman's fiction a subliterary or quasi-literary genre. The contemporary critics were particularly alert to each writer's contribution to the depiction of American social life, especially to regional differentiations in manners and character types. But on the whole they showed themselves uninterested in the story that this fiction tirelessly repeated, or its significance.

After the great vogue of this fiction had passed its practitioners were forgotten. By the end of the nineteenth century a canon of classic American writers was being fixed, and of the many active women authors only Harriet Beecher Stowe and Louisa May Alcott survived the winnowing process. Stowe, however, had written no woman's fiction until after 1870, and her reputation rested on antislavery and regional-religious literature. Alcott, for her part, presided over the waning days of woman's fiction, when it permuted into children's literature. By the early decades of the twentieth century these two women had also disappeared from the pantheon. Until recently, nothing was remembered of this great burst of feminine literary activity among readers or even scholars at large. It had no students except the cultural historians, most of whom approached it prejudicially. Recent scholarship in woman's history and literature has created both a context and a reason for reexamining this literature. I hope in this book to recapture for others a sense of what this fiction was like.

Before we can see what this fiction is, or was, however, we must put aside some of the distorting presuppositions that have controlled earlier scholarly accounts of it. The novels have been variously labeled "sentimental fiction," "fiction of sensibility," and "domestic fiction." In some literary histories the genre is called "domestic sentimentalism." This terminology is misleading, in my view, because it puts the emphasis on a presumed ambience in the fiction rather than on the implications of the basic plot. The term "sentimental" is often a term of judgment rather than of description, and the judgment it conveys is of course adverse. It means that the author is asking for more of an emotional response from the reader than the literary art has earned; or that the wrong kind of emotion is called out; or that the author's depiction of real life is heavily slanted toward the pretty and tender and hence is not a comment on reality but an evasion of it. Such adverse judgments are culture-bound, in my view; the critic of a later time is refusing to assent to the work's conventions. It is easy and amusing to imagine how, if they but had the chance, the nineteenth-century women authors would turn this criticism back onto certain highly respected literary achievements of the present moment, whose evasions, sentimentalities, and partialities their distance would plainly enable them to see.

Insofar as the claim that this fiction deals exclusively with the pretty and tender realm of experience is meant to describe it, the claim is mostly wrong. To be sure, these novels contain almost no sex, and they are not graphic about body functions (except sweat, which they attribute more freely to women than does much present-day liberated literature by both men and women), but they are full of poverty, coarseness, brutality, exploitation, treachery, pettiness, illness, exhaustion, degradation, and suffering. But it is clear that the authors deplore such aspects of experience. From their point of view, a good deal of the admired coarseness in a novel like *Tom Jones,* and the eighteenth century which it so well represented, involved the heartless tormenting of some groups by others, and a concomitant lack of respect for the essential humanity of all. The women expressed a wish to live somewhat less brutal lives than their sex had in the past. For this reason they did indeed idealize the pretty and tender, while representing many other aspects of experience. For the same reason, they assumed a rhetoric that was intended to transcend the pain and crudeness of the things they had to represent. In a world that reeked of unwashed bodies and excrement, they saw no need to remind their readers of bathroom functions. In a world where sexual encounter was likely as not to be brutal, they felt no call for four-letter words.

Sometimes the term "sentimental" is used to imply that a work elevates feeling above all else. In this sense, Ernest Hemingway, J. D. Salinger, and Norman Mailer are all more sentimental than the authors of woman's fiction. The plots repeatedly identify immersion in feeling as one of the great temptations and dangers for a developing woman. They show that feeling must be controlled, and they exalt heroines who have as much will and intelligence as emotion. Merely to feel strongly is to be at the mercy of oneself and others; it is to be self-absorbed and passive. Although committed to an ethic of social love, the authors differentiated it from self-love and linked love to wisdom, responsibility, rationality, and self-command. From their point of view, the merely feelingful person was selfish and superficial, hence incapable of love.

Sometimes the term "novel of sensibility" is used synonymously with "sentimental novel." In addition it is often utilized to assert a historical continuity between nineteenth-century woman's fiction and the earlier works of Samuel Richardson and such followers as his American imitator, Susanna Rowson. In fact, however, the women who wrote after 1820 detested Richardsonian fiction and planned their own as an alternative to it. The heroine who lived entirely in her feelings was, to their minds, a fool and a pernicious example to young women starting out in the battle with life. The woman of sensibility would—as indeed she had in novel after eighteenth-century novel—fall immediate victim in her first contest and never recover. Of what use was such a story? A graceful death that created remorse in all one's tormenters was nothing to the purpose of these authors, which was to show their readers how to live.

Moreover, they objected to the sexual center of these novels of sensibility, and not merely on prudish grounds. They were unwilling to accept, and unwilling to permit their readers to accept, a concept of woman as inevitable sexual prey. They refused to agree that women had to be victims; they insisted that male-female relations could be conducted on a plane that allowed for feelings other than lust. Although to make this point they suppressed sexuality to a degree that later came to seem psychologically destructive, at the time they were working toward a vision of woman as more rather than less fully human. They also thought that their male characters, who were often purposeful, moral men able to admire women and enjoy their company as well as their bodies, were more human than the monomaniacal Lovelaces of the Richardson tradition. Therefore, scarcely any of these novels are novels of seduction; and in the rare story where the heroine (as opposed to a minor, admonitory character) has been seduced, the result is a strengthened character and marriage with a much more desirable man than the seducer. The disappearance of the novel of seduction is a crucial event in woman's fiction, and perhaps in woman's psyche as well.

The term "domestic" for this fiction generally means that the content is largely descriptive of events taking place in a home setting and that it espouses a "cult of domesticity," that is, fulfillment for women in marriage and motherhood. Certainly there is some truth here, but the term "domestic" is not a fixed or neutral word in critical analysis. For many critics, domesticity is equated with entrapment—in an earlier critical generation, of men by women and, more recently, of women by a pernicious ideal promulgated (so the worm turns!) by men. For our authors, it meant something else. Their fiction is mostly about social relations, generally set in homes and other social spaces that are fully described. The detailed descriptions are sometimes idealized, but more often simply "realistic." And, in accordance with the needs of plot, home life is presented, overwhelmingly, as unhappy. There are very few intact families in this literature, and those that are intact are unstable or locked into routines of misery. Domestic tasks are arduous and monotonous; family members oppress and abuse each other; social interchanges are alternately insipid or malicious. Domestic setting and description, then, do not by any means imply domestic idyll.

The "cult of domesticity" that pervades this fiction is not equivalent to a later generation's idea of such a cult, as a simple injunction for woman willingly to turn the key on her own prison. The fiction does excoriate an unhappy home as the basic source of human misery and imagines a happy home as the acme of human bliss. It assumes that men as well as women find greatest happiness and fulfillment in domestic relations, by which are meant not simply spouse and parent, but the whole network of human attachments based on love, support, and mutual responsibility. Domesticity is set forth as a value scheme for ordering all of life, in competition with the ethos of money and exploitation that is perceived to prevail in American society. The domestic ideal meant not that woman was to be sequestered from the world in her place at home but that everybody was to be placed in the home, and hence home and the world would become one. Then, to the extent that woman dominated the home, the ideology implied an unprecedented historical expansion of her influence, and a tremendous advance over her lot in a world dominated by money and market considerations, where she was defined as chattel or sexual toy.

In comparison with the opportunities for personal dignity and influence promised women in this version of the cult of domesticity, those made possible by the vote or the opening of masculine occupations to women seemed relatively narrow to our authors. Politics and professions, after all, were part of the exploitive structure. A domestic organization of society would greatly reduce their power and importance. However, the women authors did not devote much fictional space to arguing with feminists, whose efforts they regarded as misguided but well intentioned and finally harmless. Nor did they attack working women, for they knew very well that women often had no choice but to work. Most of their heroines had to support themselves and often dependents as well for some period of time. Examples of professional women such as teachers and authors are found in the fiction frequently and are presented with the greatest respect and admiration, although it is generally conceded that the heroine will not follow in their footsteps. But the heroine is not developed as a counterstatement to these images. She is contrasted rather to two other feminine types. One of these was the passive woman—incompetent, ignorant, cowed, emotionally and intellectually undeveloped—whom they considered an anachronism from an earlier time. (The heroine's mother is often such a type.) However touching her ineptness and anxiety to please, she sinks quickly under life's demands to an early death or a life of apathy, debility, and obscurity. Initially pleasing to men, she has no power to hold them.

The second type, on whom the brunt of our authors' displeasure fell, is an apparent opposite to this sad case, the thoroughly "modern" woman, the so-called "belle" who lived for excitement and the admiration of the ballroom in the mistaken belief that such self-gratification was equivalent to power and influence. Unthinkingly she abetted and even stimulated the money system that was so inimical to true feminine and human fulfillment. Her needs and demands—for a larger house, luxurious furnishings, an expensive equipage, jewels and elaborate dress—required great sums of money, and the rage for money was the greatest threat to the dignity of woman's life and to the moral life of the entire nation. The cult of domesticity is a social concept that replaces the marketplace with the home, and the belle has given herself to the marketplace.

The belle herself was not entirely to blame; behind her behavior lay a sadly defective system of woman's education that encouraged her feelings at the expense of her reason, gave her mind no objects worthy of its own powers, and accustomed her to the sense of her own trivial and superficial nature. Although the cult of domesticity did involve the suppression or repression of certain aspects of the woman's personality, it put forward an unprecedentedly high view of others, and urged the development and expression of long-neglected capacities. To be sure, the cult opposed the radical demands of the woman's righters. But by assuring woman that she was a far more intelligent, resolute, and able person than was traditionally supposed, the cult, while imposing a heavy burden of good behavior on her, bolstered her self-esteem, supported her inclinations toward self-fulfillment, and justified a search for means of exerting influence that were compatible with her woman's nature. If we keep these points in mind we shall be less inclined to interpret the cult of domesticity in this fiction as a product of the authors' damaged self-esteem, as complicity in their own oppression, or as collaboration in the oppression of other women.

Woman's fiction thus represented a protest against long-entrenched trivializing and contemptuous views of women that animated the fiction of Richardson and other later eighteenth-century fiction of sensibility. The historical antecedents of woman's fiction lay not in these schools but in the novel of manners, with its "mixed" heroine, as developed by Fanny Burney, and even more in the fiction of the English women moralists—Mrs. Opie, Mrs. Barbauld, and especially Maria Edgeworth, with her combination of educational intention, moral fabulating, and description of manners and customs. Edgeworth's moral tales were the childhood reading of the first generation of American women authors, the generation active in the twenties, thirties, and forties, who led the way for the burst of woman's fiction in the fifties and sixties. The writings of these earlier women can be understood, in literary terms, as an attempt to carry over into more complex experience and into the American scene the clarity of Edgeworth's exemplary fiction blended with the accuracy of her regional novels. Drawn from these English sources, woman's fiction then developed indigenously in America, and showed itself relatively impermeable to the influence of the major women writers in England during the Victorian age. Of Jane Austen—not a Victorian, of course— there is no trace in American woman's fiction. Emily Bronte is likewise missing. Signs of George Eliot and of Charlotte Bronte can be discerned in writing of the 1860s, but not before. One might claim that a seriously compromised version of *Jane Eyre,* a plot now called the gothic romance that still flourishes widely, was in fact instrumental in destroying woman's fiction by undercutting some of its basic premises. Briefly put, Jane's goal in the Bronte novel is dominance while the goal of all the American heroines is independence—not at all the same thing. In the gothic romance the goal is to be a powerful male's only dependent— something different from what Charlotte Bronte was arguing, and different again from the thrust of woman's fiction. The only English woman author of the mid-nineteenth century who inspired American woman writers was Elizabeth Barrett, and she did so more as an example of a dedicated literary woman than for the content or form of any of her writings.

Most of the American authors were middle-class women who needed money. As a general rule—although exceptions increased as the period wore on—only middle-class women had sufficient education to know how to write books, and only those who needed money attempted it. However, the unstable financial conditions of American life ensured that there was a sizable group of such women and made their thematic concern with the problems of self-support pertinent to many readers. Some of the writers were single, others widowed or deserted, supporting themselves and family. Others, married, became chief provider when a husband failed financially or lost his health. Still others, wives of ministers, for example, provided a second income that saved their families from genteel poverty. We shall see examples of all as we proceed.

During the period between 1820 and 1870 there were virtually no satisfying and well paid occupations for women. Women did not turn to work for self-fulfillment in this period partly because no such work existed for them. Before the twenties, almost the sole vocation open to a middle-class woman was needlework in some form—seamstressing, millinery, embroidery, lacemaking. Service was not only felt to be beneath her, it was thought to be beyond her physical strength, given the realities of the wood-burning stove, home baking, well-drawn water, and the like. Around 1820, the professions of schoolteaching and authorship began to develop for women, professions obviously superior to needlework because of their greater involvement of mental powers and their opportunities for control of oneself and influence over others. Authorship promised better money and wider influence than teaching. Both professions clearly resulted from the rising standard of living and the new leisure that gave time for education and self-improvement, especially of women. Thus our authors were product of, as well as stimulus to, the changing condition of women. And, logically enough, they were strong advocates of women's education and for the appropriateness of teaching as a profession for women, causes that made tremendous progress during the period that their fiction flourished. Almost all the heroines of this fiction were devoted to books and hungry for formal education. The women authors saw cultivation of the mind as the great key to freedom, the means by which women, learning to think about their situation, could learn how to master it. Like Benjamin Franklin before them, and Malcolm X after them, they saw literacy as the foundation of liberation. Since this message was embodied in fiction, it supposed an audience already literate; but the novels constantly urged their readers to go beyond fiction. In so urging, the authors were not at all hypocritical; they were using fiction as a rung on the ladder.

During the three decades between Catharine Sedgwick's pioneering work in the 1820s and Susan Warner's first best seller, the number of women authors grew steadily. In 1848, Rufus Griswold and Caroline May each published anthologies of American women poets. In 1852, John Hart did the same for American women prose writers. His volume (Philadelphia: E. H. Butler) contained selections from forty-eight writers; the second edition of

1854 anthologized sixty-one. Many of them had written short pieces exclusively, for the annuals and gift books of the thirties and the magazines of the forties. For women, the 1850s was the decade in which the book became the predominant mode of literary packaging. Established authors gathered their sketches into volumes and shifted to longer works; veterans like Sarah Hale and Sedgwick reissued out-of-print novels from the twenties; newcomers skipped the apprenticeship and entered the profession with fictions running into the hundreds of pages. Although the novelists of this period now considered important are all male, from 1850 until well after the Civil War (some would say until the 1920s) the novel was chiefly a form of literary communication among women.

The literary women conceptualized authorship as a profession rather than a calling, as work and not art. Women authors tended not to think of themselves as artists or justify themselves in the language of art until the 1870s and after. This practical approach, along with their unclassic educations, had an inevitable effect on their work. It did not make the sorts of claims on its readers that "art" does—the dimensions of formal self-consciousness, attachment to or quarrel with a grand tradition, aesthetic seriousness, are all missing. Often the women deliberately and even proudly disavowed membership in an artistic fraternity. "Mine is a story for the table and arm-chair under the reading lamp in the living-room, and not for the library shelves," Marion Harland announced in her autobiography, while Fanny Fern dedicated *Rose Clark*, more elaborately, to the same use:

When the frost curtains the windows, when the wind whistles fiercely at the key-hole, when the bright fire glows, and the tea-tray is removed, and father in his slippered feet lolls in his arm-chair; and mother with her nimble needle "makes auld claes look amaist as weel as new," and grandmamma draws closer to the chimney-corner, and Tommy with his plate of chestnuts nestles contentedly at her feet; then let my unpretending story be read. For such an hour, for such an audience, was it written.

Should any *dictionary on legs* rap inopportunely at the door for admittance, send him away to the groaning shelves of some musty library, where "literature" lies embalmed, with its stony eyes, flesh-less joints, and ossified heart, in faultless preservation.

Fanny Fern's rhetoric here transforms "immortal" literature into a corpse and hence justifies the kind of immediate, functional writing she herself does. We see that she by no means considers herself talentless because she does not aim for permanent place-ment in the library, and in trying to assess the abilities of this group of women we are confronted at every turn by the con-straints they put on their own capacities. In fact many of them were gifted and committed writers, with narrative and descriptive talents that many a male applicant for literary immortality might have envied. One can understand that they might have found active professional life far more rewarding than the solitary struggle of the committed artist. One can even theorize that their visible success helped change attitudes toward women more than the creation of literary masterpieces might have. Yet one cannot help feeling that by dismissing work of traditional literary great-ness as outside their scope these women also foreclosed certain possibilities for themselves and others. It is undoubtedly against this foreclosure that the serious post–Civil War women artists struggled; but they had to pay the price of retreat from the active, ongoing professional life of their day. Thus one must balance loss and gain. The most serious charge that can be brought against the earlier group is that they decried a commercial ethic of success in their work while gladly permitting their own novels to be judged by it and their own lives to be shaped by it.

I use the word "novel" to refer to all their long fiction, but in fact there are several generic variants, along a scale at one end of which is the moral fable, at the other the romance, and in be-tween the novel proper, that is, a story of probability in a recog-nizably realistic setting. The moral fable arranges events in an order that displays the ineluctable operations of a principle; al-though settings may be real, they are rather implied than represented. Action and character are schematized according to the principle that is being illustrated. Generally, this principle is illuminated in two contrasting characters, one showing right and the other wrong behavior. For each of these characters, good and bad results flow inevitably and without impediment from good and bad actions.

The romance also abstracts situations from reality, projecting them in heightened character types and rhetoric against a stylized background of the gorgeous and grandiose. Landscapes are sublime, domestic settings palatial, and action presented in the exaggerated vocabulary of stage gesture. Foiled villainesses gnash their teeth and tear out hair by the handfuls; triumphant heroines roll their eyes and point heavenward; villains indulge in demonic laughs, sneering asides, and Machiavellian monologues. The romance in extreme moments looks like melodrama, but melodrama presents an old-fashioned view of women typed either as helpless virtue or foiled vice while woman's fiction by contrast, whether fable, romance, or novel, believes in effective virtue.

The novel develops events with attention to the laws of probability and actuality (always limited, of course, by the perceptions of the individual authors). The heroine's experience cannot be untangled from the particularities of her society, and the work is generally designed to provide broad and detailed depiction of regional and class characteristics including homes, dress, manners, occupations, celebrations, rituals, local speech, and so on. Hence, some thirty years before the types are supposed to have existed in America, realism and its cousin local color had accomplished practitioners. Realism certainly helped readers to identify with the protagonists, and in this way (though they have been utterly ignored by most scholars of American literature in this regard) the women authors were responding to the demands of those like Ralph Waldo Emerson who were calling for a literature faithful to the national experience.

Fable, romance, and novel are not exclusive types. Some exemplary organizing principle is at work in all this woman's fiction. All types rely on the device of pairing heroines, or pairing a heroine and a villainess. Amidst the wildest romance, passages of striking realistic description or characterization will occur—the novels of E. D. E. N. Southworth provide many examples—and even the most controlled realist will permit herself an occasional romantic episode or a melodramatic twist. And all three types develop, using different literary vocabularies, the same story of the heroine's trials and triumph.

This story itself exists in two parallel versions. In one, the heroine begins as a poor and friendless child. Most frequently an orphan, she sometimes only thinks herself to be one, or has by necessity been separated from her parents for an indefinite time. In the second, the heroine is a pampered heiress who becomes poor and friendless in midadolescence, through the death or financial failure of her legal protectors. At this point the two plots merge, for both show how the heroine develops the capacity to survive and surmount her troubles. At the end of the novel she is no longer an underdog. The purpose of both plots is to deprive the heroine of all external aids and to make her success in life entirely a function of her own efforts and character. The idea that a woman's identity or place in life is a function of her father's or husband's place is firmly rejected, not merely on idealistic but also on realistic grounds. If the orphan's rags-to-riches story caught one aspect of American life and faith, the heiress's riches-to-rags caught another. As some moved up, others fell down. When men fell, their dependent women fell with them. Several women authors began their careers as a direct result of financial catastrophe in their families; as we will see, the Panic of 1837 created a large new group of women authors. Their novels showed how women were forced to depend on themselves. They asserted that women had to be prepared for both economic and emotional self-support, but promised that the sex was equal to the challenge, even that the challenge could become an opportunity.

There are two kinds of heroine in this novel, the flawless and the flawed. The flawless are those who already possess the emotional strength and stability to function effectively when adversity strikes. The flawed are those whose characters are defective, so that triumph in adversity becomes a matter of self-conquest as well as conquest of the other. Some novels present more than one heroine. A flawed and a flawless heroine may counterpoint one another. Again, two kinds of flaws will be opposed, such as excessive dependency against excessive self-will. The overly dependent woman has to acquire firmness, the self-willed woman learns to bend so as not to break. The idea of what is, and what is not, a flaw varies according to the perspective of the individual author, yet all agree that some degree of self-control is a moral and practical necessity while total self-abnegation is suicidal. The writers' conviction that character had to adjust to limiting circumstances, their belief that suffering and hardship could not be avoided in any human life, and their strenuous insistence that such trials, because they called out otherwise dormant abilities, could become occasions for "perfecting" the character imply a deeply Victorian world view. This view is radically unlike the postmodern sensibility with its stress on the immediate, the physical, and the expressive as well as its return to the pre-Victorian infatuation with pure feeling conceptualized as identical to virtue. Hence the implications of the authors' message, evolved within such a view, may strike today's reader as inhibiting rather than liberating as they were meant to be.

The novels were Victorian also in their perception of the self as a social product, firmly and irrevocably embedded in a social construct that could destroy it but that also shaped it, constrained it, encouraged it, and ultimately fulfilled it. They told stories about the emergent self negotiating amidst social possibilities, attempting to assert and maintain a territory within a social space full of warring claims. The process was fatiguing and frustrating, but none of these authors proposed the Huck Finn solution of abandoning "sivilization" because none of them could imagine the concept of self apart from society. If critics ever permit the woman's novel to join the main body of "American literature," then all our theories about American fiction, from Richard Chase's "romance" to Richard Poirier's "world elsewhere" to Carolyn Heilbrun's "masculine wilderness" will have to be radically revised.

The heroine's "self" emerges concurrently with her growth from child to adult; as child and woman her chief relations are with those more powerful than she. We find two basic power situations: either those who have authority over the child abuse it (much the more common situation) or they are fair but unsympathetic and uncongenial. These two situations confront the child with somewhat different problems, but in both of them there are invariable conditions: home life is not happy, the child is not loved or valued, those who should love and nurture her instead exploit or neglect her. Home is more a detention camp than a "walled garden," sharing with that popular image only the walls. The romances make the point through fathers who lock up their daughters; the realistic novels prefer to show the daily wearing down of neglected and overworked orphans. The heroine's problem in these situations is, indeed, basic; it is to endure until she comes of age and at the same time to grow so that when she comes of age she will be able to leave the unfriendly environment and succeed on her own. She must learn to strike a balance between total submission, which means self-denial to the point of death, and an equally suicidal defiance. She has to learn how to comply as a practical necessity, without being violated. Compliance and inner independence are equally necessary for life.

The abusers of power run a gamut from fathers and mothers to step-parents, aunts, uncles, grandparents, guardians, and matrons of orphanages. They are the administrators or owners of the space within which the child is legally constrained. Least guilty are the mothers; often it is the loss of the mother that initiates the heroine's woes, and the memory of her mother that permits her to endure them. Most guilty are aunts, usually the mother's sisters, with whom many orphaned heroines are sent to live. These aunts are alternately hard-working and parsimonious or fashionable and frivolous. If the aunt has a family, the heroine is subject to additional mistreatment through the scorn and spite of her cousins.

As her kin fail her, the heroine meets people in the community who support, advise, and befriend her. Occasionally they intercede to remove her from the unfriendly environment. As an adult, she continues to rely on them and often returns the favors they have done her. In novel after novel, a network of surrogate kin gradually defines itself around the heroine, making hers the story not only that of a self-made woman but that of a self-made or surrogate family. Most of these novels conclude with a marriage that represents the institutionalizing of such families, for the heroine's new home includes not only her husband but all her other intimates as well. And her final "domesticity" is defined as her relations with all these adults, rather than as childbearing and childrearing, for the novels rarely follow the heroine past the threshold of motherhood. Lip service was certainly paid to motherhood as the crown of woman's joys, and no author had the courage to suggest that children might be more burdensome than pleasurable; yet the plots make it absolutely clear that although children may be necessary for a woman's happiness, they are not necessary for her identity—nor is a husband.

Between her unhappy childhood and the conclusion, the heroine experiences an interlude during which she must earn her own living. Generally she turns to some form of teaching. The heiress fallen on hard times has ladylike accomplishments in which she can now instruct others; the exploited orphan has stolen enough time from her duties to acquire a rudimentary education that she can now pass on. In this time of her life, whether through misunderstanding or other cause, the heroine is without a suitor and resigns herself to a life without marriage. She stays aloof from the husband hunting of her peers, preferring, in an oft-repeated phrase, "honest independence" to a mercenary marriage. She often rejects eligible suitors for reasons that, though sometimes far-fetched, require her to confront and accept the likelihood of spinsterhood. Although almost all the heroines do eventually marry, the stories assert that marriage cannot and should not be the goal toward which women direct themselves, that neither its inevitability nor its permanence can be assumed, and that a commercial marriage is worse by far than a single life. This message is reinforced by the important background role played by unmarried or widowed women. The proliferation and variety of such characters evokes a world in which marriage may be only an episode in a woman's life; everywhere the heroine encounters women of all ages without husbands. Few characters in this literature receive the same respect and affection as does the kind, strong-hearted widow who has brought up stable children and still finds time to mother the heroine. Too, the predominance of woman characters in most of this fiction suggests that women perceived themselves to be living in a world mostly populated by members of their own sex and recognized that, on a day-to-day basis, relations with their own sex constituted the texture of their lives.

The men in this fiction are less important to the heroine's emotional life than women. Chiefly, they are the controllers and dispensers of money, and in this way the ultimate though sometimes remote shapers of women's lives. The heiress cannot possess her wealth directly but must maneuver with men. If orphaned, she must deal with the cupidity of her guardians and suitors. An heiress with parents must combat her father's plans to dispose of her wealth, plans that generally include the disposal of her person. An heiress who is suddenly impoverished becomes so through the gambling habits of a brother or (a larger form of the same vice) the speculating habits of a father. In many novels, death of the father reveals what is called "an embarrassed state of affairs" plunging a comfortable and unprepared family into poverty. When the mother—an eighteenth-century passive and dependent woman—cannot deal with the situation, the more flexible and enterprising daughter takes charge. The brother, who ought to guide the straitened family, is absent or unable to rise above entrenched habits of idleness and attitudes of snobbery. Gambling tempts him as well as drink, and soon he becomes another of his sister's dependents. If the father survives his bankruptcy, the heroine supports him too; in effect she becomes the head of the family whatever its circumstances. But she goes beyond taking her father's place. She brings into being a new kind of family life, organized around love rather than money. Money subsides into its adjunct function of ensuring domestic comfort.

This fantasy of parental overthrow apparently owes as much to social and economic conditions as to inherent psychic needs. Society was based on money, and men had all the control—the power to make it, to disburse it, to keep it, and the terrifying power to lose it. Women had no access to the wealth-making occupations; their only financial rights pertained to inherited property, which they were permitted to will away as they wished. A woman hoping to control her "own" money in her lifetime could do so legally only if she did not marry. Daughters were economically ruled by their fathers, wives by their husbands. Thus, inevitably, in every encounter with a man, economic considerations predominated for these women. The women authors created stories in which, ultimately, male control and the money economy are simultaneously terminated. Whatever vengeful feelings they may have had modulate into the benign fantasy of rescuing the parent. Power relations are reversed, but the heroine uses her powers benevolently and rationally (the money economy, with its investing fevers and panics, is perceived as profoundly irrational), thus proving that if women had power they would be better rulers than men.

Suitors in these novels are less important than fathers, guardians, and brothers. Since the point of the fiction is the development of feminine self-sufficiency, the traditional rescuing function of the lover is denied to him. When a woman turns to marriage or elopement as escape, she finds herself enthralled to a tyrant even worse than the one she fled. Her trial is not evaded, only reformulated. And, as I have said, many heroines must endure apparently permanent separations from men they love and hence learn that they cannot depend on marriage for identity or meaning in their lives.

On the other hand, almost no marriages represent rescues of the man by the heroine. A woman will accept her obligation to save an errant father or brother, but she does not solicit like opportunities among the male population at large. She looks to marry a man who is strong, stable, and safe. She is canny in her judgment of men, and generally immune to the appeal of a dissolute suitor. When she feels such an attraction, she resists it. She is never taken in by the man's promise that he will reform after marriage, or the bait that she can be the cause of his reformation. The most famous confrontation of this sort occurs in *St. Elmo,* where Edna Earl steadfastly withstands the appeal of an irresistible blackguard and tells him to go away and save himself. In its employment of a rake hero, however, *St. Elmo* is itself a rarity. The conventional hero of woman's fiction is solid, ethical, generous, frank, hard-working, energetic, an admirer and respecter of women who likes the heroine as much or more than he lusts for her. The fiction is partial to ministers, because a minister's wife shares her husband's life to a greater degree than do the wives of businessmen, lawyers, and planters. Moreover, as a man of peace the minister is exempt from much of the more brutal and exploitive elements of stereotyped masculine behavior. Although the authors of woman's fiction all accepted certain fundamental differences between the sexes as reason for differences in social roles, they were idealizing, in their marriage patterns, something like a union of equals.

The place of religious belief in the heroine's life varies widely in woman's fiction. Some novelists are thoroughly secular; others pay lip service to conventional faith, while the books of still others are permeated with evangelical fervor. Functioning religious values are always subsumed within the domestic ideology. The writers know that God supports the principle of love and not the principle of money. Moreover they find piety an effective strategy in a woman's struggle to define herself over against social encroachment, and they present it as a pragmatic tool for their heroines' use. Finally, they permit each heroine to find her own God privately, without the intervention of masculine religious institutions—faith is thus pried out of its patriarchal social setting.

In only two novels of the entire period—Caroline Chesebro's *Isa* (1852) and Augusta Evans' *Beulah* (1859)—do the heroines have doubts of God's existence, but in most of them they have some trouble accepting his decrees. The authors insist that the universe responds to God's intentions in its general laws as well as in every particular event. However, like many more distinguished thinkers of the age, the pious among them were concerned to reconcile their certainty of God's existence (and what followed inevitably from that existence, his goodness) with the widespread human misery they saw around them. In accordance with the democratic evangelical movement of their age, they were not prepared to accept the idea of innate universal evil in all men and women; in fact, since their purpose was to convince women of their innate goodness and dignity, they had special reason for rejecting the doctrine of Original Sin. But they then had to account for the trials of the good. They interpreted trials on the secular level as occasions designed to strengthen and "perfect" (a word that recurs throughout this fiction) the faulty character. From an otherworldly vantage point, trials were sent to detach a person from earthly impermanence and turn her (or him) to God, who alone does not change or fail. The sincere heart received assurance of God's love and from this love an influx of strength that enabled it to return to its earthly struggle fortified to prevail.

Although the theology optimistically assures salvation to everyone who sincerely applies for it, the world view is bitter and despairing in some respects. Deprived of the justification of man's innate evil, God's actions are supremely cruel. The women authors rationalize that if all desires were satisfied on earth, and nothing precious ever lost, no one would care for God. By punitive measures, God makes himself necessary to his children. The proof of his existence is in suffering and deprivation; and, hard as it may sometimes seem, the mere human creature must assent to the idea that God loves us most when he most punishes us.

Evidently, the religious women authors were not prepared to class God with the other tyrannical patriarchs in their fiction. They had some hope of changing the human order, but where the divine order was concerned they considered it was wisest to accede and, if ordered to kiss the rod, then to kiss it. In return for this gesture, however, the human being received two advantages: first, the inestimable consolation of an afterlife in an era when death carried away mothers, children, and young adults in vast numbers; and second, a pragmatic strategy for dealing from a weak position with the threats and aggressions of the powerful.

As the Puritan had acknowledged his depthless iniquity and thrown himself on God's mercy to be sanctified and made good in God's goodness, the evangelical woman believer acknowledged her pathetic weakness and turned to God for strength. Such an emphasis speaks directly to the feminine situation—women are good but weak, engaged in the bootstrap operation of making themselves powerful. Their weakness was patent to themselves and others. Any fictional heroine who imagined she could succeed without help was simply untried. But since she is in a situation in which all help is denied, to whom can she turn? She has the guarantee that God will provide her with inner strength if she turns to him; thus turning to God becomes a device for calling out her own resources.

The influx of what she interprets as divine strength lifts her up in her trials and enables her to survive, to carry out her responsibilities, and to bear with deprivation and loss. It also gives her a certain calmness, self-possession, and detachment that stand her in good stead. It becomes the preliminary to or equivalent of a tact that enables her to deal effectively with others. The quiet serenity in itself wins esteem. Thus, religion becomes social strategy. When she refuses to respond to provocation and deflects aggression by good works she disarms her enemies and earns the respect of those who were previously indifferent to her. Open defiance only intensifies the hostility and ill-will of others, making her life more difficult. A soft answer turneth away wrath, and religious faith permits the heroine to carry off the victory in many complex social games for which she is radically handicapped.

The writers' religious faith coincided with their conviction that God's values were domestic, even if the concept of God himself remained masculine. During this era many aspects of American religious life were passing into women's sphere, and the churches were actively engaging in humanitarian and reform measures closely allied to domestic ideology. Moreover, in this fiction religious life has been largely severed from its institutional setting. Even though the heroines are usually churchgoers and professing Christians, their true religious life is interior. They meet God directly without the intermediate masculine power structure of the church. The heroine has many guides on her pilgrimage to a firm faith. Some of these guides are men, and some of these men are ministers. The ministers appeal to the heroine not in their official capacity, however, but as loving friends. Hence, the task of guiding souls to God is no longer restricted to, indeed becomes quite separated from, those who have been ordained in the patriarchal social institution. The most fervently pious domestic novels suggest that the women authors envisioned themselves as lay ministers, their books as evangelical sermons that might spur conversion. Finally, the language in which these books refer to God suggests that the women were more comfortable with a nonsexual than with a traditional patriarchal or erotic imagery for God. On occasion God is called the father but more often he is spoken of as a parent, combining all parental functions in an androgynous image. Christ is the friend and never the lover or bridegroom. As the women examined the concepts of father and husband most critically in their fiction, they accepted God uncritically by referring to him by such neutral terms as parent and friend. His nature, then, transcended gender.

Because its story of the development of feminine character is set in a social context, this fiction contains much explicit and implicit social commentary. Those who see in domestic fiction only the empty detailing of trivial social interactions overlook the way in which detailed presentation is controlled by social judgment and awareness. Indirectly at least, women were beginning to articulate and take a stand on some social issues in their fiction. Opinions on temperance and slavery are often expressed, but other matters are more basic to the structure of most of these novels. Besides the running attack on the predominance of marketplace values in every area of American life, woman's fiction took especial cognizance of rural-urban tensions and the class divisions in American society.

The era of massive immigration to the United States took place after woman's fiction had peaked (perhaps the resulting heterogeneity of American culture contributed to the genre's decline), but the movement of country people into the city was continuous during the period of this study, and very much on people's minds. The hundreds of melodramatic fictions of the 1840s by such popular writers as Timothy Shay Arthur, "Ned Buntline," and E. P. Roe, as well as the salacious fiction of George Lippard, all turned on the sudden growth of the city and its emergence as threat and temptation in so many American lives. The country in such fiction represented the repository of virtue and decency, and the urge to migrate to the city was interpreted as a reprehensible impulse of greed or discontent.

The women authors were more ambivalent. They saw much more clearly—or at least represented more clearly—the distressing rural conditions from which city migrants were fleeing. If the country might mean peace, stillness, rest, beauty, and harmonious nature, it did not in fact mean these to the impoverished majority that toiled on small farms and lived in dread of drought and foreclosure. The women recognized country vices: brutalizing labor, mean minds, vicious gossip. They saw women's lot on the farm as particularly hard, and country men as particularly intransigent in their opposition to feminine self-development. They observed that

the city offered opportunity for a more spacious, comfortable, enlightened life and that women especially had opportunities to
develop themselves that they lacked in the country. But they also
saw the urban evils that everyone else saw—the frenetic race for
money and status, a new kind of rootlessness, restlessness, and
alienation with its potential for casual violence, the specter of
frightful poverty and degradation at the bottom of the social scale,
the problems caused by crowding. They mourned the loss of
simplicity and the separation from natural rhythms. To resolve
their ambivalences, the writers created utopian images that
blended city and country. Some imagined a life wherein characters migrated comfortably back and forth between town and
country life, using each as corrective to the other. Others idealized
the farmer-scholar or gentleman-farmer, and his year-round country mansion wherein an urban way of life could be played out free
of all city ugliness. In a contrasting image, writers imagined the
new West as the eventual locale of garden cities, wherein urban
life preserved the greenery and natural pace of the country; an
occasional heroine was sent west to take part in this civilizing
movement, which involved taming the city as well as the
wilderness.

The women authors responded to the class system with similar
ambivalence. None of them thought to deny that a class system
existed in America, and not all of them regretted it. All agreed
that the class system presently existing was based entirely on
money ("Old New York" was apparently dead before 1830),
and most of them argued for a class system based on merit. Although they recognized that merit might exist among the poor,
they tended to believe that American society was designed to
permit such merit naturally to push itself up the social scale, and
hence that those who remained poor were the less meritorious.
Thus few of them contemplated radical social reform, much as
they detested poverty. They tended to focus, as novelists of
manners have always done, on the class-within-a-class, the meritorious who might be singled out from the merely wealthy by their

psychological freedom from money, their devotion to gracious living and virtue rather than to acquisition and display. This inner circle might contain a few virtuous poor and an occasional millionaire, but largely it was composed of people with enough money to live in comfort, but not enough to live without some kind of work. This class was profoundly middle-class, and profoundly "genteel."

Many of the women authors understood "gentility" as the social extension of domestic ideology. Insofar as she operated directly outside of her home, the domestic heroine served as a model of genteel behavior. Her behavior provided an example that the worthy poor might imitate and hence be saved, as they rose socially, from merely acquiring wealth. The heroine might also function as a stern corrective to the dissipated upper classes when she moved among them in her faultless simplicity. Although the idea of reforming a nation by correcting its manners may well seem naive or ludicrous or snobbish now, many mid-century women saw this task as a mission allied, though secondary, to their mission of overturning the male money system as the law of American life.

The acquisitive and exhibitionist behavior of the rich was not judged solely against the authors' standards of good manners, however. More fundamentally it was judged against their bitter knowledge of financial instability. In 1830, Sedgwick wrote in *Clarence* that "fashionable people, who most pride themselves on their prerogative of exclusiveness, feel the extreme precariousness of the tenure by which they hold their privileges. A sudden reverse of fortune, one of the most common accidents of a commercial city, plunges them into irretrievable obscurity and insignificance." Fourteen years later, in *Girlhood and Womanhood,* Mrs. A. J. Graves wrote that "of all countries ours should be the last, where the folly of measuring a man's standing by his riches should be found, for in no other are fortunes so ephemeral or do wealth and honors so frequently pass from one to another." These authors tended to see great or even substantial wealth as a trouble, a temptation, and because of its transience, ultimately an illusion. The "middling" class, they believed, was actually further from poverty than the very rich.

And they abhorred and feared poverty. Not one of these novels is unaware of, or fails to devote some space to, poverty as the great slough into which the human spirit sinks and wherein it is destroyed. A temporary bout with poverty might have redemptive value for a pampered social butterfly, but a lifetime of poverty was earthly hell. Our authors were, naturally enough, particularly alive to the fact that so many of the indigent were women and children made poor by undependable males and denied the opportunity to climb out of the pit on their own. Widows, the wives of drunkards or of disabled workingmen, all toiling for the support of their families at a profession—usually seamstressing—that paid lower than subsistence wages, either unprotected or abused by those who should have protected them: this vision haunts their novels, and goes far to explain why they found the shelter of the middle-class home appealing. A total reorganization of society would have to be effected before the defenseless woman could hope to hold her own in society, many of them thought; for the present, a secure position in the middle class, bolstered by her managerial abilities, was her best hope.

My comments on domesticity above have suggested, however, that these writers were thinking about a social reorganization wherein their special concept of home was projected out into the world. They recognized that home and the world were different, but unlike many male theorists of the day (and in contradistinction to the interpretation that later generations have put on them) they did not really see these as "separate spheres." Their depiction of home life showed the home thoroughly penetrated at every point by the world, dominated by man, the world's ambassador, and vulnerable to the various empty temptations of wealth as well as the possibility of poverty. If worldly values could dominate the home, perhaps the direction of influence could be reversed so that home values dominated the world. Since they identified home values with basic human values, they saw this as a reformation of America into a society at last responsive to truly human needs, a fulfillment of the original settlers' dreams.

Now in this view "home" is not a space but a system of human relations; still it is in the family enclosure that such a system can most quickly be put into practice and, since new human beings are trained there, can be lastingly learned. Woman, if she can preside over the home space, will then be not out of the world but at the very center of it. When accepting, as one's basic relation to another, obligation rather than exploitation, doing another good rather than doing him in; when books and conversation and simple comfort seem superior to ostentation and feverish pleasure—then, our authors believed, a true social revolution will have taken place, American life will have been transformed. Though not a woman's fiction, *Uncle Tom's Cabin* is permeated by this ideology, contrasting the real nation, organized on mercenary principles, with the ideal nation that might come into being, organized on the principle of familial love. The destruction of slave families by the system that considers them property is different in degree but not in kind from the destruction of white families in woman's fiction by greed, speculation, exploitation, selfishness, extravagance.

Thus our authors imagined that if each woman rose to the opportunity that history was putting in her hands, the opportunity to develop herself as worthy representative of domestic values, then women collectively would make a peaceful revolution. The decade of the 1850s was the high point of their fiction because the motives of self-development and social reform could run together so smoothly. Women could change others by changing themselves, and the phrase "woman's sphere is in the home" could appear to mean "woman's sphere is to reform the world." Some of the authors liked to use Pascal's circle, whose center was everywhere and circumference nowhere, as the image of woman's "sphere." Nor did these woman couch their reforming intentions in the language of nostalgia, although in fiction of the twenties and thirties one finds a certain longing for colonial austerity. Most authors felt that the domestic institution under whose banner they were crusading was, like woman's expanding self-confidence and self-esteem, something entirely new.

The course of history dictated that the crusade for domesticity, unlike that for woman's parity with men, would be short-lived. The liberal women who began their writing careers after the Civil War found the redemptive possibilities of enlightened domesticity to be no longer credible. The Civil War had demonstrated the feebleness of the affectional model of human relationships, and the Gilded Age affirmed profit as the motive around which all of American life was to be organized. Home now became a retreat, a restraint and a constraint, as it had not appeared to be earlier; to define it as woman's sphere was now unambiguously to invite her to absent herself permanently from the world's affairs. When Marion Harland turned from writing fiction to writing cookbooks in 1871, she made a significant gesture. Domesticity and feminine heroism had parted company. The various departments of domestic science—nutrition, health, child development, household management—proliferated between the Civil War and the First World War as ways of making woman's life more rational and more endurable, but they did not embody the happy certainty of the domestic fictionists, that in her home relations woman was going to change the world. Nor did such disciplines encourage women along the road of spacious education and self-development as the educational crusades of the novelists had. Hence, after the Civil War, the idea of expanding woman and her world began to oppose the domestic ideology rather than cooperate with it. Women continued to write, in ever greater numbers, but the "woman's novel"—that is, the novel designed to succeed with a mass audience of literate women—changed its form and ideology.

3

Catharine Sedgwick
and Other Early Novelists

The most popular novels of the early national period were *The Power of Sympathy* (1789), *Charlotte Temple* (1794), and *The Coquette* (1797). All three were about women and the last two were written by women. *The Power of Sympathy,* an epistolary novel by William Hill Brown, has two plots, the first concerning a narrowly averted marriage between half-siblings (one illegitimate and hence not identified as kin until the catastrophe) and the second concerning the seduction of a virtuous woman by her sister's husband. Both plots end in the violent deaths of their protagonists. *Charlotte Temple,* by Susanna Rowson, tells of the simple, trusting heroine's seduction, subsequent abandonment and sufferings, and ultimate death from poverty, exhaustion, and fever. *The Coquette,* by Hannah Foster, tells much the same story about a spoiled and artful flirt who refuses good marriage offers and dies disgraced in childbirth after she has succumbed to a seducer far more artful than she. Together the novels present an unqualified picture of woman as man's inevitable dupe and prey. The woman invariably succumbs to male arts, and dies as a result. From a woman's point of view, this is a demoralized literature.

It is a sign of woman's improved view of herself that the seduction novel largely disappeared from her reading and writing in the next generation. (Seduction continued to be a staple of sensational men's fiction.) Women who theorized on fiction, like Lydia Maria Child in *The Mother's Book* (1831), looked for novels that would expand and strengthen the young girl's mind, giving her the fortitude to accept what was inevitable in her lot, and the energy to change what was not. "A real love of reading is the greatest blessing education can bestow, particularly upon a woman," Child writes. "It cheers so many hours of illness and seclusion; it gives the mind something to interest itself about, instead of the concerns of one's neighbors, and the changes of fashion; it enlarges the heart, by giving extensive views of the world; it every day increases the points of sympathy with an intelligent husband, and it gives a mother materials for furnishing the minds of her children." Child recommends books of history, biography, and travel, to expand the restricted young woman's knowledge; she also finds that recent novels, a great improvement over old-fashioned sensational fiction, may be read with profit. She compiles a guide to allowable novels according to the reader's age, and discusses those books and authors that are dangerous for young minds. The fiction of Byron, Charles Maturin, Monk Lewis, and Anne Radcliffe falls into the latter category; ignoring Richardson altogether, Child singles out *Charlotte Temple* as especially vicious. "I dare say [it] was written with the best intention; yet I believe few works do so much harm to girls of fourteen and fifteen."

The world view of these pernicious novels is "false," she says, and yet their "horribly exciting" events can act on the inexperienced imagination as a literal intoxicant. By this means, such novels can make a young girl into the silly victim they claim she is. This implicit acknowledgment of the immense power of fiction over the developing character suggests, in part, why fiction became so important a tool for those who were concerned with woman's development and growth. Good fiction would strengthen her powers of reason, will, and judgment, just as sensational fiction inflamed her uncontrolled feelings and ignorant imagination.

Good fiction did not disapprove of feeling and imagination, or hold up for emulation heroines who lacked these qualities but took it for granted that the reader possessed feelings and imagination in natural abundance and had no need for them to be further developed.

Lydia Child (1802–1880) did not create any fiction of the sort she recommended to mothers. She was a productive literary professional whose life is important in any history of nineteenth-century woman's growing independence; her forte was the essay. She wrote extensively on a variety of topics and achieved recognition as an early abolitionist. Her newspaper columns for the *Boston Courier* were collected in the mid-forties as a two-volume series called *Letters from New York;* these essays contain a broad range of social commentary, went through many editions, and were widely discussed and quoted. In all, she published more than fifty works, including three historical novels: *Hobomok* (1824), set in Colonial times; *The Rebels* (1825), a story of the Revolution; and *Philothea* (1836), a romance set in classical Greece. The only American woman recommended on her list in *The Mother's Book,* a list including such English women writers as Maria Edgeworth, Mrs. Barbauld, Mrs. Opie, and others of their school, is Catharine Sedgwick. And, indeed, Sedgwick is the author of the earliest examples of the new kind of American woman's fiction.

Catharine Maria Sedgwick (1789–1867) is accorded a place in some literary histories for her two historical romances, *Hope Leslie* (1827) and *The Linwoods* (1835). These historical romances feature women protagonists and establish the tradition whereby, in the more fanciful setting of a remote time, women are endowed with heroic capacities unrestrained by probabilities. Hope Leslie, for example, in the novel named for her, daringly rescues the saintly Indian maiden Magawisca from prison. Sedgwick's four other novels, rarely discussed in criticism, are contemporary woman's fiction wherein women display heroic traits within the limits of nineteenth-century social possibility. These novels are *A New-England Tale* (1822), *Redwood* (1824), *Clarence* (1830), and, much later, *Married or Single?* (1857).

Sedgwick's career was not typical, in that she turned to writing as diversion and psychological therapy rather than for economic reasons. Her father was a self-made success, a lawyer who served in Washington's Congress, and her mother, who was his second wife, was descended from two prominent New England families. Sedgwick attended school briefly but was educated mainly at home. Her mother died in 1807 and her father (who in 1808 had married a woman uncongenial to his daughter) in 1813. Thereafter, Sedgwick lived with her brothers; two sisters and four brothers survived with her into adulthood and they, with their spouses, formed a close-knit group, all of them settling in or near Stockbridge, Massachusetts, where they had grown up.

Sedgwick seems to have begun to write in order to alleviate boredom and severe depressions, to which she and her sisters (like their mother, who had suffered serious mental illness) were susceptible. She achieved considerable prestige in her own time, was ranked with James Fenimore Cooper for her historical writing, and continued to produce actively for more than thirty years, turning after 1835 from adult fiction to moral tales, juveniles, and etiquette books. The didactic purpose that dominates her later writings is evident in her earlier fiction, where it merges with astute description of manners and customs. Although Sedgwick often pointed her plots with melodramatic incident and decorated them with digressive episode, she achieved fundamental coherence in each novel by following the life of one young woman who, self-mastered, achieved independence from circumstances and control over her own life.

A New-England Tale was undertaken to illustrate the bad effects of old-style Calvinism, but this intention became secondary to its story of an exemplary orphan. Jane Elton's once-rich father dies bankrupt when she is twelve; her pious, passive mother, unequal to the demands of impoverished widowhood, follows a year later. Jane, happily, combines her mother's piety with a more energetic character and is able to succeed in a difficult life as her more traditional mother could not. She goes to live with an aunt, Mrs. Wilson, who has no interest in the child besides the free labor she will provide. An old-school Calvinist, Mrs. Wilson occupies herself with religious formalities and neglects good works. Her badly raised children are lazy, self-indulgent, and dishonest. Jane submits to exploitation in this nasty household but refuses to be morally intimidated. She discovers that, however distasteful the tasks assigned her, constant industry drives away melancholy. She prevails upon her reluctant aunt to send her to the local school. A star pupil there, she is offered the position of assistant teacher but turns it down since she is not yet of age. However, when Mrs. Wilson accuses her of stealing—a deliberately face-saving accusation designed to shield the true, known culprit, her son—Jane responds to this aggression by moving out and taking the teaching job.

Edward Erskine, a promising young lawyer who is the community's most eligible bachelor, despite or because of his rather loose living habits, helps Jane settle herself in lodgings, and when he proposes to her she accepts him, partly from gratitude and partly because he is considered such a good catch. She excels as a teacher and soon becomes disenchanted with Edward. Realizing that she cannot respect or love him, she breaks the engagement, resisting his promises to reform and his pleas for her support. Her gesture repeats her earlier repudiation of a conventional dependency and her assertion of moral autonomy. Having no other husband in view, she prepares for a single life.

The story ends with her marriage to Mr. Lloyd, a wealthy, middle-aged Quaker widower who had settled, with his two daughters, in Jane's village, buying her parents' house. All at once Jane gets husband, comfort, children, and the home of her childhood with its implicit opportunity to recover what has been lost and rectify her parents' errors. The point is not that, by marrying a father-surrogate, Jane remains a little girl; on the contrary, by marrying an older man with children, Jane becomes a mother and

an adult. She and Mr. Lloyd will provide for his children the
home that Jane's parents did not provide for her.

Lloyd, for his part, has been attracted to Jane by the strength
and independence she showed when she left her aunt and broke
her engagement. The gestures that showed she was willing to live
alone have won her a good husband. Three points emerge from a
reading of this story. First, because moral principle is the core of
Jane's nature, principled action becomes the source of self-respect,
and Jane's insistence on maintaining her self-respect, even when it
leads to such "unwomanly" behavior as leaving her aunt and
breaking an engagement, is applauded by the author. Second,
self-regard leads Jane to demand an education, which is presented
as the practical path to independence for women. Finally, the
love story is deliberately antiromantic, rejecting a conventionally
attractive male whose very conventionality disqualifies him for a
mutual marriage relation. Mr. Lloyd lacks Edward's appeal, but
he shares Jane's values and behaves toward her with consistent
respect as opposed to Edward's alternating idolatry and tyranny.

Sedgwick narrates this simple story in the effectively plain style
that she maintained throughout her career, even though her
novels grew larger and more complex. *Redwood* has many more
characters and several subplots and aims for a wide social picture
encompassing rich and poor, rustic and urban. Its core story is
another version of the exemplary heroine's triumph, contrasting
a young woman who is morally principled and self-dependent
with an antiheroine, whose dependent vanity changes, under
pressure, into spite, deceitfulness, and evildoing. The story begins
in medias res as a carriage accident forces Mr. Redwood, a
middle-aged man of Byronic mannerisms, and his spoiled, frivolous
daughter, Caroline, to take refuge in a Vermont farmhouse where
Mr. Lenox lives with his unmarried sister, "Aunt Debby." The
heroine, Ellen Bruce, is living temporarily with Farmer Lenox,
and the group is soon augmented by the arrival of the socialite
Mrs. Westall and her paragon son Charles. Redwood and Mrs.
Westall hope that their children will marry, but Charles compares

Caroline's petty egoism to Ellen's large-souled nature and falls in love with the latter, despite her obscure parentage.

Ellen's mother, who had died in the girl's infancy, had concealed the father's identity in a letter not to be opened until Ellen came of age or got engaged. She left Ellen to a friend, Mrs. Allen, a plain, practical farmer's wife. A wealthy, childless neighbor also took an interest in the girl, and the two women shared Ellen's upbringing. Between them, Sedgwick explains, "there was a system of checks and balances that produced that singular and felicitous union of diversity of qualities which constituted the rare perfection of Ellen's character. Mrs. Harrison communicated her taste and skill in drawing, her knowledge of french and italian and all those arts of female handicraft that were the fashion of her day" along with an interest in history and poetry. "When she might have been in danger of an exclusive taste for the occupations of those who have the privilege of independence and leisure, she returned to Mrs. Allen to take her lessons in practical life, to share and lighten the domestic cares of her good friend, and to acquire those household arts that it might be the duty of her station to perform, and which it is the duty of every station to understand." The phrase "checks and balances" conveys Sedgwick's bias against the self-indulgent heroine of sensibility.

Ellen spends little time contemplating her own feelings; she has learned to be happy in advancing the happiness of others. As one character says of her, "instead of talking about her own feelings and thinking about them, you would not know she had any, if you did not see she always knew just how other people felt." These words are spoken by a servant, and the admiration and affection of servants is always taken, in fiction of this type, as a sign of a character's moral worth. In a series of incidents, Ellen shows her benevolence and magnanimity: she persuades a blind girl to submit to a delicate operation that restores her sight; she rescues Caroline from a boating mishap; and, in an extended subplot she and Aunt Debby rescue one of Mrs. Allen's daughters, who has run away to join the Shakers and been abducted by the community's embezzling manager. Unconventional but unwaveringly moral, she is in every sense a "hero."

The worthier Ellen seems to Charles and to Redwood, the angrier Caroline becomes; finally she unscrupulously enters Ellen's room, breaks into the girl's trunk and opens the letter from Ellen's mother. To her great distress, she reads there that Ellen is Redwood's daughter by an early, secret marriage. Horrified by the realization that Ellen is not only her rival for Charles but for her father and half her fortune as well, Caroline removes the letter and reseals the empty envelope. Thus, when Ellen, having accepted Charles's proposal, prepares to read her letter, she finds nothing. Of course she is deeply disturbed, but since her parentage means nothing to Charles, Caroline's scheme does not achieve its intention. Subsequently, the truth comes out and Caroline's conniving is exposed. Contrite but unimproved, she marries a fortune-hunting army officer and goes with him to the West Indies, soon to die of a fever. Ellen gets husband, father, name, and fortune; she repays her father's abandonment of her mother with filial affection.

In this gesture she shows the superiority of the nineteenth-century morality to that of the eighteenth, and of a world managed by women to one ruled by men. For the striking point about her upbringing is less that it consisted of checks and balances than that it has been exclusively carried out by women. Her dying mother, hiding her father's identity from her until maturity, had deliberately removed his influence from her life. We see what that influence might have done to her by observing the character of the daughter he has raised. Mrs. Allen, Mrs. Harrison, Aunt Debby—these strong, independent, variously talented women have been Ellen's mentors. She has been rescued from the patriarchy. When united with her father, she accepts him into her home and her world, rather than becoming an inhabitant of his, and Redwood for the first time in his life finds peace. The mythos is clear: the modern age is to be woman's age, an age of virtue, family harmony, and love.

After writing her acclaimed historical fiction *Hope Leslie,*

Sedgwick returned to the contemporary scene and woman's fiction with *Clarence,* which like its two predecessors centers on a self-dependent and stable woman. *Clarence* embodies a double contrast, between the heroine Gertrude Clarence and her friend Emilie Layton, and between Gertrude and Emilie's mother. Gertrude's active, decisive, practical nature is contrasted to Emilie's timid and self-destructive passivity; her solid value system to Mrs. Layton's mercenary worldiness. Rather than opposing a matriarchal to a patriarchal ethos, *Clarence* opposes the urban, commercial world to the rural world of natural values. In a long prologue, the country-city dichotomy is expressed in the story of Mr. Clarence's tragic acquisition of wealth. For as he gains a great fortune he neglects his family; he ignores the illness of a beloved son, and the son dies. When his wife dies soon after, the embittered man retires with his daughter Gertrude to the country, determined to save her from the temptations that ruined him.

As a young woman, Gertrude has become an ideal character, "a fit heroine for the nineteenth century; practical, efficient, direct, and decided—a rational woman" who yet "loved to abandon herself to the visions of her imagination" and "gave her faith to the poetry of love." Like Ellen the product of checks and balances, Gertrude negotiates between the poetry and prose of existence. Her country rearing has given Gertrude the moral acuity to see through the artifices and pretense of complex city life. Her great fortune poses no temptations to her, and she perceives and deals with the attractions it holds for others. Her view of human nature is realistic without being bitter; like Ellen, she enjoys doing good for others. The novel gives many instances of her capabilities and her magnanimity in both the country and the city; its chief story concerns Gertrude's rescue of her unfortunate friend Emilie from a mercenary marriage engineered by her spendthrift parents. Heavily in debt to him, the Laytons agree to the suit of Pedrillo, an alleged Spanish nobleman who has taken credulous New York by storm. (In a revised issue of the novel in 1849, Sedgwick observed that New Yorkers had grown too sophisticated to be taken in by this sort of imposture.) Emilie loves a deserving young southerner, but lacks the fortitude to oppose her parents. Her behavior, which might have been praised as filial virtue, is treated by Sedgwick with contempt, although she pities rather than blames Emilie. Observing her friend's inability to act for herself, Gertrude acts for her, first by offering to pay the Laytons' debts and then, when Pedrillo refuses the money, by literally abducting the girl away from him at a masked ball. As in *Redwood*, the conventionally male prerogative of rescue is given to a woman.

Like Mr. Clarence's tragedy, Emilie's plight illustrates the incompatibility of a system of love and one of money and exploitation. Mr. Layton is a contemptible character while his wife is charming and intelligent, but both are so corrupted by worldliness that they have forgotten their responsibilities to Emilie as their daughter and as a human being. At first attracted to Mrs. Layton's wit and beauty, Gertrude quickly comes to perceive the calculation that underlies the older woman's actions, and withdraws from her. (She is not so obtuse as Isabel Archer, in a similar situation.) She observes on repeated social occasions that there is no happiness in a society organized to acquire and display wealth, but only excitement, a miserable substitute. The emptiness and insecurity of fashionable life are satirically exposed in *Clarence* and the family system strongly affirmed. But even more strongly the novel affirms the independent self.

Emilie's story also shows that male lust is inherently an exploitive passion. Pedrillo's purely lustful attraction to the young girl is contrasted with the respectful affection of her southern sweetheart. This proper feeling is not the same as romantic love, which is broadly satirized in a subplot involving the obsession of a romantic painter, Louis Seton, for Gertrude. Romantic love, like lust, is an egotistic passion and it is dismissed in Seton's example as a mental illness. Right feeling implies appreciation of and respect for the integrity of the other. Such feelings are a tribute to the woman who inspires them, as lust and romantic infatuation are not. A woman is rather insulted than flattered by expression of lust in a man and responds appropriately with distancing, self-protective behavior.

At the end of the novel Gertrude marries a young lawyer, son of a rich man who died bankrupt. Determined to make his way back to economic security on merit, this young man adamantly refuses to approach any rich, marriageable woman. The "romance" of the novel follows Gertrude as she successfully conceals her identity until this man, whom she desires for a husband, comes to love her for herself. In the management of her love life, as in everything else, Gertrude is in complete control.

The three woman's novels that Sedgwick wrote within eight years share a strong heroine who has much to teach her readers but nothing to learn herself. The novel's events show her character to readers but leave that character unaltered. Though the background of each heroine is different, all share the core of moral firmness that makes them responsive to but independent of circumstances. These heroines are rational rather than pious, and clearly developed as an alternative to the legacy of sensibility. Woman's fiction written after Sedgwick tended to be influenced by a romantic ideology; although it did not revert to sensibility, it put a stress on psychological struggle and the inner life completely lacking in these novels by Sedgwick. Typical woman's fiction of the fifties featured a faulty heroine who worked through to a strength and composure she did not have at the outset. In her last novel, *Married or Single?*, published some twenty-seven years after *Clarence*, Sedgwick showed an awareness of the trend in woman's fiction and created, for the only time, a flawed heroine.

When the novel opens, Grace Herbert, eighteen years old, passionate, and self-centered, is living with her sister Eleanor (who is older by a year) in an odd household made up of their worldly stepmother Mrs. Clayton, her equally worldly daughter Ann, and their uncle William, an unworldly widower. The novel begins by surveying the unhappy marriages of the parental generation:

Uncle William's sickly wife had neglected their child, who died early; Aunt Sarah married a handsome profligate who, in a state of drunkenness, killed himself and their son by overturning their carriage (drunken driving appears to have been as common in the nineteenth century as it is today). The first marriage of Grace and Eleanor's father had been happy, but he had little in common with Mrs. Clayton, his second wife, and his death left her in charge of two girls whose temperaments were more complex, and values more sound, than her own. This survey picks up the question posed in the novel's title and answered in its preface: ought one to marry? The answer is, better no marriage than a bad one.

However, the real story of the book dwells less on the question than perhaps Sedgwick intended. It follows Grace as she learns to overcome her fondness for material luxury and social status, and tells how, in so learning, she becomes capable of a good marriage. Though not rich, the sisters are of good family, and have a busy social life. Eleanor is a pattern of sweetness and self-discipline—rather a more submissive character than Sedgwick would have approved of earlier—and she contrasts with her tempestuous sister who naturally assumes the center of the stage and feels that she belongs there. An example of her self-absorption is Grace's assumption early in the novel that the popular young minister Frank Everly is coming to the house to court her, when in fact he is in love with Eleanor. But her essential goodness and flexibility are manifest in her ready, generous acceptance of the truth and her rueful amusement at her own folly.

Eleanor marries Frank and sets up house with him, carrying out the role of conventional wife to perfection. Grace continues to live an idle showy social life for several years. Since she has no money of her own, she must either make a wealthy marriage or drop out of society, and though its empty rituals do not content her, she is too fond of status and display to accept obscurity. (Here, as elsewhere in Sedgwick's writing, we locate patterns that were to influence Henry James.) With mixed feelings, she consents to marry Horace Copley, the city's most eligible bachelor. The reader knows, but Grace does not, that he has seduced a number of servant girls; one particularly pathetic episode of this sort has formed a subplot. Grace does learn, however, of his dalliance with a wealthy woman, Mrs. Tallis, who, overcome with remorse when her neglected little girl dies, enlightens Grace as to Copley's character. Sedgwick endeavors to show that Grace's immediate repudiation of Copley is not jealousy but instinctive morality. Most young women in New York would not censure such behavior in a man. But Grace sees at once that such tolerance implies profound social corruption. Her sympathies are rightly with the victimized woman, and she tries to console Mrs. Tallis and encourages a reconciliation between her and her husband.

She withdraws from society now and goes to live with Eleanor, giving music and drawing lessons to support herself and to contribute to the economy of her sister's growing family. Since she gets a fine husband at the end, the purpose announced in the preface—to dignify spinsterhood—is not carried through in *Married or Single?*, although to be sure Grace is in her mid-twenties when she marries. *Married or Single?* argues rather that a woman should never marry for social prestige or financial security, and asserts that by developing the emotional independence and practical skill to support herself, she will be free to marry only for motives of affection and respect. Because good men appreciate strong and independent women, such behavior is paradoxically more likely to lead to a good match than orthodox husband hunting.

Although no other woman writing in the 1820s and 1830s achieved Sedgwick's stature or rivaled her accomplishment, these decades were marked by the entrance of many women into the profession of literature. However, publishing at this time was a risky business, and novel-publishing especially so. The chief places to publish were in the gift-books, annuals, and magazines; hence women who were writing for money would more likely produce short pieces than novels. Two of the most successful prose writers—Emily C. Judson (1817–1854), who wrote as "Fanny Forester," and Sara Jane Lippincott (1823–1904), who signed herself "Grace Greenwood,"—composed exclusively in short forms; their collected sketches—*Alderbrook* (1847) and *Greenwood Leaves* (1850) respectively—were best-selling books. Sarah Josepha Hale, widowed and with five children to support, began her literary career with a very good local-color novel, *Northwood: A Tale of New England,* in 1827. (Its 1852 reissue added material on slavery and changed the subtitle, misleadingly, to "Life North and South.") A year after this promising beginning she took an editorial position and, though she wrote an occasional long fiction, her energies turned away from novels. As editor for several decades of *Godey's Lady's Book* she was one of the most important literary figures of her time—but not as a novelist.

One other woman, Margaret Bayard Smith, wrote significant novels in the twenties. She was a Washington wife and hostess known in her day for lively letters that were later collected and that constitute a primary source of information about social life during Jefferson's administration. Her two anonymously published novels, *A Winter in Washington* (1824) and *What is Gentility?* (1828), articulate a conservative feminine ethic strikingly different from Sedgwick's. Smith is one of the very few woman writers of the time who looked for a pattern of feminine behavior in the past. *A Winter in Washington* combines set descriptions of social life in the capital city during Jefferson's presidency, with an episodic and melodramatic plot loosely cohering around the Seymour family. Its organizing theme is the threat posed to republican virtue by the importation of foreign social life. Since women manage the social life, their behavior has national as well as personal significance. Mrs. Seymour, who is likened to a Roman matron in virtue, contrasts to her niece Mrs. Mortimer, a modern, free-living belle.

When Mrs. Seymour objects to her frivolous and indecorous conduct, Mrs. Mortimer responds, "Is not this the grand purpose of all the labour bestowed on our education? From our very infancy, are we not taught the necessity of *pleasing?* and why is this so? Because nature has so ordained it. To please, is to govern. Beauty was given to *our* sex—strength to the other; it is ours to please—it is theirs to protect. . . . Let us not complain of our weakness, since kind nature has attached to it a charm more powerful than masculine strength could impart." In turn, Mrs. Seymour answers that beauty is a "fragile" power. If they wish lifelong influence over men, she says, women must secure masculine respect and esteem by virtuous behavior. "By this would they establish that equality, for which they now contend in vain; and instead of being the toys, the playthings, and the victims of men, would become their companions, their friends, and their advisers." Mrs. Mortimer may think herself a liberated woman, but beneath the superficial social freedoms she continues in the traditional relation to men: dependent and scorned.

The belle's behavior is nationally as well as personally destructive, for "importing the fashions, we import the manners of European courts; and if the evil is not checked, it will sap the very foundations of society, and injure not only our social, but even our political institutions." This looks progressive enough, except that in the context of resisting European influences, *A Winter in Washington* calls for a return to old-fashioned Colonial patterns of feminine behavior rather than making new claims for education, moral independence, and autonomy. The author suggests therefore that woman's proper place in society has already been defined and attained.

This argument recurs in her second, better constructed novel. *What is Gentility?* asserts that the great opportunity of American life is the chance to become educated rather than the chance to make money, and that education is the appropriate criterion for assessing social rank. But then it argues against educating women. "In the arithmetic of society, woman is a quantity—man is the denominator, which gives to that quantity its value," Smith writes, finding nothing wrong with the situation thus described.

Her novel contrasts the effects of education on two children of the newly-rich McCarty family, Charles and Catharine. After four years away at school, Charles returns home an educated, sensitive, democratic man. He hunts out congenial friends regardless of their wealth, and marries the lovely Lydia Tilton, sister of a self-educated carpenter. In due time he becomes an ambassador, and at each stage of his progress Lydia acquires the social and intellectual graces that are necessary for her station.

At the same time, boarding-school education has turned Catharine into a superficially accomplished but restless and snobbish young woman who spends all her time shopping for clothes, attending fashionable parties, and searching for a socially prominent husband. The upper ranks resign themselves to her presence at their parties, but scorn her pretentions; she is finally left a discontented old maid. "Women are domestic creatures," Smith writes, "and unless their habits and their tastes are conformable to their condition, the acquisition of knowledge, in itself valuable, often proves a source of more suffering, than enjoyment." But Smith does not prove her case, for Catharine is clearly as ignorant after her education as she had been before it. The author does not note that Catharine's "fashionable" education, specifically designed for the current conception of the feminine mind, was altogether different from Charles's, and that her contrast between the effect of education on women and on men is therefore invalid. The type of education Catharine received may well have been responsible for her later frivolity and discontent—this general point was perceived and acted upon by many of the educational reformers who argued that women should be educated in precisely the same way as men. Smith, however, argues that women should receive their education at home, so that their home-roots will never be disturbed. Her work provides a contrast by which we can better perceive the progressive element in most woman's fiction. Unlike most of the woman authors, she was not a true professional and she did not write for money—facts that may somewhat account for her rather different approach to woman's situation, although of course Sedgwick's example shows that progressive attitudes toward education were not confined to the needy.

To try to succeed financially with a long fiction in the 1830s and 1840s was to take a great risk, and hence the women who wrote novels either did not need money (like Sedgwick and Smith) or—much more common—also engaged in other literary tasks: writing short pieces and verse, compiling anthologies, producing domestic manuals, cookbooks, or books of etiquette. One such multifaceted professional who wrote some interesting longer fictions was Caroline Howard Gilman (1794–1888), a New Englander by birth and upbringing who relocated after her marriage in 1819, to Charleston, South Carolina. Gilman had been raised by relatives (her father died when she was three and her mother when she was ten). After a decade of constant childbearing—she had seven children, three of whom died in infancy— she founded the *Rose-Bud*, a children's magazine, in 1832. This developed into a general magazine, the *Southern Rose*, in 1835 and ran for four more years. Gilman wrote most of the content of these magazines, as well as additional short stories, verse, travel literature, and the like. She edited several compilations and wrote three novels, two of which were quite popular: *Recollections of a Housekeeper* in 1834 (retitled *Recollections of a New-England Housekeeper* in a later edition) and *Recollections of a Southern Matron* in 1838. In an autobiographical sketch that was anthologized in Hart's *Female Prose Writers of America* (1852), she observed that "on the publication of the 'Recollections of a New England Housekeeper,' I received thanks and congratulations from every quarter, and I attribute its popularity to the fact that it was the first attempt, in that particular mode, to enter into the recesses of American homes and hearths, the first unveiling of what I may call the altar of the Lares in our *cuisine*. . . . My ambition has never been to write a novel. . . . The story is a mere hinge for facts."

And indeed the *Housekeeper*, a small-format volume running to 155 pages in its first edition and supposedly authored by "Mrs.

Clarissa Packard," has very little story. Narrated in the first person, it gives a brief account of Mrs. Packard's girlhood in a New England village and then follows her to Boston when, at age seventeen, she marries a rising young lawyer. The book's focus, implied in the title, is on the wife's work of running her husband's house. Written in a style of exquisite clarity and spareness, the work gives a vivid picture of domestic routines in the early nineteenth century. (Like Sedgwick and many other women writers, Gilman wrote in a style nothing like the florid and rhapsodic rhetoric attributed to women writers of the time by later male critics.) The *Housekeeper's* attitudes toward housekeeping are ambivalent. In part the book joins the developing movement to give housework the status of a profession, by assuring the housewife that what she does is a work of dignity and importance, and also by giving her extensive advice on how to manage her household rationally and efficiently and thus lighten her labors. In part, however, it counters this very movement by idealizing a society in which housework would be carried out by catering companies, window-washing services, laundries—trained people located outside the home.

Such a system would free the housewife from chores and leave her to her more important domestic responsibilities as wife, mother, companion, and hostess. Even more important, it would free her from servants.

Even with two servants—necessary in an era of wood-burning stoves, pumped water, and daily bread baking and pudding making—Mrs. Packard had to do a great deal of work herself. And she invested many frustrating hours in supervising a succession of servants who demonstrated varying temperaments and training. The *Housekeeper* unfolds as a sort of domestic picaresque, in which a parade of unruly and incompetent servants files through the orderly setting of Mrs. Packard's tidy Boston home. Because she manages as well as any woman can, her call for the true professionalizing of household services is meant to convince. A wife "has enough to do, with the agitating responsibility of her maternal cares; her little ones may be sickly, her own health feeble. Many a woman breaks and sinks beneath the wear and tear of the frame and the affections." Servants, who should lighten the load, often impose additional burdens. We may put these remarks in the general context of bad diet, indifferent hygiene, lack of exercise, and poorly designed clothing within which the nineteenth-century woman had to carry out her role. And we may put them in the context of Gilman's own experience as a woman who had lost her mother when she was ten, and three of her children before they were ten. A housewife can learn, to be sure, to manage her chores, her time, and her servants efficiently; but at its lightest, hers is a heavy lot.

The importance of servants in Mrs. Packard's life reminds us of the middle-class orientation of the women authors. Although they often show servant women as strong, admirable, and necessary auxiliary characters, they never use them as protagonists. Upward mobility is the heroine's destiny, but the upward rise of servants when it occurs is an occasion for satire rather than celebration. Our authors are not selfishly motivated here by the wish to keep servants in their places—they believe that circumstance or inherent capacity have created real differences. Some authors seem to believe that most people in the working classes are inherently coarse-textured (although exceptions are always possible), while others attribute to environment the shaping of the working-class character. But whether nature or nurture, it takes a strong hold on the personality. The servant girl who comes from a background of abysmal poverty, learns habits of order and efficiency from her middle-class mistress, and goes on to marry a rising tradesman, replicates the heroine's progress to some extent but on a far more modest scale: class exercises a greater limitation on potential than gender. A range of virtues is permitted to the servant woman: fidelity, bravery, stoicism. She may be endowed with acuity and pithy rhetoric. Her relation to the heroine may often be an important source of comfort and support for the latter. She herself, however, cannot become a heroine, although the possibility is not foreclosed for her daughters or granddaughters. She will best succeed in life herself not by aspiring upward, but by aspiring to be a good servant. Was this attitude snobbery, social realism, or self-fulfilling prophecy? Whichever it might be, it meant that women's aspirations had to be appropriate to their original station in life—their class.

The title *Recollections of a Southern Matron* suggests that it is a companion to the *Housekeeper*, and so it may have been intended. But it is much more a novel, a story of girlhood on a southern plantation that breaks different ground from Gilman's earlier work. Most southern fiction before Gilman's novel, by such authors as Robert Montgomery Bird, John Pendleton Kennedy, and William Caruthers, was thoroughly masculine in its orientation, with the women in minor, stereotyped roles. With *Southern Matron*, the novel of southern womanhood came into being. The prefatory intention, "to present as exact a picture as possible of local habits and manners," is subordinated to the presentation of a young woman growing up through the agency of three loves. In childhood she idolizes her saintly Christian tutor who dies of tuberculosis; in adolescence she is briefly drawn to the passion and impetuosity of the neighboring planter's son; in womanhood, she falls in love with and marries a man who tempers his masculine force with morality and control. This tripartite division of men is rare in woman's fiction; women far more often than men are assigned the role of holy invalid. However, fiction regularly represents the stages of woman's growth by the men she loves; and the contrast of men along the lines of passion and control is characteristic of American Victorianism.

Gilman's third novel, *Love's Progress* (1840), begins as a sort of fictionalized text on child development, depicting the phases of a child's maturing in a New England village. But the chronicle of Ruth Raymond's normal development veers abruptly into melodrama when she reaches the age of eighteen, for then her mother dies and her father becomes a maniac. As a devoted daughter Ruth must dedicate herself to her father even though it means sacrificing her fiancé. The action climaxes at Trenton Falls (a favorite scenic spot in early woman's fiction—Sedgwick had also staged exciting scenes here) where father and lover battle for the girl. Ruth and her father fall into the water and the father is swept away.

This bizarre plotting depicts a father's attachment to his daughter so intense that she cannot marry without a violent sundering of ties. Some might wish to see in this fantasy the projection of a woman's unconscious incestuous wishes onto the father, but the story is better interpreted as the intensified representation of a father's possessive jealousy and the basic equivalence, from the woman's point of view, of the father and the husband. The book closes with these significant words of comfort spoken by the fiancé: "I have traced the self-sacrificing *progress* of your heart's *love* through life's varied duties, and I know that the tender *daughter* will be the faithful *wife*." The identity of father and husband is asserted in the suitor's paternal tone and in the balanced phrasing. Although the tyranny of fathers over daughters is a staple in woman's fiction, only Gilman attributed that tyranny to love. In most cases, the father's tyranny represents a failure of love, his habit of regarding his daughter as a thing, a possession, rather than a human being to be esteemed.

The great Panic of 1837 gave new impetus to the developing idea that women needed preparation for more than home and marriage. After that terrible year an episode of financial reversal and an interlude of self-support became virtually obligatory in woman's fiction. Many works of the years immediately following addressed themselves directly to the Panic. Hannah Farnham Sawyer Lee (1780–1865), who had been widowed at the age of thirty-six and left to raise three daughters, began a successful literary career as author of instructive fictions when she was fifty-two. Her timely *Three Experiments of Living* (1837) was an enormous success. It is a sequence of three tales showing the rise and fall of the Fulton family. "Living within the Means" shows Jane and Frank living frugally while he establishes himself as a

72   WOMAN'S FICTION

physician. In "Living up to the Means" their growing success has
engendered worldly ambition and consequent lavish spending. In
"Living beyond the Means," Dr. Fulton gives up his practice and
turns to the more lucrative fields of business and speculation; the
Panic ruins them on the eve of their daughter Elinor's social
debut, an event that had been planned as the capstone of the
social season.

Hannah Lee blames both Fultons equally for greed and poor
judgment. Financial disaster is a just punishment, and thus the
Panic becomes a rational event instead of an irrational catastrophe.
The little volume—143 pages in its first edition—went through
thirty American and English editions, and its sequel, *Elinor
Fulton*, of more concern to this study, called for eleven editions
before the year was out. *Elinor Fulton*, also published in 1837,
equalled *Three Experiments* in length. It demonstrates the heroism of the daughter—she whose debut was never held—as she
rises to the needs of her distressed family. Dr. Fulton has gone
west to resume his profession and accumulate the means to pay
off his creditors; Mrs. Fulton and her two daughters live in lodgings. Mrs. Fulton, passive and complaisant, provides occasion for
another critique of the alleged eighteenth-century feminine ideal.
Women like her are "frail barks, made for the smooth waters of a
summer's sea. Woman has her part to perform as well as man,
nor is it one of less vigorous principle." The younger daughter
Julia is still a child, so the burden of running the family falls
entirely on Elinor. The young woman's character unites "resolution and firmness with the yielding disposition of her mother, but
her strength lay in her uncompromising sense of duty." Aided by a
servant of about her own age, whose intractable temper had been
turned to firm loyalty by fair and friendly treatment, Elinor
manages the household finances and gives piano lessons that bring
in enough to maintain the little establishment in frugal respectability. After several years Dr. Fulton returns, clear of debt, to
resume the headship of his family, and both his daughters make
good marriages. But the focus of the story is its community of

women, functioning without men as an economic unit and a complete family. Although the author sees no professions open to women beyond teaching and running boarding houses (she strongly advises that women be trained for business) she manages to make financial exigency appear as a challenge to feminine abilities.

Although her achievement was slight, Emma Catherine Embury (1806–1863) was a well-known literary figure in her time. Married to a successful New York banker, she ran a literary salon that included Poe, Rufus W. Griswold, and others, until an illness in 1848 put an end to her social life. Her most famous work is the long story *Constance Latimer, or The Blind Girl* (1838), which retells Elinor Fulton's story in a more emotional mode. The story was written to benefit a newly founded institution for the blind, and featured a blind heroine, but Embury used this popular image, developed (for example) in Lydia H. Sigourney's poetry as a type of protected, passive, and spiritual femininity, as an example instead of woman's capacity for strength and independence. The Latimers are an immensely wealthy family suddenly undone by tragedy. Scarlet fever kills the older son and blinds Constance, the daughter, when she is six; a few years later the Panic makes them poor. The first event destroys the health and mental equanimity of the mother; the father is similarly afflicted by the loss of his fortune. Constance, who had been sent to a school for the blind before the family became poor, now shows her mettle. She assists her father with his accounts as he tries to make sense of his disordered finances; she weaves and works household decorations to beautify their poor lodgings, and she gives music lessons that earn $1500 per year. Gradually, Latimer works his way back to comfort—not affluence—and Constance is relieved of her burden. Refusing marriage because she is blind (though a most eligible young man proposes), she has demonstrated that even the seemingly most helpless woman need not be protected from the real world or consigned to lifelong dependency.

Eliza Lee Cabot Follen (1787–1867), a Bostonian, lived with

her parents and then with two sisters until her marriage in 1824, when she was thirty-seven years old. Her husband, Charles Follen, nine years younger than she, was a political refugee from Germany who taught at Harvard until his abolitionist views cost him his job. After his death in a steamboat accident in 1840, Follen devoted herself to a literary career. She wrote many books for children, and edited the *Child's Friend,* a juvenile magazine, from 1843 to 1850. Her best known work for adults, *Sketches of Married Life* (1838), argues that feminine independence is not incompatible with, indeed is necessary for, a good marriage. She contrasts, in the mode of a moral tale, a good marriage between two equal and self-respecting people with a bad one based on the traditional submissive-dominant pattern where deceit and withholding is the norm.

Fanny Herbert and William Roberts are both wealthy; their happiness has no external impediments, but secretiveness and role-playing lead to increasing coldness, distrust, and virtual rupture. On the other hand, Amy Weston and Edward Seldon encounter every sort of external obstacle before and after marriage, but their self-respect and mutual esteem keep them intimate and happy. Amy, who "was so heterodox as to believe that mind was of no sex," devotes herself to useful projects, her most important being the establishment of a day-care center so that poor mothers whose husbands are "dead, vicious, absent, or sick" can go out to work. Edward—who had lost his money, settled with his creditors, and then earned his fortune back again—searches out his creditors and repays them cent for cent. In their active and benevolent lives, each values the other; and unlike Fanny, Amy thinks highly of herself. She does what she thinks right regardless of how it looks to the world, and is not afraid to let herself be known as she is to her husband. In turn, he values her for her strength and honesty. Fanny, who lives the conventional foolish life of a fashionable woman, craves affection but fears that her husband will reject her if he should know her "whole foolish heart," her "whole whimsical and faulty character." But she finds no peace in the thought that he loves her for qualities she only pretends to have. The message seems to be that only the woman with a strong ego can have a happy marriage. This too is Sedgwick's message, and it signifies a changing view of women.

Sarah Hale, whose authorship of *Northwood* has been noted above, turned in 1828 to editorial work, to short pieces, and to anthologies. Her writing career eventually produced more than twenty-five books and unnumbered uncollected pieces. *Flora's Interpreter* was one of the most popular of many dictionaries of floral meanings and quotations, with more than twenty printings; her *Complete Dictionary of Poetical Quotations* also circulated widely. She wrote gift books for children, a household manual, a cookbook, etiquette books, several volumes of short stories, and the ambitious *Woman's Record,* an encyclopedia of famous women and their achievements from ancient times to the present. It is no wonder that she had little time for long fiction; three little moral tales for women comprise her total output.

The Lecturess, or Woman's Sphere (1839), is the earliest anti-feminist fiction that I have found. In the first part of the 124-page novel, the woman's righter Marian Gayland wins a noble husband, William Forrester, even though she is a "lecturess" and he has a particular prejudice against the type. At first she rejects his proposal, but when her previously successful lecture tour meets hostility in the South, and she lies sick in a hotel room, it appears to her that her motives after all were not to "raise her *sex,* but to manifest her *own* superiority." Chastened by this insight, she retires from public life to become a good wife.

In the second part of the story she destroys her marriage by stubbornly attending a series of lectures delivered by a woman despite her husband's disapproval. Her husband rejects her; defiantly, she returns to lecturing herself. Forrester thereupon leaves her permanently and she dies, lonely and sick, with these words for other women who might be tempted to behave as she did: "Approaching death taught me that true pride, true independence in a woman, is to fill the place which her God assigns her; to make her husband's happiness her own; and to yield her will to his in all things, conformable to her duty to a higher power. By such conduct will a woman attain her *rights*—the affection of her husband, the respect of her children and the world, and the approval of Heaven." Forrester is faulted for his stiff-necked coldness toward his erring wife—forgiving warmth would have brought her back to him, contrite and happy to be forgiven. Yet much the greater blame attaches to Marian for her stubbornness. The model husband-wife relationship requires forebearance from the husband and obedience from the wife, carrying into adulthood the pattern of a parent-child relation.

The Lecturess is structurally discontinuous, since its second part, concerned with the principles of a good marriage, could have used any kind of wifely defiance as its occasion. Even more important, however, Marian's dying words do not address themselves to the issues she had raised as a speaker on woman's rights. For the stimulus to her early career had been the situation of her widowed mother, a seamstress. Marian "could not understand why a man should receive so much larger compensation for his labor than her mother, who rose daily with the sun, and worked incessantly till night, and then received in payment a paltry sum, scarcely enough to furnish them with bread." Clearly the right of a woman to her husband's affection is of no use to the poor exploited widow. Logic has been distorted by two of Hale's strong convictions: first, public display is inappropriate and counterproductive for women; second, agitation for suffrage was premature. For her, education for women was the more important and more timely cause. "We have said little of the Rights of Woman," editorialized the *Lady's Book* in January 1850. "But her first right is to education in its widest sense, and such education as will give her the full development of her personal, mental, and moral qualities. Having that, there will be no longer any question about her rights, and rights are liable to be perverted to wrongs when we are incapable of rightly exercising them."

In a pair of novellas, *Keeping House and Housekeeping* (1845) and *Boarding Out* (1846), Hale treated the profession of middle-class wife. In the first, she shows that a woman who ignores her domestic obligations is far less free than one who attends to them rationally. Mrs. Harley, the fashionably raised protagonist, leaves her household entirely to unsupervised servants who turn her home into chaos and severely strain her budget. As her home life deteriorates, she finds the pleasures of social life (to which all her time is devoted) increasingly empty. A large party that was to have established her as a social leader is a humiliating fiasco; home life is the only source of true pleasure. Under the guidance of her husband's aunt, Mrs. Harley takes control of her house and with it, her life. In *Boarding Out,* Hale shows dire consequences ensuing on the abandonment of home. When the Barclay family, previously affluent and happy, moves into lodgings to save Mrs. Barclay from the trials of running a household, personal tragedy and financial ruin follow almost immediately. At first a comedy of manners with the depiction of a variety of amusing mishaps in boardinghouse life, *Boarding Out* becomes a melodrama when a child dies and Mr. Barclay plunges into debt. Tampering with the family and home structure produces inevitable catastrophe.

One of the most technically accomplished of the morality fictions so common in the late thirties and early forties is *Girlhood and Womanhood* (1844), by a Mrs. A. J. Graves. Mrs. Graves (I have been unable to determine her dates) also wrote a popular treatise called *Woman in America,* which appeared in the same year. This is a fine example of the merging of a progressive view of woman's abilities and a stress on the need for education, self-respect, and self-dependence, with the conviction that woman could most effectively fulfill herself and realize her mission, in the home. The work celebrates feminine potential and attacks the training of women for instilling "errors, weaknesses, and foibles" in them from infancy. While *Woman in America* looks to a future when women will attain a far higher position in society than they now have, *Girlhood and Womanhood* is a gloss on the present that shows how miserable their current condition is.

"It is woman's lot to minister unto others. To fulfill this lot, she must learn to bear pain, sickness, and disappointment with patience and fortitude. . . . The numerous and pressing duties of domestic life, must be attended to, though her strength may fail under her constant and fatiguing exertions. . . . Let every mother think of these things, and . . . provide for [her daughter's] after duties, by instilling into her mind the necessity, and inculcating the practice of unshrinking fortitude and unwearying activity, of patient, uncomplaining endurance of pain." Whatever woman may hope for in the future, this is her reality in 1844 according to Mrs. Graves.

The work opens in a southern boarding school run by the admirable widow Mrs. Norville. The characters of a group of the schoolgirls are sketched and then a series of short narratives chronicle their later lives. The whole is unified by a first-person narrator who is one of the students. Orphaned on the eve of her graduation, this wealthy girl, Ellen Maitland, elects to stay with Mrs. Norville and, when the beloved teacher dies, assumes responsibility for educating her two sons. Ellen's happy spinsterhood and contented personality form the touchstone against which the various narratives of married misery are displayed, for whatever Mrs. Graves's intentions with this book may have been, she succeeds in showing that marriage, which is woman's destiny, is also her doom. Married life is a combination of fatiguing cares and dissatisfying encounters with men who, in general, are tyrannical, indifferent, or both. Only two of ten schoolgirls make happy marriages; for the rest marriage is a brief, convulsive nightmare from which they awaken when they are widowed or abandoned to build life anew with other stranded women— sisters, friends, or mothers. Because men on the average are selfish, shallow, and insensitive, Graves does not suggest that marriage will be improved if woman educates herself as a moral and intellectual being. On the contrary, the more large-souled the woman is, the greater her marital sufferings will be. "My mind became possessed of a settled conviction," Ellen writes of her decision to stay single, "that men as a race, are very fickle and capricious, and that their hearts are not worth the trouble of winning. . . . The fear of being called an 'old maid' has been the cause of more domestic misery than many are aware of. . . . The reasons for remaining unmarried are in many instances creditable to the head and heart of those who continue so." By sponsoring Mrs. Norville's boys (an opportunity available to any woman who desires it, because the world is so full of orphans) Ellen assures herself of the pleasures of motherhood and a home in her old age, without having to endure the miseries, frustrations, and submissions of wifehood. Graves's view of woman's lot leads to spinsterhood.

The writer of this time whose work probably most approximates the stereotype of the liberated woman author scourging other women back within limits is Louisa C. Tuthill (1799–1879). She was married at eighteen, widowed eight years later (during her marriage her husband was constantly in poor health), and left with four young children to support. Attracted to a writing career in girlhood (an attraction she had consciously resisted), she now turned to it for personal solace and livelihood. Eventually she wrote more than thirty books, a mix of household manuals, etiquette books, juvenile and moral tales, as well as, surprisingly, a *History of Architecture from the Earliest Times* (1848). Among her works are three fictions for women.

Each segment of *The Belle, the Blue, and the Bigot; or, Three Fields of Woman's Influence* (1844) contrasts appropriate and inappropriate feminine behavior. The belle makes her heartless conquests and ruins men's lives while the true-hearted woman thinks of the man's welfare and happiness before her own; the "blue" writes for personal fame while the true authoress writes for needed money and to do good. When she becomes successful enough to earn a surplus, she disburses it in charities. Finally, the bigot practices a formal and self-centered religion while the truly religious woman ignores forms and concentrates on the moral training and support of her children. In every case, self-serving behavior contrasts with behavior in the service of others. Whenever a woman does anything for herself or her own self-aggrandizement, she exceeds her sphere and dishonors her sex; the result is disaster to others and eventually to herself.

My Wife (1846) contrasts a terrible marriage contracted by husband and wife on the basis of money and beauty, with an idyllic one based on mutual respect and shared values. Unlike Follen's ideal in *Sketches of Married Life,* however, this one resembles John Ruskin's famous walled garden in its division of roles. The exemplary husband writes to a friend that "when I am absent during the day, and perplexed with the multitudinous cares of an extensive mercantile concern, my home rises before my mind's eye, like a beacon-light to the tempest-tossed mariner. The sweet, consoling thought, that I have such a haven of peace and love soothes and hushes my perturbed spirit." (Later in her career Tuthill read and admired Ruskin and edited two selections of his works.)

In 1856, on the tide of woman's fiction, Tuthill assayed a full-length novel, but *Reality, or The Millionaire's Daughter* retains such characteristics of the moral tale as synoptic narration and characters displayed only through their behavior and hence the work has an antique air. The story utilizes an "Elinor Fulton" formula. The heroine, Irene Hazlehill, with a dishonest, worldly father and a self-indulgent, morbidly religious invalid mother, is plunged into poverty and disgrace when her father commits suicide and leaves his wife and daughter bankrupt. This fall is a blessing, of course, for Irene finds that she can forget her own misery and experience active happiness by devoting herself to others. She moves herself and her mother into a rural cottage that she furnishes with exquisite taste on a minimal budget. The mother recovers her spirits and putters happily in the dairy and garden, while Irene diffuses her genial and refined influence around the neighborhood, instructing the local poor in needlework, domestic economy, religion, and morals. Irene's fall is greatly cushioned by the fact that she is not forced to work, and instead of becoming what it promised to be—a story of feminine independence and self support in the face of the "reality" of economic need—the book becomes a pastoral fantasy of woman's genteel influence.

In the second half of *Reality,* after Irene has married a talented architect, Tuthill's traditionalism takes over entirely. Woman's choice of a husband is, apparently, her last choice; thereafter her will must be subject to his. If she makes a bad choice—as does Irene's close friend Mary, who marries a drunkard—she must suffer until she dies; if she chooses well then she has no reason to wish for the right to assert her independence. The principle of woman's independence, Tuthill says, is absurd. "If a woman is governed by right principles, and acts conscientiously, a strong and cultivated intellect, and even a strong will, can do her no harm. . . . The female Quixotes, [however,] who have a 'special mission' to change the natural order of things, and assume dominion over our heads, instead of our hearts, are guilty of almost as great a folly as angels would be, were they to come down to earth, and mingle in the strife of one of our Presidential elections." These words, spoken by Irene's husband, receive the author's approval. Since the self-direction Irene has mastered in the first half of the novel is incompatible with blind submissiveness, she must spend the final chapters unlearning her earlier accomplishments. Although Tuthill's picture of marriage is happier than Graves's, it gives the like (though probably unintended) impression that the single woman lives a richer, fuller, and freer life than her married sister.

Susan Fenimore Cooper (1813–1894) achieved a critical success with her nature diary, *Rural Hours,* published in 1850. Daughter of the famous novelist, after his death in 1851 she devoted her literary energies to the perpetuation of his memory. In 1846 she published her only novel, a two-volume work called *Elinor Wyllys; or The Young Folk at Longbridge.* Pseudonymously

attributed to "Amabel Penfeather," it was said to be edited by
J. F. Cooper, who provided a tactless and characteristically bel-
ligerent preface, interesting for the bias it imposed on his
daughter's work. The author, he wrote, "has seen much of that
portion of the world with which a lady becomes acquainted, and
has seen that much under the most favorable circumstances. As
usually happens in such cases, her book will be found free from
exaggerations of every sort, and will be more likely to be well
received by persons of her own class, than by those who are less
familiar with its advantages." An insipid study of manners among
upstate New York gentry, the book features a heroine who is said
to be exemplary, but we see her only at balls, dinners, and parties,
and get little opportunity to judge.

Elinor is an orphan living with a wealthy and indulgent grandfather and aunt; her only trouble in life is that her cousin Jane is
very beautiful while she is very plain. Many heroines of domestic
fiction must number relative plainness among their handicaps, but
Susan Cooper is the only novelist who made lack of physical
charm the sole hardship. It is difficult to imagine that this minor
disadvantage could have enlisted the fierce reader sympathy that
most woman's fiction demands, and one is not surprised to find
that the book had no particular popularity.

Another book in the boarding-school genre was *Ida Norman;
or, Trials and Their Uses,* by Almira Hart Phelps (1793–1884),
a schoolmistress, a leader in woman's educational reform, and
younger sister of Emma Willard, who founded the Troy Female
Seminary in 1821. Phelps achieved considerable reputation as the
author of popular textbooks in science. Her botany text, published
in 1829, was the best known. She was principal at the Patapsco
Female Institute at Endicott's Mills, Maryland, from 1841 to
1856, a school of the same caliber as her sister's. *Ida Norman* was
originally written in 1846, in weekly installments to be read to the
students as lessons in moral instruction. It was published in 1848,
and reprinted in 1855 with a second volume.

Ida is the daughter of wealthy and worldly parents who have

totally neglected her education; consequently, she is a spoiled, self-indulgent young lady with atrocious manners and incapable of self-control. When her parents go to Europe on a diplomatic mission, she is sent to a boarding school run by the virtuous widow Mrs. Newton. The discipline she reluctantly undergoes there and her exposure to more democratic and egalitarian ideas serve her well when her mother dies abroad and her father, ruined and disgraced, runs off with an intriguing Frenchwoman. While her brother Louis goes to Europe to locate the disappeared father, Ida remains with Mrs. Newton and becomes a teacher in her school. Later, when Louis has brought Mr. Norman back and succeeded in vindicating his reputation and recovering his lost fortune, Ida takes her place as companion and support. (Much as Ida has improved over her former self, we may note the gulf between the possibilities open to her and those permitted to her brother.)

Like other fictions of the thirties and forties, *Ida Norman* asserts that a woman can depend on nothing but her own moral character, but it shares with only a few works of that time the device of a flawed protagonist whose character is changed for the better by her trials. Trials really do have their uses, as the subtitle suggests, in such fiction. The 1855 edition of the novel added a second, short volume, giving Ida a husband; but its advocacy of the single life for women is carried forward in a new character, Julia Selby. Julia had been a heartless coquette in Volume I but she is transformed into a reputable "blue" and teacher in Volume II. The futile quest for ballroom supremacy is followed by an awakening, and Julia funnels her personal ambition into a useful and self-satisfying form. Julia gets the novel's last words, as she writes to a friend about the general condition of women and her own particular situation. "I assert the right of every woman to marry, or not to marry; if she decides on the latter, I protest against her being considered as a victim to be commiserated;— would that it were not too often the case that pity is needed by the suffering ill-treated wife, who, in her servitude, loses all power to feel, much less to assert that she has any rights. Let those who are expending their sympathies upon southern slaves, think of the households where the unhappy wife is concealing in her heart's core wrongs known only to her Maker, and to him who inflicts them."

As a final example of the minor fiction of these earlier years we may look at Eliza Leslie's only novel, *Amelia* (1848). Leslie (1787–1858) was known for her children's works, her short stories, etiquette manuals, and above all for one of the earliest and most successful American cookbooks. First published in 1828, it ran to 520 pages and had more than a thousand recipes in the 1857 edition. *Amelia*, subtitled "The Vicissitudes of a Young Lady," tells the story of an innkeeper's daughter, brought up as her own by a wealthy woman, Mrs. Cotterell. When they move to New York, Amelia is everywhere courted; unfortunately, Mrs. Cotterell has never legally adopted Amelia and her sudden death, apparently intestate, returns the heroine to her father's control. Therefore Amelia, with her refined sensibilities and lady's training, cannot work as she had planned to, giving music lessons, but must drudge in the inn, subject to the hostility of her stepmother and the brutal exploitation of her crude father. Thus Leslie makes the point—she is the only author of the period to do so, because no other uses a working-class heroine—that the middle-class, with all its artifices (or perhaps even because of them), is a much better place for women to be than anywhere else. Amelia's father treats her like chattel, is interested only in the work to be exacted from her, and is delighted to get rid of her when she comes of age and his legal power over her is ended. In the middle class, the power of strong men to exploit weak women is held in check by the conventions of respect and admiration. If, in order to receive this respectful treatment, women must submit to a training in refinement and delicacy that partly unfits them for robust activity, the gain is worth the loss. Happily for the heroine, Amelia's genteel upbringing shows through even in the tavern, and she catches the eye of a gentleman who believes in an aristocracy of manners rather than money. He employs her as a companion for his mother and later marries her. Although it is in no way an antifeminist story, *Amelia* sounds a note of strategic warning to middle-class women: in a world where women and men are inherently unequal by virtue of different physical strengths, woman is lucky to be protected by gallantry and the mystique surrounding her imputed delicacy and refinement. (Perhaps this explains in part the tremendous interest of women in etiquette books.) To relinquish her penumbra, and reject chivalric protection, is to invite inevitable defeat in a much more brutal system of power relationships.

4

Maria McIntosh

The novels of Maria Jane McIntosh (1803–1878), bridging the decades of the 1840s and 1850s, show the increasing focus on the inner life in woman's fiction. One finds McIntosh's name neither in general literary histories nor in specialized studies of the domestic or sentimental genres; yet she was the first of the popular women novelists of the mid-century. *Two Lives* (1846) went through seven editions in four years, and *Charms and Counter-Charms* (1848) had eight with a total sale of about 100,000 copies. She was born into a wealthy and distinguished Georgia family. Her mother was a widow when she married Lachlan McIntosh, whose fifth wife she was (as in our own century, though for different reasons, lifelong marriage was more an ideal than a reality). The father died when McIntosh was three, and the little girl grew up with her mother on the McIntosh plantation, a gracious mansion with extensive grounds and beautiful views, which figures as the setting in many of her fictions.

After her mother's death when McIntosh was twenty, she managed the estate for twelve years. In 1835 she sold the property and went to New York to live with a half-brother. She invested her money in New York bank stock and lost it all in the Panic of 1837. In his 1852 anthology John Hart tells her story in the mode of woman's fiction: "The lady awoke from a life-dream of prosperity in a strange city, totally bankrupt. . . . By an almost universal dispensation of Providence, which ordains means of defense and support to the frailest formations of animal life, with the new station was granted a power of protection, of pleasure, and maintenance, unknown to the old." McIntosh's life story is a model of moral and intellectual growth in the face of adversity, the image of woman's fortunate fall. The author lived through a version of the story that she wrote and rewrote.

The "means of defense and support" that was given to McIntosh was, of course, authorship. She began her career as writer of moral juveniles, pseudonymously issued between 1841 and 1843 as "Aunt Kitty's Tales." Aunt Kitty was their narrator, a kindly maiden aunt, and their titles define them: *Blind Alice, A Tale for Good Children; Ellen Leslie, or the Reward of Self-Control; Florence Arnott, or Is She Generous; Jessie Graham, or Friends Dear, but Truth Dearer; Emily Herbert, or The Happy Home*. (A last work intended for this series, *The Cousins*, appeared separately in 1845; and a kindly maiden lady figured as the narrator of a popular volume of adult short stories, *Evenings at Donaldson Manor*, a literary success of 1851). McIntosh also wrote two longer moralities for adolescent boys. *Conquest and Self-Conquest, or Which Makes the Hero* (1843) is about a young midshipman who does not drink, gamble or duel, and whose manly self-control wins him respect, success, and a bride. The foil character, succumbing to every temptation, ends his brief career by being permanently crippled in a pointless duel. *Praise and Principle, or For What Shall I Live* (1845) follows the same formula, contrasting one law student who succeeds through honesty and hard work with another who fails through lack of discipline.

Her first woman's fiction, *Woman an Enigma*, was published anonymously in 1843, by Harpers. In setting and incident the work seemed a romance, but the story of the development of feminine character transcended its conventions. The didactic certainties of the work are tempered by McIntosh's knowledge that

woman lives in an uncertain world. The supports that she has
been led to rely upon are insecure, and her training in dependence
is hence unfunctional. Adversity, which she had not expected, uncovers capacities previously unsuspected in her. Yet McIntosh
could not embrace adversity wholeheartedly; partly she mourned
the loss of an imagined world where women were protected and
cared for all their lives and hence did not have to develop com-
bative qualities. She believed that certain inherent feminine
qualities—dependent tendencies, physical weakness, inertia—
would prevent women from ever reaching the same height of
individual development as men; there would always be a back-
ward pull toward submission and irresponsibility. Often events
forced women to go much further on the road to independence
than they wished to go. How could a woman tell when she had
reached her limits? How could she know what obstacles, both
inner and outer, really defined her boundaries, and which were to
be challenged and overcome? These questions are treated in each
of McIntosh's six woman's novels, yet each reaches a solution for
a particular character and together they do not present a single
answer. The first four, written in the 1840s and early 1850s,
imply an aggressive and expansionist view of woman's potential,
asserting that women underestimate and undervalue themselves;
the last two, published in 1857 and 1862, appear to suggest that
women have become overreachers and need to remember their
limitations. Perhaps McIntosh became more conservative as she
aged; perhaps an unchanged ideology looked different in a
changed world.

McIntosh's principal novelistic gift is her narrative ability. She
has a fine command of story line and can weave a variety of incidents and a large cast of characters into a single dynamic fabric.
Her plots are complex and ambitious, with clearly interrelated
parts. The stories are appropriate vehicles for their themes; their
didactic intentions seem germane. She can describe and illuminate
inner processes and mental conflict; her stories achieve a psychological depth that none of the earlier women writers had sought.

Her accounts of the inner life are often provocative and insightful in a way that her handling of behavior and conversation are not; she relies too readily on disruptive melodramatic plot devices, on stock characters, and formulaic rhetoric. Her style confuses intensity with hyperbole and her characters tend to orate at one another rather than to talk. There is an evident gap between purpose and accomplishment in her fiction, but it would be wrong to say that she attempted more than she achieved. One has a recurring sense that, in fact, she achieved more than she attempted. Her facile reliance on formula suggests that she intended to manipulate received elements of plot, character, and style into pleasant, exciting, moral, and useful novels; instead, however, she shaped this standard material into variations on the theme of woman in search of herself.

One observes this gap particularly strikingly in *Woman an Enigma,* where the romantic materials of a convent upbringing, revolutionary France, intriguing aristocrats, and other shopworn properties are worked into the shape of a novel of feminine character development. McIntosh announces a purpose in the opening paragraphs of the novel: she will show that woman's behavior, reputedly inconsistent and erratic, acquires coherence and demands respect when we understand its motives. Her approach is psychological—explaining outer behavior by inner causes. She hopes to persuade the reader to revalue womankind by showing him or her how properly to perceive the sex. Since in all probability her readers will be mostly women, the overall result will be to help women think better of themselves.

The story develops beyond its announced intention. It does show a pattern to some apparently erratic feminine behavior, but it also shows a woman maturing through adversity. Fresh from a convent, where she has been sequestered since childhood by indifferent and indigent aristocratic parents, Louise de la Valière is betrothed to the Duc de Montreval, brother of an older woman who has been her only friend. This friend dies, and Louise is sent to Paris by Montreval "to gratify his taste and to win the world's approval of his choice." Louise is beautiful but exceedingly naive; Montreval wants her to acquire social polish. "Would it not have been both wister and kinder in Montreval," the author asks, "to become himself her guide and teacher?" Because she is a woman and wants to please her fiancé, Louise resolves to become the sophisticated women he wishes her to be, even though her own natural temperament goes against it. So Louise is untrue to herself, paradoxically "urged on her dangerous path by the deepest and truest impulses of her nature." When Montreval arrives in Paris after six months, ready to announce his betrothal, he finds in his fiancé what he takes to be an accomplished flirt, and although he had scarcely been deeply in love with Louise before, he is now bitter and outraged. He withdraws from his engagement, leaving Louise a handsome income in trust, which she refuses to accept.

Montreval's facile misjudgment of her nature teaches Louise that there is no security in love. "Sorrow was doing its appointed work with Louise. The loving woman's heart was there still—but she was learning that in this was not her life." Additional tribulations come with the Revolution: as an aristocrat Louise is in danger of her life; moreover, her father and a vicious suitor plot together to possess themselves of the money Montreval has left for her. In pursuing the legal and financial details of the trust, McIntosh displays technical knowledge that one might have supposed inappropriate for women and beyond their understanding at that time. Clearly, however, since she is very explicit in laying out the terms and conditions of this income, McIntosh expects her readers to know what she is talking about.

Eventually the father and suitor abandon their attempts and flee to Geneva with all the family possessions, leaving Louise and her mother penniless and threatened in Paris. They escape to England, where a friendly banker meets them and again urges Montreval's money on them. Although Louise's mother would be happy to accept the money, Louise insists on supporting them by working. She begins with needlework and music, and later becomes a governess in the banker's home, where she finds a certain tranquility and learns to take pleasure in simplicities and in nature. Here, many years later, Montreval meets her again and finds neither the flirt he imagined her to be nor the clinging vine she actually had been. She has become queenly and self-assured, "an awakened and developed nature." In every respect she is Montreval's equal, and she awakens in him a deep response that her earlier, more superficial self could not have hoped to inspire. The marriage that did not take place would have united a male supremacist to a timid, trusting, submissive girl. Louise would have lived out her life as her husband's pet and plaything—if he had not tired of her. The marriage that concludes *Woman an Enigma* is the marriage of two regenerated beings, each respectful of the other's dignity and integrity.

Louise and her story evolve through four stages. She appears at first as a particularly appealing example of the traditional woman, whose natural affections and dependent tendencies have been encouraged by a convent upbringing that ignores her intellectual and moral capacities. Soon she experiences the greatest disappointment that such a woman can know, the failure of the love in which she has trusted, and which she has been trained to require. This disappointment makes her aware of the defects in her education and spurs her development. Without it, development would not occur because it would not be required. On the other hand, it is almost inevitable that such a woman will be disappointed, for her superficial nature does not inspire a deep love. In the last stage, Louise has grown into an individual who can live without love but is able to inspire a lasting, mature passion. The ability to love and be loved stems from the same self-respect that underlies her independence. Out of the ashes of the traditional woman emerges the new woman or the true woman who is, in effect, woman as a fully realized human being.

Two Lives; or, To Seem and To Be (1846) is the first novel McIntosh published under her own name, and the first of the new wave of woman's best sellers. It uses a pair of contrasting heroines; with one it pursues the theme of the dangers of dependency, with the other it shows the dangers of independence. Grace Elliott and her orphan cousin Isabel Duncan have been brought up by Grace's widowed father and his sister on the family estate in the South. The story opens with the death of Mr. Elliott when the girls are in their teens. They are sent to New York to live with another uncle, to be educated and introduced into society.

The differences between the girls are emblemized in their appearances; Isabel is tall and erect, with a high white forehead and dark hair worn in a severe style while Grace is small, fragile, drooping, low-browed, and blondly ringletted. The contrast of straight line and curve implies the opposing conventional images of the deep-rooted independent tree and the dependent, clinging vine. Isabel is self-aware and analytic, Grace impulsive and emotional. Isabel acts on principle, Grace acts for effect. Craving the approval of others, she changes her behavior to suit the company. Her innately compliant nature has been exaggerated through her upbringing; slightly more dependent than Isabel to begin with, she has been petted and admired in response and now requires continual flattery and attention. The New York Elliotts are fashionable people; Mr. Elliott is preoccupied with making money and Mrs. Elliott with displaying it. Offended by the emptiness of this life, Isabel withdraws into herself. In Grace, "a plant which has no independent root," the desire for love quickly degenerates into "a thirst for admiration," and "selfish vanity" becomes her ruling passion.

Although Isabel's firmness is much more admirable than Grace's shallow compliance, it has limitations and dangers. Because Isabel had promised her dying uncle that she would make every sacrifice for the weaker cousin, she rejects the proposal of a man she loves, a young minister from the South named Falconer, mistakenly believing that Grace loves him too. Since Falconer has no interest in Grace at all and is well suited to Isabel, McIntosh sees the girl's behavior as more pigheaded than admirable, the manifestation of spiritual pride in an independent nature. Life may require self-sacrifice, but some self-sacrifice is merely self-indulgence. Falconer leaves town and Grace quickly gets engaged to someone else; Isabel undergoes the torment of loss augmented by the realization that she has sacrificed her own and Falconer's happiness for a pointless scruple.

Leaving Isabel to suffer, McIntosh takes up the stormy course of Grace's engagement, for her fiancé soon becomes disenchanted with her flightiness—she cannot even resist the temptation to attend a dance, so weak has she become—and breaks with her. In vengeful pique, she marries a dissolute marquis and goes off (with Aunt Elliott) to be the toast of Paris. In the meantime, Mr. Elliott loses all his money and Isabel has the regenerating satisfaction of going into lodgings with him and giving music lessons for their support. At this point, the author stops her narrative to contrast the two pictures: the belle of Paris and the hard-working independent woman, to show how much better off, despite appearances, Isabel really is. The story then continues, showing Grace abandoned by her husband and Isabel married after all to Falconer. Grace comes home to die in Isabel's happy home. This ending is an unnecessarily obvious underscoring of the idea that the woman who lives for the esteem of others gets nothing, while the one who lives so as to merit her own esteem gets everything. Dependency, which has for so long been presented to women as good strategy for their weakness, is in fact bad policy. Independence, when it means following principle instead of fashion and when it does not degenerate into inflexibility, is more than its own reward.

Charms and Counter-Charms (1848) was McIntosh's longest and most successful novel to that date. It is an ambitious, unconventional treatment of the theme of destructive feminine dependency. It introduces two heroines, as in *Two Lives*, but neglects the stronger to trace the development of the weaker. Mary Raymond, secretly in love with Everard Irving, who in turn is betrothed to her cousin Evelyn Beresford, goes to live with an older friend in Baltimore and quickly learns the lessons of independence, self-esteem, and satisfaction through service. Her friend points out that feminine dependency is less loving than selfish; disinterested true love is possible for a woman only when she does not need constant approval and affection from the beloved and this can only come about if she is, in some measure, detached from him. A woman can transcend dependency, the friend asserts, because chiefly it "is the result of education rather than nature—of an education which has taught her to draw her impulses and her rewards from others rather than from her own heart and from Heaven." McIntosh had expressed the same idea in her own voice earlier, when she commented about Evelyn's defective education that "woman was not intended solely as an embellishment to the life of man. . . . However they may have been neglected or even repressed by her education, she has aspirations as high, desires as vast as he, and powers fitting her at least to follow his lead, and sympathize with his noblest efforts." And she repeats it later at more length:

To please the objects of her affections; to sacrifice herself to them; to make her life a ministry of love, demanding only love as its repayment—these were [Evelyn's] principles of action. How often are they the only principles with which woman is sent forth to her combat with the powers of earth! The distinction made by Milton between our first parents, seems to be recognized as just by their descendents. Man is taught to draw his motives from above . . . while from her very cradle woman's heart is linked to earth as the source of her motives, hopes, rewards, and if she lives for God, it is "for God in" some earthly object.

Having learned this lesson quickly, Mary leaves the action; Evelyn's more tortuous route to independence forms the subject of most of the novel. She does not marry Everard Irving after all (he is saved by the author for Mary), but falls under the spell of a fascinating older man, one Euston Hastings, whom she meets at the home of Mrs. Mabury, an older friend with whom she is temporarily living. Hastings courts the young girl partly because her open infatuation flatters him, and partly to annoy Mrs. Mabury; rather to his own surprise, his flirtation leads to marriage. Once married, the couple's relationship quickly deteriorates, and McIntosh's analysis of the decline is subtle and acute. Evelyn's exacting dependency irritates her husband, and he begins to neglect her deliberately. Instead of responding with dignity and self-command to his provocations, Evelyn creates self-abusing scenes; her cry, "Love me; only love me," literally hounds him out of the house. "Her injudicious efforts to chain him to her side—her passionate remonstrances—her tearful appeals, drove him further from her. . . . She rather exaggerated his sovereign influence over her life. Hourly she found some new mode of making him feel her entire dependence on him for every enjoyment." One night she stays up waiting for his return, "demonstrating to him most conclusively, the lonely suffering to which his absence condemned her. . . . No book beguiled the weary time— no employment made it less tedious; but there she sat—passionate longing, sad memories, and sadder anticipations making the whole sum of her being—jealousy eating into her heart, and an indignant sense of wrong embittering every thought." This and other episodes disgust Hastings to the point of abandoning her, and within a few years of their marriage he goes off to Europe with Mrs. Mabury.

In reaction, Evelyn shifts from selfish dependency to total self-abnegation. She follows her husband to Europe, finds him again just as he has grown tired of Mrs. Mabury, and begs for reconciliation on any terms. Cruelly, Hastings demands that she live with him as his mistress, under an assumed name. She is to make no claims and accept gratefully whatever he gives her of his time or affection. Evelyn agrees, but in the ensuing interim of abasement her deeper nature revolts and she begins to develop some true self-esteem. Isolated and unhappy in the house where Hastings "keeps" her, she becomes more thoughtful, more religious, and more independent. As McIntosh has already made clear, piety and independence are closely allied, because the woman who depends on God does not need to depend on men.

After nursing Hastings through a near-fatal illness (which

turns the tables and makes him dependent on her) she leaves him. Her new strength and seriousness impress Hastings; he begins to respect her and finally to love her. Now it is his turn to beg for reconciliation. Under Evelyn's guidance, the couple begins to aspire to what the author terms a Christian marriage, by which she means a marriage in which each partner lives according to moral principle rather than as slave or master of the other. The final, brief section of the novel traces Hastings' religious conversion, an event that effectively perfects their marriage. Womanlike, Evelyn had lacked self-trust; manlike, Hastings is too self-reliant. He becomes a Christian when their adored little girl dies and he is faced with the obvious limits of his power. (Women, in general, do not need lessons on the limits of their power.) It is worth noting that although Evelyn prepares the way for Hastings' conversion, she is not the cause of it. McIntosh does not want men to be the masters of women nor women to be the masters of men: equality of the sexes under God is her ideal.

In 1850, McIntosh published her only work of nonfiction, *Woman in America: Her Work and Her Reward*. For the first time she goes beyond the issue of self-development to the question of woman's possible influence on the world around her. Conventionally, she divides public life into its political and social spheres and assigns woman hegemony in the social sphere. The national significance of social life has been undervalued, she says, and the content of social exchange trivialized. Social life displays and shapes the national character no less than politics; in shaping it to embody such democratic principles as the aristocracy of merit, the dignity of labor, and the immorality of extravagance, woman has "her work and her reward." When women see the opportunity that the social sphere offers their abilities, they will be content in it. In the West, woman's mission is to Americanize an ignorant immigrant population (to McIntosh the Germans, Danes, and Swedes were barbarian hordes); in the South, to Christianize the slave and combat the artistocrat's contempt for honest labor; in the North, to counter the insecurities and ostentations of a money-centered life with a serene, stable domesticity. These opportunities may appear banal but they require heroism: "With eyes uplifted to a protecting Heaven, she must walk the narrow path of right—a precipice on either hand."

McIntosh speaks exclusively to one segment of the American female population: white, middle-class, and native-born. Her argument is as much genteel as feminine and indicates how the two can merge into a single cultural concept:

Not by laying aside the distinctive character of our sex to enter the halls of legislation, as petitioners or otherwise,—not by banding into societies to debate and harangue on social evils and their redress—shall we win this high honor, but by ruling in the little realm of home, our legitimate domain, in the spirit of wisdom and of love, by cultivating every feminine grace and charm which may secure for us a wide social influence, and by using this influence to command truth and holiness, to allay the animosities of party and the prejudices of caste, and to prove to the world that there is no civilization so high-toned and of such true refinement, as that which is based on Christian principles.

From the woman's point of view, *Woman in America* defined the territory where McIntosh's expansive ideology of feminine self-development met her much more contracted social philosophy. Her next three novels operate in that territory. *The Lofty and the Lowly; or, Good in All and None All-Good* (1853) is an ambitious attempt to sketch all of American society, and its regional settings are a welcome change from the stylized, high-society atmosphere of balls and dinners that had dominated *Two Lives* and *Charms*. Running to just over six hundred pages, it is much longer than anything she had produced earlier—in their first editions, *Woman an Enigma* was 238 pages long, *Two Lives* was 318 pages, and *Charms* 400 pages. Because of the complexity of its social portraiture, it is probably the most rewarding of her books, despite its length, for the twentieth-century reader.

In her preface, McIntosh puts her social intentions ahead of the woman's story. Her tale is about the North and the South, and in telling it she is consciously assuming the traditional feminine role of peacemaker, hoping "to remove some of the prejudices separating the North and South United States, by a true and loving portraiture of the social characteristics of each. . . . Relying upon the privileges accorded to her sex by the chivalry of every age, she stands between the contending parties, bearing the olive branch, and desiring only to pour balm into the wounds given by more powerful hands." Almost certainly she means to contrast her own womanly writing behavior with the unnatural militancy of Harriet Beecher Stowe. Ironically, to the extent that Stowe inspired McIntosh to expand her range and attempt the broad social canvas, her influence on the lesser author was entirely beneficial.

McIntosh's regional typology is standard: she sees the South as passive and undisciplined, and the North as energetic and self-controlled, with greater potential for evil and heroism. The putative hero of the novel is a northerner, Robert Grahame, son of a ruined factory owner, who pays off his father's debts, gets the mills working again, makes a fortune by the machinery he invents, and comes to the aid of his southern friend Donald Montrose when the latter's typically southern foolishness involves him in heavy debts. To be sure, Donald is indebted to a pair of northern swindlers, but he must bear the responsibility for his predicament because he is a careless, undisciplined pleasure-seeker. Robert and Donald epitomize the gentleman of the North and South, one responsible, able to defer present pleasure for future good and to deny self-gratification to help others, the other erratic, selfish, and susceptible to sensuous temptations. For all his "machismo" or perhaps because of it, the southern male is a weak character and the southern woman suffers accordingly.

The Lofty and the Lowly develops the stories of three pairs of brothers and sisters: Robert Grahame and his sister Mary: Donald Montrose and his sister Isabelle; and their Boston cousins, Charles Montrose and his sister Alice. The Bostonians, with their widowed mother, take up residence on the Georgia plantation owned by

Donald and Isabelle's father, and the four children grow up together. These lives intersect when Donald is victimized on a
northern vacation in a gambling episode by two schemers, one of
whom is Robert's ne'er-do-well younger brother. McIntosh's
handling of Donald's downfall oddly blends melodramatic fantasy
and pragmatic detail; she chronicles with relentless exactitude the
stages by which a gambling debt for $5,000 grows into a lien
against Montrose Hall for $50,000, showing once again that she
knows quite a bit about money and expects her women readers to
understand her.

Too proud and too careless to concern himself with his debts,
Donald permits them to accumulate while expressing scorn for
Robert Grahame as a plebeian working man. Eventually Donald's
folly implicates his mother and sister, for the plantation that is
their home must be mortgaged to meet his obligations. The villainous mortgager would like to see Isabelle thrown in as
collateral. The two women, who understand money and have no
distaste for hard work, must be the passive victims of a man's
financial obtuseness and aristocratic preference for idleness. In the
meantime, the death of the elder Montrose, the coldness of Mrs.
Montrose, and the financial difficulties at Montrose Hall cause
Alice to return north with her mother (Charles has joined the
Navy and is out of the action). Alice's is the increasingly familiar
story of the timid, ladylike, hesitating girl developing under trial
into a woman of strength.

On her earlier visit north, Alice had been profoundly impressed
by the young women who were employed in Robert Grahame's
factories. She learned that "some are working that an old father,
or feeble, helpless mother, may die beneath the roof which they
love, because it sheltered their happier life; some that a young
brother may not want the culture which his mind craves." Alice
was inspired by the example: "I should like to feel that I was
capable of doing as they do." Returning to the South, she
assuaged this feeling by teaching the slaves to read, an enterprise
which is quickly emulated by others around the countryside.

(Despite the fact that it was illegal to teach slaves to read, many southern women novelists showed their heroines engaged in this activity.) Now she is called to work for necessities rather than ideals.

McIntosh recounts Alice's career in self-support and financial management with care. Alice's mother can do nothing for herself; Alice and a servant must bear all the responsibility. The servant (this is a twist) is an elderly male slave named Cato, given to Alice by her uncle, who insists on following his mistress to the North. He does the laborious housework while Alice earns money. She embroiders, gives music lessons, and cultivates flowers that she arranges into bouquets which Cato takes to market. She also learns to negotiate with tradespeople, to make a budget and live within it, and even to bargain with the landlord, who becomes an ardent though gentlemanly admirer. Practical wisdom and business capability accrue without loss of gentle feminine dignity; thus Alice can negotiate with the men who rule the financial world without offending them. Her femininity is good strategy in a man's world, for a woman has little recourse against a male enemy, as Isabelle's unfortunate experience with the wicked mortgager demonstrates. Thus, even as McIntosh shows the need for independence she shows the need to curb it by realistic assessment of the requirements for survival. The so-called self-supporting woman in fact depends on men because they control the economic world. Whether men should or should not have this control is beside the point when one has to earn a living. Moreover, their control is inevitable regardless of whether it is right because men are physically stronger. The disarming gestures of weakness by which women invoke the chivalric responses of men represent pragmatic adjustment to inequality.

In such an economy women and slaves share common disadvantages and develop a common realism. As Cato says when abolitionists try to lure him away from Alice, "Free bery good ting, but free ent all; when you sick free won't make you well, free won't get you clo'es, nor hom'ny, let 'lone meat. Free bery good, but free ent every ting." Thus when brother Charles returns and takes over, saying to Alice, "You are no longer to make bargains and hire yourself out as if you were free; you belong to me now," Alice responds, "I like that a great deal better, but I am not sorry to know that I can help myself." We are not meant to be shocked by her answer. All her resourceful toil can bring Alice little more than subsistence, while a man can make millions. Women need feel no shame in accepting the support of men who have reserved for themselves all the avenues to wealth. No better future is realistically imaginable for Alice than that which McIntosh bestows on her—marriage to Robert Grahame and access thereby to his fortune and his social status as millionaire manufacturer.

From time to time in *The Lofty and the Lowly* the author attributes the existing social and sexual divisions in society to the determinations of a beneficent God. Her arguments come down to these: it is right that some be stronger than others, and right that power and possessions belong to the stronger. Her actual story shows that these conditions are cruelly unjust; her expression of piety is at bottom an expression of resignation to what she believes inevitable. Women are disadvantaged; realistically considered, their possibilities in the world are enormously limited. McIntosh is on the brink of perceiving feminine self-development less as the means to enter the world than as solace for being denied participation in it. But she stops short of this, and her next novel, *Violet; or The Cross and the Crown* (a popular success of 1856), exploits the fear and paranoia of powerlessness. Its schematic and violent story displays woman at the mercy of male aggressors with no defenses. "She could suffer and be still;—in this lay her woman's power," McIntosh writes, but her story mocks the platitude or shows its true meaning: women have no power of any kind.

Violet opens with an impressive description of the bleak, rocky New Jersey coast, where a community of scavengers lives by plundering wrecked vessels. On one of these wrecks they find a living infant next to the body of its beautiful young mother. The mother is buried, the infant is adopted by Dick Van Dyke (leader of the scavengers) and his wife, and a trunk with some baby clothes and other identifying papers is hidden. When the infant, Violet (called Mary by her adoptive parents), is about eight or nine years old, her real father, wealthy Captain Ross, with his older child, a boy, happens to visit the odd community of castaways. Attracted to "Mary" by her remarkable resemblance to his dead wife (he knows nothing of the birth of a baby) he pays the Van Dykes to let him adopt her informally. They cannot resist Ross's money but rightly suspect that she will be refined out of her station, and thus lost to them as a daughter.

Called to nurse her sick "mother" after seven years of living with Captain Ross, Violet must bear the cross, as McIntosh believes it to be, of waiting on a woman so manifestly her inferior, and of enduring the coarseness and brutality of her surroundings. Partly to behave like a Christian, but as much to maintain herself as a lady, Violet gives religious instruction to the local children. Thus, *Violet* is also a story of class differences, with Violet buffeted between two worlds and given much credit by the author for what strikes a modern reader as snobbish fastidiousness. The struggle between Violet's two fathers to possess and dispose of her is the most significant aspect of the class struggle. The working-class father restrains her by physical force, the upper-class by psychological pressure. Equally selfish, they are equally insensible to Violet's claim, as a human being, to be her own person. In accordance with the general melodramatic atmosphere of *Violet,* McIntosh makes the heroine's marriage the arena of combat. Captain Ross wants her to marry his son. Though unaware that they are siblings, the two young people have always regarded one another as brother and sister and are profoundly opposed to marriage. Van Dyke's candidate is a coarse, flashy person from the city who likes Violet's gentility and offers a large sum of money to Van Dyke in exchange for his "daughter." One father is motivated by love, the other by greed, but to both Violet is property.

In this world of powerful and egotistical men, Violet's efforts to assert herself seem pathetic. She tries to withstand her fathers in vain; her example has no effect on the demoralized women of the lower classes; an interlude of governessing in the South comes abruptly to an end when Van Dyke has her kidnaped. Tied up in the hold of a ship that is returning her to New Jersey, Violet must face the irrelevance of any female ideology to the reality of male dominance. In her helplessness she sees beyond the threat of physical violation to the fact that her exquisitely defined person-hood is not real to those who control her; she experiences the negation of herself as a self. In this context, McIntosh's earlier adjuration to suffer and be still becomes especially ironic, for the physically restrained girl can do nothing else.

The improbable happy ending of this unlikely story is consistent with its theme of woman's weakness. Violet's destiny has been postponed as the fathers argued with each other over who had the right to select her husband; in this interim she had attracted the attention of a handsome young Englishman who had known her mother, who had in fact come to America expressly to find the daughter. Now, the ship on which Violet is held captive is wrecked. She is saved by the fathers of those children whom she had instructed in religion. And the Englishman uncovers the secret of her identity (which he had intuitively penetrated) and proposes to her. The paranoid world reverses itself, and every-thing conspires to rescue and exalt the heroine.

Despite its lack of realism in the story line, *Violet* is consistent in its demonstration that woman is inherently too weak ever to hope to prevail, in any matter, by direct action. It is far less so in its auxiliary intention of showing that woman has an indirect power that will ultimately prevail. The idea of power of any sort for woman seems a forlorn hope in this novel, its improbability underscored by the grandiose, self-indulgent fantasy at the end, when Violet's Englishman turns out to be an enormously wealthy landholder, and she becomes mistress of a vast estate.

Seven years passed between the publication of *Violet* and of

McIntosh's last fiction, *Two Pictures; or What We Think of Ourselves and What the World Thinks of Us* (long after they had become archaic, McIntosh continued to use moralistic subtitles). Published in 1863, it suggests that McIntosh had revised her view of the message that women needed to hear. She tells them not be to more independent, but to be less so. This conservatism seems deeply tied to the personal nostalgia that pervades *Two Pictures,* for its haplessly independent heroine has been thrust out of her lovely and beloved childhood home, in the confines of which she had been free and happy. "Home," therefore is identified not with a sphere in which woman rules, but one where she is irresponsible and protected, enjoying liberty to be sure, but the child's liberty. Perhaps McIntosh felt the fatigue of age; certainly she felt the threat, in 1863, to the physical integrity of the South.

Whatever the causes, her last fictions take a different approach to woman's dilemmas. Her earlier works had said that life would inevitably thrust woman out of her home and force independence on her, and that this event would be beneficial to feminine growth and maturity. In *Violet* she implied, and in *Two Pictures* asserts, that life may do this, but it may not; and if it does not, the woman who willfully leaves the circle of love and protection in search of independence is worse than a fool. Thus, she denies the value system of the fortunate fall, on which so much "trial and triumph" literature depends. The self-dependent, morally developed woman is not superior to her untested sister; she is simply a battle-scarred veteran who has had a bad time:

Thus has God made woman. The sense of power which is a delight to man weighs like a heavy burden upon her. Like the vine, it is only when the tendrils which have sought to attach themselves to a stronger and less pliant object have been again and again torn away, cut down to the stalk, that she learns to stand unsupported, to live an independent life; and in doing so, like the vine, she loses much of her own native gracefulness. She may be useful; she may bear abundant fruit to man's good and God's glory, but some of that loveliness which charmed the imagination and won the heart is lost.

The statement above is taken from *Violet; Two Pictures* goes beyond it when it considers the story of a willfully independent woman who, so to speak, cuts down her own tendrils and thus engages, in the author's view, in acts of self-mutilation. The novel begins with the first-person account of her childhood by the heroine, Augusta Moray. An orphan, she lives on the beautiful Georgia plantation of her kindly but distant great uncle whom she adores, tended by her devoted black mammy, Charity. Although she has intervals of loneliness and occasional fierce cravings for love, Augusta revels in the freedom of her uninhibited natural existence and the beauty of her surroundings. In her solitude and unconstraint she develops into an undisciplined, outspoken, intensely honest, and feelingful person.

Her blissful childhood ends abruptly when Uncle Moray decides that he wants to find a male heir to leave his property to, and hence institutes a search for distant relations. Augusta must prepare to share her Paradise with usurpers and face what she cannot interpret as other than disownment. Beyond her hurt at being cast aside, there is the pain of the virtually certain loss of the home she loves so well. Her situation captures the ironic circumstances of many young women of her time—she is trained to love her home, and forced to leave it when she marries, while the boy is brought up to go out in the world, with home ties accordingly slighter than hers, yet comes into possession of the homestead.

Moray's search uncovers two families of distant kin in the North, both named Moray and each with a young son. The two youths are invited to live on the plantation, to be educated by Moray and assessed as heirs. Hugh Moray, the older of the two, comes from a poor but large-souled family; his father is a naval officer, his mother an exemplary homemaker. Hugh himself is a serious, hardworking, responsible person; in him and his cousin Charlie, McIntosh makes her regular contrast of male types, between the industrious, self-sacrificing man and the idle self-seeker. Charlie arrives at the plantation with his mother, a scheming widow who intends to win the estate for her son. Her manipulative nature is masked by perfect manners, and she quickly manages to make the outspoken Augusta seem continually in the wrong. The young girl is forced into the first dissembling of her life; to please her uncle, she must pretend to love this aunt, whose hostility she intuits behind the facade. She does not respect Charlie, but cannot help liking him. Hugh she loves at once and forever.

Unwilling to risk his future on the possibility of becoming his uncle's heir, and convinced that no man should rely on inheritance for self-definition, Hugh persuades his uncle to finance his study of the law, and when he has completed his studies (years pass quickly in this novel) he returns to New York to help support his family. Augusta is sent to New York for schooling at this time, and becomes a daughter in Hugh's home, where she finds at last the family circle she has always longed for. The nascent romance between Hugh and Augusta is thwarted by Charlie's mother, who wants Augusta to marry her own son. Charlie, in the meantime, remains on the plantation developing the vices of the southern aristocrat (a fact that does not escape his uncle's notice): a distaste for work, a predilection for expensive pleasures. It seems most likely that Charlie will not inherit, and his mother is driven to desperate and dishonest measures to secure the plantation for him: she tampers with Moray's will.

Thus, the will that is discovered after his death leaves the estate to Charlie, asserts that Hugh has already drawn his portion of the inheritence in the money spent on his legal training, and leaves to Augusta nothing beyond a recommendation that she marry her propertied cousin. Estranged from Hugh by Mrs. Moray's interference, and intensely offended by the will's disposition of her person (in this, Mrs. Moray miscalculates, attributing to Augusta the same sort of mercenary nature she herself possesses), Augusta determines to become entirely self-sufficient. She takes a job in New York as a governess, acquitting herself nobly although she hates the work.

At this point McIntosh separates right from wrong in Augusta's behavior and response. She was right to leave the plantation and to refuse to marry Charlie. Given the deception that has been practiced on her (forged letters and the like) she is probably right to break off with Hugh, although a less proud and suspicious nature might have been slower to condemn someone she knew so well. But to leave the loving home of Hugh's parents for the home of strangers, to substitute relations of money for those of love, is altogether inexcusable. Augusta languishes in her work as governess precisely because she has undertaken it in the wrong spirit and for the wrong reasons. As time wears on she becomes increasingly bitter and alienated from all around her, possessed all the while by a demon of self-righteousness. Not until Hugh's father dies does she perceive her behavior in its true and awful light. "How magnanimous had seemed her conduct in withdrawing from all on whom she could be supposed to have any claim, in resting only on her own resources, relieving them of all draft on their sympathies and their aid. Now, this magnanimity was dwarfed into the littleness of selfish passion." Beside herself with grief and guilt, Augusta tries tardily, and desperately, to go to her relatives. A nightmare sequence of missed train connections and empty depots culminates when Augusta arrives at the home of some friends, soaked through in a tremendous downpour, and suffers a complete physical and mental breakdown. (Like other woman's novelists, McIntosh rarely uses the faint except for minor, comic characters; but nervous collapses and extended physical illness are the frequent lot of heroines.)

As she slowly recovers, Augusta for the first time since childhood attains a right relation to the universe. Reconciled to the Morays, she returns south for the climate, living quietly in the home of the local minister near the Moray estate. In this same year of turmoil Charlie has neglected the upkeep of the plantation and made it the scene of continuous fashionable parties; in numerous gambling episodes he has acquired a debt equal to the value of the entire plantation. Mrs. Moray, in a frenzy to thwart the social rival whose property the plantation will become, confesses that Charlie had inherited through an illegitimate will; then she collapses in a violent, ultimately fatal, illness. Since Charlie has no legal title to the estate, it cannot be attached to pay his debts. Augusta, self-transcendent, nurses Mrs. Moray through her final illness; Hugh, arriving in Georgia to claim his estate, claims his bride as well. At the end, Augusta has become mistress at last in her own house; her cold uncle has been replaced by her loving husband, and Charity is still around to dote on her. The child and the woman's life merge and thus the role of traditional dependent woman is shown as the defiant arrest of time. Arrest, and rest: these are the values of the world of *Two Pictures*.

The critique of feminine independence proceeds not from fear of male strength, as had been the case with *Violet*, but from exhaustion and nostalgia. As a woman who had now been supporting herself for thirty years, McIntosh perhaps knew exhaustion at first hand, and as the war threatened to destroy the childhood home she had left many years before, the plantation presented itself to her imagination as the abode of happiness and repose. Independence is after all no country for a woman. One year of independence sufficed to wear out the strength of so vital a character as Augusta had seemed to be:

Resting, indeed, she was, as she had never rested before. . . . Where was her pride, her independence now? All exchanged for the sweetness of entire trust in the large heart, the clear judgment, the firm will of him whom she had chosen for her earthly guide. She had exercised wisely her woman's right of choice, and the result was this ineffable peace. What could the poor, vain ranters about woman's independence have given her in exchange for it? Ah! They know not how sweet it is to "obey," when obedience has been preceded by "love and honour." Only see that he whose rule you accept bears the lineaments of the Divine Master, and be assured your highest happiness and truest dignity in this, as in every relation, will be found in obedience to God's arrangements.

How different these closing words of the novel are from McIntosh's earlier insistence that women must live directly for

God, and not for God in some man. Her first books for women had urged them on to moral and intellectual development and independence and warned them to be prepared for financial self-support. Now she is afraid that they have gone too far. She reminds women that there are practical limits on achievement, limits that take many forms but derive ultimately from the man's strength and the woman's weakness. McIntosh was not hypocritical in her exposition of these limits, forbidding to others what she had claimed for herself; she had taken her own path not from choice but necessity. Now she points out the hardships of that path. Speaking as a veteran, she cautions the young girl not to overestimate her own strength.

The nostalgia in *Two Pictures* fantasizes marriage as an idealized parent-child relationship. This fantasy is not only restricted to women, it is almost certainly restricted to unmarried women. The man who regrets his lost childhood is unlikely to imagine that he will find it again in marriage, because marriage is represented to him by the culture as the assumption of adult responsibilities. No matter what the culture has promised her, the married woman knows very well that for her, too, marriage means responsibility and care. McIntosh's image of marriage at the end of *Two Pictures* is one reserved for the unmarried woman—the young girl afraid of life or ignorant of it, or the older single woman weary of it. At the same time, however, the nostalgia of *Two Pictures* transcends its gender reference. The wish not to grow up is pervasive in our major literature, and in *Two Pictures*, McIntosh demonstrates that women as well as men are vulnerable to the desire.

5

E. D. E. N. Southworth
and Caroline Lee Hentz

E. D. E. N. Southworth and Caroline Lee Hentz were two immensely popular writers who became widely known at the end of the 1840s. Both composed romantic novels set in the South, and were esteemed by their contemporaries for their freedom and spontaneity of conception and expression. If there were unwritten laws constraining the woman author, directing her to conceal ambition and confine her stories to idealizations of decorous gentility, then these women were flagrant transgressors, with such high spirits and good humor in their lawlessness that they largely escaped criticism. Their literary pecadillos only increased their popularity.

Emma Dorothy Eliza Nevitte (she came by all her initials validly, but her use of them was a characteristic flourish) was born in Washington, D.C., in 1819. Her father died when she was three (few of these authors enjoyed the presence of their parents until maturity) and her mother, who had been his second wife, remarried two years later. The stepfather, Joshua L. Henshaw, was a New Englander in Washington at the time as secretary to Daniel Webster. He later resumed his profession of schoolmaster, and he educated Emma in his academy, from which she graduated in 1835. She then taught school until her marriage to

Frederick Southworth in 1840. She moved with him to Prairie du Chien, Wisconsin, but returned to Washington four years later without him, pregnant and with a small child. The causes of her marital break-up are not known, nor do we know who abandoned whom. From time to time, she contributed something to her husband's support, but they never lived together again, and he contributed nothing to hers. In need of money, she taught at first in the Washington public schools, but the pay was inadequate and she began to supplement teaching with writing. Her stories found ready publishers. Her first novel, *Retribution* (1849), was serialized in the *National Era,* where its success led Harpers to republish it in the same year. This was the beginning of an extraordinarily prolific career.

Between 1849 and 1860, Southworth wrote eighteen novels, and though they are certainly full of faults, not one of them shows a trace of fatigue. It is certain that she enjoyed her career and the recognition it brought her. She cast her own experience into the form of a heroine's triumph, all the more glorious because of the depths from which she had emerged. These are her own words, as culled from autobiographical statements in the *Saturday Evening Post* and republished in John Hart's 1854 edition of *Female Prose Writers of America:*

Let me pass over in silence the stormy and disastrous days of my wretched girlhood and womanhood—days that stamped upon my brow of youth the furrows of fifty years—let me come at once to the time when I found myself broken in spirit, health, and purse—a widow in fate but not in fact, with my babes looking up to me for a support I could not give them. It was in these darkest days of my *woman's* life, that my *author's* life commenced. . . .

The circumstances under which this, my first novel, was written, and the success that afterwards attended its publication, is [*sic*] a remarkable instance of "sowing in tears and reaping in joy;" for, in addition to that bitterest sorrow with which I may not make you acquainted—that great life-sorrow, I had many minor troubles. My small salary was inadequate to our comfortable support. My school

numbered eighty pupils, boys and girls, and I had the whole charge
of them myself. Added to this, my little boy fell dangerously ill. . . .
It was too much for me. It was too much for any human being. My
health broke down. I was attacked with frequent hemorrhage of the
lungs. Still I persevered. I did my best by my house, my school, my
sick child, and my publisher. . . . This was indeed the very *melee*
of the "Battle of Life." I was forced to keep up struggling when I
only wished for death and for rest.

But look you how it terminated. The night of storm and darkness
came to an end, and morning broke on me at last—a bright glad
morning, pioneering a new and happy day of life. First of all, it was
in this very tempest of trouble that my "life-sorrow" was, as it were,
carried away—or *I* was carried away from brooding over it. Next,
my child, contrary to my own opinion and the doctor's, got well.
Then my book, written in so much pain, published besides in a
newspaper, and, withal, being the *first* work of an obscure and
penniless author, was, contrary to all probabilities, accepted by the
first publishing house in America, was published and (subsequently)
noticed with high favour even by the cautious English reviews.
Friends crowded around me—offers for contributions poured upon
me. And I, who six months before had been poor, ill, forsaken,
slandered, *killed* by sorrow, privation, toil, and friendliness [*sic Hart*,
for friendlessness], found myself born as it were into a new life; found
independence, sympathy, friendship, and honour, and an occupation
in which I could delight. All this came very suddenly, as after a
terrible storm, a sun burst.

I quote this passage at length to show that Southworth not only
took pride and pleasure in being rich and famous, but that she
had no fear in saying so and that her popularity did not suffer
for her fearlessness. Southworth was not a moralizing writer and
her plots lack the educational organization characteristic of much
fiction of the fifties. But one message does animate her fiction—
do not be afraid. Her fearless heroines, and the fearless author
behind them, conveyed this message to many hundreds of thousands of feminine readers.

One should note some characteristic habits of expression and

attitude in the passage quoted above. There is first the avidity
with which Southworth appropriates and employs conventional
rhetoric: sowing in tears and reaping in joy, the battle of life,
morning after night, sun burst after storm. The intensity that she
puts into these platitudes pushes them beyond formula into felt
experience; she uses clichés when she uses them, not to avoid
experience but to control it. There is also her habit of weighting
each moment with the passions of a lifetime; the bitterest sorrow,
the great life-sorrow of the second paragraph, becomes "life-sorrow," ironically put in quotes and swept away in the third. This
habit of immersing her characters and readers in the moment
without thereby committing them to it conveys the sense of character at once caught up in life and yet detached from it, a sense
of resiliency that need not be purchased by avoiding experience.
Finally, note her ready exaggeration: "furrows of fifty years,"
"too much for me," "*killed* by sorrow," "after a terrible storm,
a sun burst." Life comes across as full of excitement, drama, force,
great highs, and great lows, every minute intensely interesting.
It is really no wonder that her readers went away rejoicing and
that each of her books exceeded its predecessor in popularity.

Although Southworth was by no means a great writer or a
great stylist, like the other authors of woman's fiction she certainly
had her own style. In her works there is a consistency of elements
such that all—story line, characterization, language, message—
reflect her boldness and energy by their pervading ornateness.
Southworth is a writer whose work is shamelessly decorative. A
modern reader might interpret all this embellishment as equivalent to that gushing rhetoric which is supposed to be particularly
feminine. It seems to me rather to represent the genderless impulse
that plain people have toward exuberant decoration as a counterstatement to a bare life. In an age of feminine restraint, such
exuberance would be decidedly unladylike—thus Sarah Hale
admonished her (in *Woman's Record,* quoted by Hart in the
1854 edition of his anthology) for going "beyond the limits pre-
scribed by correct taste or good judgment." Southworth's writing

constitutes a flamboyant rejection of the expected literary behavior of women writers. Not for her were such feminine values
as the spare, the self-effacing, the decorous, the understated, or
the unobtrusive.

The exact extent of her popularity is difficult to gauge, although
Frank Luther Mott believes that for overall sales she was the
greatest publishing success in nineteenth-century America. Hard
numbers seem to be lacking and in any event book sales would
tell only part of the story, since all her works were first serialized,
and sometimes more than once. In 1857, Robert Bonner, editor
of the enormously popular fiction magazine, the *New York Ledger,* put her on exclusive contract; she published her novels in
serial form in the *Ledger* but retained the copyright for book
publication and thus made a fortune. Because some of the novels
were so popular, however, Bonner serialized them more than once
before they were published as books. *The Hidden Hand,* for
example, which is said to be her most popular work, was serialized
in 1859 and twice more before it appeared in its first edition as
a book in 1889. It is confusing to speak of a "popular book" of
1859 when, in fact, the "book" did not appear until thirty years
later! Nevertheless, it seems fair to say that Southworth's fiction
was widely known and widely read in America for some forty
years of the nineteenth century, between the publication of
Retribution and her death in 1899.

There are also difficulties in calculating the exact number of
novels she wrote, because a serial work was frequently given a
new name when it appeared as a book (*The Hidden Hand* was
published as *Capitola's Triumph, The Curse of Clifton* as *Fallen
Pride* as well as, in another edition, *The Mountain Girl's Love*),
or published as two works instead of one. *Self-Made,* serialized
in 1863 and 1864, was serialized a second time and then published as two books in 1876: *Ishmael* and *Self-Raised.* All of
these titles have led critics habitually to assert that she wrote more
than she did. It seems safe to suggest that she wrote about fifty

novels in all, the last copyrighted in 1894. This number is less than tradition allows her, but it is still a formidable output.

Southworth's habit of exaggeration means that none of her characters can be called realistic, although this same habit also frequently makes them seem alive. Within the constraints of the woman's formula, her work contains a proliferation of feminine characterizations. Nothing could be further from her work than the reductive and tedious male dichotomizing of women into evil-dark and angelic-fair (a polarity actually rare in most woman's fiction of the period); Southworth's women are all shapes, sizes, and colors, all equally beautiful. Some of her types are conventional, but others are thoroughly individual. Contrasting to this prodigality of females, she has only two basic representations of the male, both unamiable: the tyrannical and hypocritical father or father-surrogate and the impetuous, self-centered suitor. (The popular *Self-Made* featured a paragon hero, but it is an exception to the tenor of her fiction.) In the fourteen novels from the fifties that form the subject of my analysis, I have found only one thoroughly good man, the father in *The Lost Heiress*. Most are of limited intelligence and overwhelming vanity. There are wicked and scheming women who cause trouble for the heroines, but these women are subordinate to the men whose folly licenses their wickedness. The major, repeated, varied story is that of the struggle of good women against the oppressions and cruelties, covert and blatant, of men. Among Southworth's favorite situations are daughters disinherited by jealous or materialistic fathers; hasty, secret, and disastrous marriages into which inexperienced girls are forced by importunate suitors; misunderstood wives abused, harassed, or abandoned by self-righteous but deluded husbands.

After her first couple of novels Southworth settled into a structural formula. She began with a sequence of terrific melodrama, in which a child and her mother are separated. The child is brought up in a "home" that travesties the ideal—it is patched together out of the fragments of a family and, far from being a

female preserve, is dominated by a male. He, ruling in what culture supposes to be the woman's sphere, gives her no room to live
or breathe and is nothing like the culture's ideal of man. The man
in the house—passionate, immature, unreasonable, uncontrolled,
and uncontrollable—is rather a rampaging beast than a protector,
provider, or model of the rational will. In his obsession with
property, with fantasies of owning and transferring estates that
often actually belong to the women, he rather deprives his women
of security than provides them with it.

The goal of the heroine in such a situation is far more primitive
than "woman's rights"; it is to construct the traditional sphere
that some woman's righters found constraining and wanted to
leave behind. Southworth's women want to make a place for
themselves where men can be distanced and controlled. Given
the fact that men have all the advantages as the outset, the realization of this wish is enormously difficult. Ultimately it called for the
transformation of the male so that he saw woman as a human
being entitled to possession of herself, to respectful treatment,
rather than an object for use, pleasure, or exploitation. He will
come to see women differently only if he is deeply impressed by
the example of a "true woman," which, to Southworth, is nothing
more than a true human being. When he realizes how he has
underestimated women, man will be so overwhelmed at his previous stupidity that he will become in a basic sense a new man.
This new man is the embodiment of woman's image of ideal man.
Only when such men exist can there be homes, families, and
woman's place. When woman has her place, it will be time to
decide whether that place is fully satisfying.

Taken one way, these novels imply a glorification of the cult
of domesticity; taken another, they represent a severe criticism,
because they show that the defective male nature makes the ideal
of the separate sphere generally unrealizable. But either way,
woman's need to struggle for her survival and her dignity was
the base of Southworth's writing; and if in novel after novel she
showed woman gaining this victory, she might be conveying some-

thing more than entertainment to her vast feminine readership. Given her popularity in the *Ledger,* which was not a woman's magazine, men must have read her fiction in great numbers too; perhaps her work helped both sexes to look on women more favorably.

Southworth used her formula in a series of ingenious variations. She set most of her fiction in rural Virginia and Maryland and embellished it with highly wrought descriptions of landscape. She set forth the manners of a rude aristocracy and the traditions of a rough society down to poor white and slave. She depicted magnificent plantations and log cabins and the kinds of life lived in each. In her own time she was especially praised for her depictions of slaves, and they do seem strikingly free from stereotype: they are strong-minded, self-respecting, highly verbal, intelligent, versatile people; not rebellious, craven, childlike, or shaped according to pro- or antislavery sentiments; they are beings in every way the equal of the whites, making the best of an abominable situation with wit and grace. (Technically a southerner, Southworth was always against slavery and says so repeatedly in her fiction. Her "best" white characters always free their slaves.)

Her novels are usually several hundred pages long, partly because of the large cast of minor characters, partly from stylistic redundancy, and partly because each work develops the stories of two or more heroines simultaneously. She could veer from absurd melodrama to strong naturalism in a single novel, indeed in a single sentence. A wife is tricked into a convent and into leaving her son to be brought up as her evil sister-in-law's child in *Vivia;* but in the same work the daily routines of a lame young widow trying to run a farm and support herself and three elderly, useless female relatives is followed from crop-planting to credit-forestalling, cooking, and ironing. Southworth did not reject false or purloined wills, forged or intercepted or lost letters, storms, floods, fires, droughts, kidnapings, mock murders, feigned marriages and suicides, carriage accidents, shipwrecks, poisonings. Yet her imagination is too spacious and robust to be called gothic, and similar incidents appear in most of the fiction of her time; she differs from the more realistic authors in the frequency of such melodramatic devices, and from the melodramatists in that she uses them in a spirit of fun rather than of high seriousness.

Retribution is her most austere and shapely novel and probably conforms more to twentieth-century taste than any other she wrote. It opens at a boarding school where the heroine, Hester Gray, plain like her name but rich, meets Juliette Summers, who is penniless, scheming, charming, brilliant, and beautiful. (Juliette had an Italian mother, which explains her propensity for intrigue.) Overwhelmed with a merited sense of inferiority and hungry for love, Hester is an easy prey to Juliette, who cultivates the friendship because it might later be useful to her to have a rich friend. After a few years Hester is called home by her guardian, a middle-aged censorious man named Ernest Dent, who seems to have no calling in life that gives him more pleasure than instructing the girl in her duties as mistress of a huge estate.

The relationship that develops between Hester and Ernest is treated by Southworth with a cold and incisive eye: Hester, abject, guileless, inept, and Ernest, lofty, paternal, critical, distant —he appropriating to himself the role of lawgiver and judge, she humbly acquiescing. Each enjoys this role-playing, but even though Hester is demeaned by the exchange she actually likes it better, for her nature is satisfied to remain a child, while much in Ernest remains unengaged by the transaction between them. The harsher he is, the more she reveres him; and yet Ernest does not know that he is being harsh, he only thinks he is being fair. Finally they marry, Ernest rationalizing his greed for Hester's estate under cover of the good that he can do as its master and Hester blind, perhaps willfully, to his ulterior motives and his basic indifference to her. "I admire his STRENGTH," she tells a rejected suitor, "moral, intellectual, and physical. . . . I love to feel myself sustained by a strong arm, powerful enough to protect and defend me . . . [to] fold my wings upon some broad bosom that would love and shelter me . . . [and give] protection, security, and repose."

Instead of protection Hester gets neglect, betrayal, and an early death. Soon after her marriage, Juliette arrives for a long visit and Ernest quickly becomes infatuated with her. It takes all Juliette's skill to keep from becoming his mistress while maneuvering for his affections, and she manages this difficult task not out of loyalty to Hester but because she knows that if she becomes Ernest's mistress she will never become his wife. And Hester's health is obviously failing. She suffers increasingly from a sense of her worthlessness and from ill health—hysterical blindness, which clears up when her daughter is born, is followed by fatal consumption. On her deathbed she thinks about her marriage; in view of the realities of the situation, her reflections take on an irony that must have been intended by the author:

I love where I venerate, and that is the great necessity of my life. . . . This is in accordance with the laws of God and of nature. . . . Just so far as a woman's soul possesses the distinctive lineaments of her sex, does she feel the force of these instincts. Talk of woman's bondage, and woman's chains; the bondage is a bondage of protection, the chain a chain of love. . . . Talk of woman's rights; woman's rights live in the instincts of her protector—man.

After Hester's death (Hester "the loving but unloved, the gentle, yet oppressed, the confiding, though deceived, was dead at last. . . . Hester was dead, *and out of the way.*") Ernest and Juliette marry. The second part of the novel chronicles the deterioration of their relationship as each, distrustful and contemptuous of the other, becomes increasingly bitter and recriminatory. Yet neither feels remorse for their treatment of Hester; Southworth will not permit feminine self-effacement any gratification, even posthumously. After fifteen miserable years, spent mostly in Europe, Juliette elopes with a corrupt Italian; as she disappears we realize that Southworth has modulated her into a fiend whose role was to punish Ernest for his cold, hypocritical assumption of superiority over Hester. The chastened old man returns to the South and joins his daughter, who has grown up with Hester's good heart but much more strength. They free all Hester's slaves (an act intended by the mother, but precluded by her death before she came of age), thereby impoverishing themselves, and then go west to begin a new life.

The Mother-in-Law (serialized in 1850, published 1851) is Southworth's third novel. Uncharacteristically, it lacks a strong male antagonist, but its prodigality of plot and character is typical. It develops seven major female characters: the mother-in-law Mrs. Armstrong, a proud, domineering, unbending woman who is the evil force in the story, and six varieties of heroine. These include her daughter, Louise, a totally passive and compliant person, the end product of a ferociously repressive education; Zoe, a foundling and a "dove," that is, a gentle, domestic woman; Anne, a noble, intellectual mulatto slave; Susan, her mistress, a serene, self-dependent, benevolent person; Brittania O'Riley, Louise's governess, a self-centered, luxury-loving, high-spirited, energetic woman; and finally Gertrude Lion, a nordic beauty who is six feet tall, rides, hunts, eats roots and berries, cannot bear to be indoors, and generally upsets every notion of conventional femininity while remaining a woman with the "majesty of Juno and the freedom of Diana."

For each of these women Southworth plots a different, exciting story; since all are neighbors and close friends, their stories intertwine. Most interesting are her stories for the unusual heroines, Gertrude and Brittania (Brighty). Brighty's wit and dash attract an elderly military man, General Stuart-Gordon, who owns the estate next to Mrs. Armstrong's and whose son is married to Louise. Brighty has no use for young men, but an experienced, weatherbeaten, rich older man is another matter, and so she marries him and gets land, mansion, luxury, and love—everything she wants. This marriage precipitates a crisis for poor Louise, for her mother, who had engineered her marriage to young Stuart-Gordon, now engineers a divorce. Gertrude, ranging about the landscape and performing many daring rescues of a sort generally reserved for men, meets her own true love when she saves him from a carriage accident. When this beautiful young man is chosen by Mrs. Armstrong as Louise's second husband, Gertrude rescues the pair at the altar, claiming Louise for her first husband, and Louise's new spouse for herself. Far from resenting her aggressiveness and vigor, the beautiful young man is enthralled by it. Between them, these two female characters break most of the rules of conventional femininity and are rewarded for it. Each is true to her own self, enjoys life in her own way, and has her desires gratified. The passive, weak-willed, and conforming women, above all Louise, suffer. Self-expression and selfishness—providing they stop short of the point of exploiting others—are healthy and condonable. No special restrictive ethic applies to women.

The main plot of Southworth's fourth novel, *Shannondale* (serialized in 1850, published 1851) follows the monstrous behavior and character of Squire Darling, who disowns his daughter Winifred when she elopes with her tutor and takes to drinking and lechery with her scheming governess. Winifred (physically wounded when she intercepts a blow her father intended for her husband) and her spouse pass a miserable winter of poverty and cold, she ill and he unemployed. The stock situation of young people made to suffer by the old gets a certain life through the graphic detail with which Southworth develops their "poor white" situation and the counterpointed degeneration of Squire Darling into a sexual beast. The story attacks the image of the southern patriarch, showing that his unbridled command of others results in total lack of self-command.

The Discarded Daughter (serialized in 1851 and 1852, published 1852) was the author's seventh novel, also known as *Children of the Isle*. It tells another version of the evil-father story. General Garnet is the villain (like most of Southworth's male antagonists, he has a military title), a calculating adventurer whom the heiress Alice Chester had been forced to marry by her father. Garnet can be debonair and charming when occasion calls for it, but he loves only his (really Alice's) estate, and his life-dream is to unite it to the one adjoining. Since the heir to that estate, Magnus, is a noble fellow, Garnet's daughter Elsie has no objection to the marriage that is required for the fulfillment of this dream. But matters change when a nearer heir turns up, a scoundrelly person, and Garnet orders Elsie to marry this newcomer instead. She refuses, and from that point to the end of the novel, the plot develops as an exposure of the injustice of the property laws and other legal advantages of husbands and fathers, and as a denunciation of men's psychological and physical power over their wives and daughters. The property laws encourage the male sex to put property ahead of persons; the patriarchal system represents the legalized swindling of women, and its "domesticity" is sham. The novel concludes when all the sympathetic characters make a new home for themselves in the West, which stands for salvation from the feudal South.

The Curse of Clifton (serialized in 1852, published 1853) was Southworth's eighth novel, said to be her most popular until eclipsed by The Hidden Hand six years later. Its story of a group of splendid women and defective men contains several simultaneous plot lines. There is one vicious woman in this novel, Georgia, the young and beautiful fourth wife of Major Clifton. But her power derives from male obtuseness and gullibility. Her husband fatuously elevates her above his daughters; the hero believes her slanders and distrusts his own wife. These two men represent a favorite Southworth configuration of males—the old and the young fool.

They contrast to the several virtuous women in the novel, above all to the chief protagonist Catherine Kavanagh, who, with the intellect of a genius and the will of a Cromwell, is one of Southworth's strongest affirmations of feminine capacities. But as a poor mountain girl Catherine has no better fate than to wait for Archer Clifton to lower himself (in his own eyes) to marry her, and then to suffer his distrust and neglect. While he disports himself in the city, punishing her for misdeeds that Georgia has imputed to her,

Catherine runs two plantations and retains her courage and integrity. (Southworth details her management in a way that might have inspired Ellen Glasgow to attempt the same kind of specificity seventy-five years later.) She persists in good works until her husband is enlightened and thoroughly contrite. This story varies the patient Griselda plot, which traditionally ends when the husband is satisfied that his wife is good enough for him. Here, Archer Clifton comes to understand that his wife is far too good for him. This insight initiates a reformation, or more properly a regeneration. Clifton's new admiration for the good woman transforms him into a man that such a woman can live with happily.

India (serialized in 1853 as *Mark Sutherland,* published 1855), also known as *The Pearl of Pearl Island,* was Southworth's ninth novel and is identified in some criticism as an antislavery novel. It does open with the protagonist's gesture of freeing all his slaves, thereby making himself a poor man and losing the affection of both his mother and fiancée. But in the main it is the story of how he and his angelic wife, Rosalie, whom he marries after his first engagement is broken, build a new life in the West. Without Rosalie, the good loyal woman, the transition from southern patriarch to western freeman could not have been accomplished. She keeps his house, helps him edit his newspaper, teaches school, cheers his spirit, and plays a dozen parts to his one. Here as in *Retribution* and *The Discarded Daughter* Southworth shows that the democratic ideal for her means equality for men and women, and she places her democratic hopes in the West. On the frontier the corrupt South will be replaced by a society that permits women an equal participation in all the affairs of the commonwealth. This society will be just and good in theory as well as fact: in theory, because it is based on the premise of equality; in fact because the activity of good women will make it good. The author's criticisms of the South and of men are intertwined, because the South has institutionalized the patriarchy, which means the domination of men.

Southworth's tenth novel, *The Lost Heiress* (serialized in 1853,

published 1854), tells the story of a heroine rescued by a long-lost
father from the importunities of a domineering suitor—a twist
to the conventional story of heroines rescued from fathers by
suitors. This father is a magnanimous man, but the suitor, with
his absurdly high self-esteem and his unblushing, unearned assumption of every masculine prerogative, is a satire on the male
character. Her next novel, *Miriam the Avenger* (serialized in
1854, published 1855), also known as *The Missing Bride* and
The Fatal Vow, has a similar type, Thurston Wilcoxen, a young
man full of himself, impetuous, exacting, and unreasonable. He
pressures the heroine, Marian Mayfield—a noble independent
woman who runs a small farm, where she takes care of an invalid
friend and the friend's daughter—into a secret marriage and then
mistreats her abominably. In a mysterious incident, Marian
appears to have been murdered by a passing stranger. Thurston
is left for a decade with a gnawing sense of guilt that transforms
him into a decent human being while Marian in reality has spent
those ten years in England, recovering from her grief and regain-
ing her shattered self-esteem:

A little while ago I did not know Thurston—my life was perfect in
itself without him. I stood upon my own feet—strong, happy, calm,
self-possessed and self-reliant—supporting myself and supporting
others—needing no comfort, yet able to comfort others—lone but
free!—now, heart and soul and spirit—all that is best of me—have
gone out of my own possession, and into another's—and peace that
nothing could disturb before, is now at the mercy of another's smile
or frown. Should this be so? Is this worthy of an intellectual—an
immortal being? No.

By virtue of the hero's transformation, Marian eventually gets a
worthy mate.

Within a frame even more melodramatic than usual, *Vivia, or
the Secret of Power,* her thirteenth novel (serialized in 1856, published 1857), follows the lives of three young women, Helen
Wildman, a passionate, self-willed vixen; Theodora Shelley, a
fragile, pensive, passive young woman with artistic talent; and

Vivia (Genevieve) Malmaison, a sunny, energetic, life-loving and love-inspiring heroine. Genevieve is worshipped by a mountain youth, who, fired by love for her, makes himself into a successful writer. But Genevieve will not have him until he outgrows his dependency on her. Helen, whose impulsiveness is self-destructive, first tricks a man who does not love her into marriage and then, disgusted with herself and him, deserts him. The main story line follows Theodora, who wishes only to be left alone to dream and paint but is dragged roughly into life by a forced marriage. She is wedded while drugged to Helen's brother Basil Wildman, an honest but oafish farmer (their relationship foreshadows that of Dorinda and Nathan Pedlar in *Barren Ground*). Basil, on whom a deception has also been practiced, respects and loves his wife and does not force himself on her when he understands what has happened. His behavior earns Theodora's respect in turn, but their relationship does not blossom into love. His accidental death in a flood puts the burden of the farm, and the support of his grandmother and two aunts, all on her. Despite her retiring nature, and a lameness acquired in a riding accident that was Helen's fault, Theodora learns to farm, to hire and fire, to keep accounts, to haggle and borrow. After a while, the grandmother dies and the two aunts go to live elsewhere; Theodora moves to New York alone, where, with Genevieve's help, she pursues a successful career as a painter. In time both of these women marry happily: Genevieve weds her mountain boy, now an independent man; and Theodora marries her first love, who had been tricked earlier into marrying Helen.

Southworth ended the decade with her most popular serial, *The Hidden Hand*, serialized in 1859 and not published in book form until 1889. It was her sixteenth work; she had been writing for just ten years. The novel is set largely in the city (a departure for Southworth), where Capitola, the independent, self-support-ing, and self-rescuing heroine, has run away from her villainous guardian uncle. Capitola proves as resourceful and effective in the city as other Southworth heroines had been in the country, and carries the fantasy of feminine preeminence further than any previous novels had, for she dresses as a boy and successfully acquits herself in such masculine exploits as fighting duels. But like those of all Southworth heroines, her story ends with a good marriage. One would wish that, in her repeated depictions of strong and superior women, Southworth had left an occasional heroine unmarried, as sign that glamor might adhere to a single woman, an old maid. Perhaps she felt that her public would be disappointed if she failed to reform the man; more likely, since she seemed to write as she pleased, she found confirmed spinsters irrelevant to her interest in the conflict between men and women. Perhaps for the same reason, she uses few important auxiliary characters who are spinsters or widows.

Such figures are common in Caroline Lee Hentz's fiction, and so are antagonist women, whose place in Southworth's fiction is rather decorative than structural. Four of Hentz's eight novels pit the heroine against another woman; in *Linda,* a stepmother; in *Rena,* a jealous rival; in *The Planter's Northern Bride,* a former wife; in *Helen and Arthur,* an older sister. Like Southworth, Hentz preferred active, enterprising, strong-willed women to passive and fragile types for her heroines; but she tended to make these women more ladylike and "ethereal" than did Southworth. Southworth preferred interesting to beautiful faces, while all Hentz's heroines are exquisite as angels, though not invariably blonde. Rena, in the novel that bears her name, has straight, heavy dark hair and a frank, open disposition; it is her clinging and duplicitous antagonist who is blonde. But Hentz preferred simple contrasts to the variegation characteristic in Southworth's novels. Just as her heroines are more delicate than Southworth's, her style, though in the same decorative mold, is more subdued, and her range more restricted. Her writing is deft and light; she is often successfully comic and occasionally surprisingly graphic.

Tyrannical fathers do appear in her fiction, but the important male characters are mostly young, and her depiction of men follows its own polar scheme: there are overzealous, undisciplined suitors—typical southern males as we have seen them in Gilman, McIntosh, and Southworth—who have never been trained to self-denial or self-discipline—and magnanimous, noble heroes whose passions are held in check by respect for the woman and by an ideal of appropriate manly behavior as protective rather than exploitive. Some recent discussions of Hentz have suggested that *all* her men are jealous and overbearing and attributed these traits to the alleged character of her husband. Although a man of this type does figure importantly in Hentz's novels, he appears as one of a pair developed according to a conventional duality.

Hentz had been born Caroline Lee Whiting in 1800; she was a Massachusetts native, one of eight children whose father, a bookseller, died when she was ten. In 1824 she made what looked like a good marriage to Nicholas Marcellus Hentz, a French immigrant, who was an accomplished linguist, engraver, painter, and entomologist. From 1826 to 1830 they lived at Chapel Hill, where he was Professor of Modern Languages at the University of North Carolina, and she bore four children, one of whom died. Then he resigned his position for reasons unknown and commenced an erratic career, establishing a succession of girls' schools in different southern towns. Caroline Hentz assisted in teaching and administration at these schools and also took total responsibility for the boarding operation of these establishments. At Chapel Hill and in the first years of their wanderings, she had written plays, stories, and short novels. Two collections were published, *Aunt Patty's Scrap Bag* and *The Mob Cap,* in 1846 and 1848 respectively. In 1849, when her husband's health gave way, she turned full time to writing. From then until her death from pneumonia in 1856, she was the family provider and a very busy writer, producing eight novels and several collections of short stories.

In her day, Hentz was found to balance "spontaneousness and freedom" with "refinement, delicacy, and poetic imagery." She was praised too for her wit and humor; hers, one critic observed, was a "merry muse." The impression that persists in her books is of high spirits and good fun, less earthy than Southworth's. It was at least partly her intention to show that the ideal of womanhood did not require continuous self-suppression, passive compliance with the demands of others, and a life of suffering and self-sacrifice. Her heroines suffer when they have to and sacrifice if necessary, but they all have a capacity for enjoying themselves and manage to find much pleasure in life. On occasions when they strike particularly high-minded attitudes they do so partly in a spirit of self-parody. They approach life as a test and trial, of course, but also as adventure and entertainment.

Hentz's first and most popular novel, *Linda* (1850), went into its thirteenth edition within two years. It combines a story of domestic persecution with a series of perilous adventures and escapes, a formula that evidently pleased many. Linda, who has led a happy child's life as the pet of the plantation, enters a new era when her mother dies and her father remarries a cold-hearted and domineering widow, Mrs. Graham, who has a son five years older than Linda. The father, a good-natured, phlegmatic man whose "will was easily shaped by the will of others," quickly falls into the background and permits his new wife to slight Linda and favor her spoiled, willful son outrageously. A mercenary woman, she dislikes Linda but wants her to marry her son, Robert, so that he can have her money and estate.

Linda gets a respite from persecution when she goes off to a ladies' school run by the virtuous Mrs. Riviere—given her personal history, it is hardly surprising that Hentz used schoolmistresses in supporting roles regularly, and often chronicles the details of boarding-school life. On the way to school with her father, Linda is involved in a carriage accident from which she is rescued by Roland Lee, the exemplary son of a reduced widow who is making his way back up in the world. Four years later, the steamship on which she is returning from school with her father blows up. Her father is killed (Hentz describes his "crisped and blackened body" with surprising relish), and again Roland, now the steamship pilot, rescues her. His magnanimous, open, disciplined nature contrasts to the Byronism of Robert Graham, who is self-absorbed, erratic, turbidly and turgidly emotional. Linda has not a splinter of the Byronic in her nature. She is drawn to Roland and repelled by Robert. Without her father on the plantation to protect her, Linda finds the ceaseless attempts of her stepmother and stepbrother to hound her into marriage intolerable. "I am living in sin and strife," she reflects, "in an atmosphere of passion, withering to my soul's life. I am becoming a creature of wild impulses, which might urge me on to deeds of madness and crime." Desperate, she runs away.

Now follows an assortment of gory adventures wherein Linda, a noble Indian named Tuscarora, and a former schoolmaster escape several villains. These events culminate in a tremendous brain fever for the heroine, who lies ill for many months while a report comes to Robert Graham and his mother that she is dead. Robert turns on his mother, driving *her* into a fever, and suffers agonies of remorse that lead to a religious conversion, and ultimately to his becoming a minister. This reformation does not win Linda away from Roland, and when she recovers and returns to the living, Robert is so magnanimous as to perform the wedding ceremony.

Linda in some ways represents an example of the kind of "doublespeak" that popular novels are supposed to capitalize on. It makes use of storm and suffering while insisting that passion or uncontrolled emotion is selfish and destructive. The device of using stormy incidents to advocate peace and quiet continues in Hentz's subsequent novels. Yet in these books, the novelist's stock defense that she depicts certain scenes to warn against them is ultimately convincing. Hentz tries and succeeds in making storm and suffering seem unattractive; one might contrast her here again to Southworth, for whom all strong emotions are enjoyable. Hentz's heroines are afraid of passionate men, and for good reason—theirs is not a fear of the sexuality of the male, but of the male "animal"—that kind of man who in imperious pursuit of his own gratification thinks nothing of how he treats the object of

his supposed desire. Hentz's women are both traditional and untraditional in this respect: traditional in that they are searching
for men to look up to and respect, so that the marriage vow of
obedience may be freely and willingly fulfilled; but untraditional
in that they do not respect men who make them suffer. For Hentz
there is an ideal of true manhood as well as of true womanhood.
Her ideal man is not timorous or effeminate, but his force is
controlled by respect for the rights and needs of others. Hentz
saw such a man as even more admirable than the self-disciplined
woman, because she thought that men had inherently greater
force and consequently needed greater will power to achieve self-
control. In her view the passionate displays of the uncontrolled
man revealed weakness rather than strength, a weakness close
to insanity.

In a sequel to *Linda, Robert Graham* (1855), Hentz permitted
Robert to marry Linda after a series of events showed how thoroughly he had mastered himself. After years as a missionary in
India, Robert returns to find his love for Linda, now married and
a mother, as strong as ever. He sublimates it into brotherly protection when Roland is away at sea; he even proposes to another
good woman, determined not to let a useless passion warp his life.
Linda and the author take this gesture as a sign not of an unfor-
givable infidelity, but of maturity and realism. When his bride
dies of consumption and Roland is lost at sea the way is cleared
for a marriage that now will be ideal. One observes that Hentz
has no qualms about second marriages or second loves.

Hentz's second novel, *Rena, the Snowbird* (1850), has a New
England setting. Its characters are Rena, the black-haired tomboy
of the title, her Aunt Debby, a prosperous farmer widow who
brings her up because her hypochondriacal mother cannot cope
with her vitality, and Stella, a beauteous blonde orphan from the
poorhouse. Through Rena, Hentz makes the statement that the
wild girl who longs to be a boy is just the girl who will mature
into the best type of womanhood. In contrast to the angelic-
seeming Stella, who wishes to be petted and admired but has

nothing beyond her physical beauty to offer, Rena combines the attractions of honesty, competence, good nature, and enthusiasm, and is loved by all. Of course she gets the hero, Sherwood Lindsay, and Stella's connivances scarcely disturb the smoothness of her life.

True opposition originates in the hero's father, Ernest Lindsay, for Hentz's pair of good and bad men in *Rena* are father and son. This man had abandoned Aunt Debby at the altar when a better opportunity came along; he had sired Stella secretly and let her disgraced mother die in the poorhouse; he is mercenary, snobbish, autocratic, ambitious, and passionate. He forbids Sherwood to marry either Rena or Stella, the former because as a farmer's daughter she is too plebeian, the latter because it would be incest (although he doesn't give Sherwood reasons). Sherwood loves Rena and prepares to disobey him, but since Aunt Debby is also opposed to the match, it is postponed. Through the wicked Lindsay, Hentz continues her crusade against uncontrolled passion. When his political ambitions are disappointed through the loss of an important election, he kills himself in a fit of rage—making Hentz's point about the nearness of passion to insanity, and freeing the lovers to marry.

The most interesting character in *Rena* is Aunt Debby. After anguishing for several years over Lindsay's desertion of her, she pulled herself together and married a prosperous older farmer, whose death left her with a handsome property. Now, by astute managing of the farm, and clever investing of her income, Aunt Debby has become, on her own, far more successful than her husband had ever been; putting her money out to interest, she is the only woman moneylender in all this fiction. She is a fully independent person, one of a type "with whom we never can associate the idea of love—who have such perfect unity of character, we never can imagine them as forming a *half* of another." Hentz's prose conveys her approval of Aunt Debby, a self-dependent woman, strong and often bitter in her prejudices, immovable in her ideas of right and wrong, blunt and generally cold in her

manners, with the "absoluteness of a queen, rectitude of a judge."
It is an unconventional portrait, and the author unconventionally
praises the type she has portrayed.

Her guardianship of Rena is a mutually beneficial relationship,
for Aunt Debby is not a person to train a woman in artifice, and
she preserves the basic energy of Rena's character while training
her in industry and self-control. In turn, Rena's affectionate disposition makes life a good deal more pleasant for Aunt Debby
and softens the harshness of her character. She remains strong
and independent but loses her bitterness and the self-protective-
ness that had been caused by disappointment.

I pass over Hentz's *Marcus Warland* (1852), which has a male
protagonist, to *Eoline,* published in the same year, which has
another interesting portrait of a single woman. This is Miss Manly
(certainly deliberately named), headmistress of the boarding
school where Eoline, the heroine, takes a position as music teacher
after running away from her father and a forced marriage. Once
again Hentz develops a contrast of men, between the passionate
young Creole who takes a job in the school just to be near Eoline,
and the man to whom Eoline had been plighted, who turns out
to be an ideal man after all. In keeping with Hentz's comic attitudes, the two young lovers, having stoutly resisted marriage on
the principle that marriages contracted by parents are degrading,
find that they love one another, and their marriage is a joke on
everyone, including the fathers.

Eoline's character is a mix of adolescent Byronism and practical
sense. "I was born to look up—up—high as the eagle's eyrie," she
says. "It is this upward-reaching spirit that makes me joy in the
warring clouds of the rushing winds. They are high and powerful,
and I love them." Still, when she runs away, she runs to a teaching job that she has already made certain of, and she packs her
bags with care. Her teacher, Miss Manly, is a more substantial
character. She has elected her schoolmistress's life as a vocation,
and not out of need or in recoil from disappointed affections. Her
great faults are transfigured by the sincerity of her ambition, her

rather ludicrous posturing is redeemed by the underlying dedication. As Eoline comes to know her better, she increasingly respects her and (in a reprise of the Rena-Debby relationship) her affection does the lonely woman good. "There was much in her of the material of which martyrs are made and heroes moulded," writes Hentz, who gives to her, and to her school, Magnolia Vale, the last scene in the book:

"I have chosen my vocation, and never shall abandon it. It has its thorns, but it has its roses, too. Let others seek happiness in the exercise of domestic virtues. . . . I have entered a broader, and I say it with modesty, a nobler, more exalted sphere." . . . A deep and gentle seriousness shaded the blooming countenances around her, for they felt, as she spoke, the truth of their immortal destiny. The sun which had been hidden behind a white, fleecy cloud, now rolled its silver wheel on the clear, blue, ether, and a flood of light bathed the bosom of Magnolia Vale.

The writing here probably exemplifies what the critics called her poetic imagery and seems florid to today's taste. But we should not overlook Hentz's purpose. In celebrating a girls' school, she celebrates the movement to educate women and the women dedicating themselves to that movement; and her point goes beyond the acquisition of knowledge to the fact that the structure of this experience, which takes young women seriously as people and their education as a divine charge, has the result of making the young women themselves feel "the truth of their immortal destiny."

Helen and Arthur (1853) develops yet another single and singular woman character. Aunt Thusa is both figuratively and literally a spinster. She had kept house for a bachelor brother and been left poor when he died. Now she boards around the community, spinning each household's flax in turn and enthralling children and servants with her storyteller's gift, a gift that runs to the supernatural and morbid. Introduced as a minor character to bring out the hyperimaginative faculty of the heroine,

Helen, she develops beyond the requirements of the story line, as Hentz herself observes in an aside:

We acknowledge a preference for Miss Thusa. She is a strong, original character, and the sunlight of imagination loves to rest upon its salient angles and projecting lines. When we commenced our sketch, our sole design was to describe her influence on the minds of others, and to make her a warning beacon to the mariners of life, that they might avoid the shoals on which the peace of so many morbidly sensitive minds have been wrecked. But we found a fascination in the subject which we could not resist. A heart naturally warm, defrauded of all natural objects on which to expend its living fervor, a mind naturally strong confined within close and narrow limits, an energy concentrated and unwasting, capable of carrying its possessor through every emergency and every trial— these characteristics of a lonely woman, however poor and unconnected she might be, have sometimes drawn us away from attractive themes.

The main plot of *Helen and Arthur* uses Hentz's favorite contrast of feminine types, between the natural heroine whose open personality is a lodestone and the designing heroine whose calculating personality alienates. Unlike Southworth and others who endowed the manipulative woman with immense attractiveness, Hentz permits her little drawing power. *Rena* had opposed a dark-haired honest beauty to a clinging blonde conniver; *Helen and Arthur* contrasts the more conventionally fair, affectionate Helen to her scheming, passionate older sister Mittie. Hentz like other women authors sees a near relationship between scheming and passion; beneath the calculations of this type of woman is seething emotionality. This submerged passion is the source of her attraction, in the writings of many women authors; but Hentz finds a passionate woman no more appealing than a passionate man.

Mittie has fallen in love with Bryant Clinton, a friend of her brother who is visiting their home; Bryant, something of a womanizer, responds at first but soon succumbs to Helen's more traditional femininity. Helen is appalled by what she considers his dishonorable advances and repelled by his insinuating masculine style. She much prefers Arthur Hazleton, a physician some fifteen years or more older than she, and many times wiser and firmer. Between Clinton's advances, Mittie's jealousy, and the instability of their brother Louis, Helen finds home life unbearably turbulent and takes refuge in the home of Arthur's widowed mother and blind sister.

We must pause to observe here how very often in woman's fiction the young heroine responds to her dilemma by running away, how that gesture earns the author's approval, and how it leads to improvement in the heroine's circumstances. In contrast to Richardson's Clarissa, whose flight led to imprisonment and death, flight in woman's fiction implies a movement toward freedom. But, in contrast to the flights of Tom Sawyer and Huckleberry Finn, the women run successfully because they know where they are going and because running away is not a final gesture but a beginning. Tom Sawyer runs away only so that those he leaves behind will mourn him. Huck Finn runs from, but not to. The heroines of woman's fiction spend no time at all wondering how their loss will be taken (too often, as they fully know, they will not be missed at all), and they run toward goals that are clearly visualized, that involve greater freedom but also greater responsibility. From their very different perspectives, both Richardson and Twain interpret flight as an intrinsically histrionic and ultimately futile gesture. Oddly, for our supposedly homebound women, running away had its uses.

Helen's two women protectors are characteristic examples of admirable single women in Hentz's fiction. All ends well for the heroine and her allies, of course. Helen marries Arthur. Clinton is jailed for forgery and embezzlement ("white-collar" crimes to which weak male characters are often driven in this sort of fiction, when they run into debt). Mittie, after agonizing in the throes of passion until her health and beauty are lost, resigns herself to a single life. We see again Hentz's intention of conveying antiromantic sentiments through the medium of romance. Perhaps her method is duplicitous, but how else would she be more likely to reach devoted romance-readers?

The Planter's Northern Bride (1854) is now Hentz's best-known work because it was intended as a counterstatement to *Uncle Tom's Cabin*. It chooses, for its purposes, a heroine from the North, daughter of an intransigent abolitionist, who marries a wealthy planter for love even though she is both prejudiced against and ignorant of the South. As mistress of a plantation she finds grace and energy, morality and taste, in the region and decides that the slave system is appropriate to the Negro character. As Eulalia, the heroine, attaches herself to the South, the author expounds on the fearful threat to southern whites and their property created by abolitionist agitation. Finally, the book is less a defense of slavery than a frantic plea to the North to curtail abolitionist meddling with southern life before it initiates a bloodbath.

Women's issues in *The Planter's Northern Bride* are subordinate, though not absent. Planter Moreland has divorced his vicious first wife, who, unable to accept his patriarchal marriage attitudes and chafing under what she considered restraints on her freedom, had behaved indiscreetly as a means of rebelling. Eulalia must make up her mind to a marriage that, because the first wife is still alive, many would consider adulterous. Hentz argues that when an earlier wife has failed to carry out her responsibilities, divorce is legitimate and a second wife need have no moral qualms. In fact, her marriage is a virtuous undertaking; she brings order to a deteriorated household, rears and loves the neglected children, and restores her husband's faith in women. Hentz recognizes that patriarchy is an institution affecting women as well as slaves; but since she is defending it for the slave, she must defend it for women as well. Hence Eulalia is her most conservative and traditional heroine, fulfilled in the most traditional kinds of wifely behavior and happy to be ruled by Moreland. The first wife dies, ill, poor, and insane.

Hentz's last novel, *Ernest Linwood* (1856), subtitled "The

Inner Life of the Author," has been inaccurately assumed by some to be autobiography. It is, rather, Hentz's only fiction narrated in the first person, and the only one in which the heroine is permitted to marry an unreclaimed passionate man. The story refutes the heroine's naive belief that marriage can change a man's nature. When *Ernest Linwood* opens, the heroine Gabriella lives with her impecunious, abandoned, adored mother and a loyal servant. Gabriella, who must expect to earn her own living later in life, plans to be a schoolteacher, but her poetic nature longs for a romantic destiny. In an epidemic her mother and the servant die; Mrs. Linwood, a wealthy village aristrocrat, takes Gabriella into her home and brings her up as a daughter.

In time, the Byronic son of the house appears, and he and Gabriella immediately fall in love—this love, thinks Gabriella, will be the romantic fulfillment she has longed for. Mrs. Linwood warns Gabriella that Ernest, like his father, is mentally unstable, with a morbidly suspicious nature that manifests itself toward women in irrational jealousy. Gabriella is more stimulated than repelled by the idea of the single-minded devotion implied by uncontrollable jealousy; she feels sure that her love is so great, and her conduct will be so exemplary, that she will assuage and cure her husband. Of course she is wrong. Their marriage gives Ernest scope for his pathology and is a disaster for her.

First, he will not go out socially nor permit them to entertain company. After about six months of enchanted idleness in the splendid New York mansion that he fits out for her in oriental style, Gabriella realizes that she is bored. She discovers that though Ernest wants her to be happy, "I must be made happy in *his* way, and by his means. . . . Though he covered the iron bed with the spirit of love, the spirit sometimes withered under the coercion it endured." No matter how carefully she watches herself, untoward events keep taking place that arouse Ernest's jealousy, and eventually in a frenzy he shoots her. Recovering from a long illness, Gabriella learns that Ernest has disappeared. Thus within a year or two jealousy has been shown to be insanity;

the ideal of romantic marriage has been exposed as a travesty of marital harmony. "A union so desolated by the storms of passion as ours has been," Gabriella tells her husband shortly before the catastrophe, "must be sinful and unshallowed in the sight of God." Now our poetic heroine, fully enlightened, yearns for a life of mundane, domestic content.

She achieves this kind of life when her lost father enters her life. He is not the hypocritical deceiver Gabriella's mother had thought him, but a good man separated from his family by a series of mistakes and deceptions on the part of others. He is very wealthy, and he makes a home for Gabriella. "The bliss of confidence, the rapture of repose, the sublimity of veneration, the tenderness of love, all blended like the dyes of the rainbow, and spanned with an arch of peace the retreating clouds of my soul." In this passage Hentz attaches to quietude the adjectives of romantic intensity: confidence is bliss, repose is rapture, veneration is sublime. To those who have undergone the romantic agony, bourgeois content seems an ecstasy.

When Ernest reappears again several years later, apparently cured by his own excesses, he is integrated into a household dominated by Gabriella's father. Hentz goes beyond her earlier advice that women should avoid falling victims to the glamor of romance; she says in *Ernest Linwood* that when they admire the Byronic male they invite their own destruction. Mrs. Linwood and Gabriella have both made a mistake in complying with Ernest's insane demands; had they resisted him, they could not have made him sicker and they might have helped make him well. When woman plays the man's game, he simply plays it himself all the more intensely. In such a world it takes another male to guarantee that the romantic male will behave himself: Gabriella's father is her security.

In this image of a world finally integrated under the rule of a benevolent patriarch (the same image functions in *The Planter's Northern Bride*) we see the chief difference between Hentz and Southworth. Hentz was critical of romantic patterns and of the patriarchy; yet in each novel she found a mate for her heroine whose appreciation of good women assured that he would rule benevolently; thus she combined feminine self-expression and self-development with a traditional hierarchical view of the relations between men and women. But Southworth found men so invariably inadequate to the responsibilities of patriarchy that she had to imagine a different system altogether—sometimes a matriarchy, sometimes a western democracy. Her novels are at once much more enthusiastic in their romanticism, and much more cynical about the patriarchal ideal, then Hentz's.

6

Susan Warner, Anna Warner, and Maria Cummins

Late in 1850, in time for the Christmas season, a book called *The Wide, Wide World*, bearing an 1851 copyright date and pseudonymously published under the name Elizabeth Wetherell, made a kind of publishing history. The volume and speed of its sales altered the expectations of all publishers and authors thereafter; it is alleged by some historians to have initiated the very concept of the best seller. A success of this kind—though certainly not of this magnitude—was what the author, Susan Warner, had hoped for. She had written it out of great financial need, to make money. Later, after her authorship became known, she made it clear that she would not have undertaken to write for any other reason. She was born in 1819 into a comfortable, even luxurious, home. Her father had worked his way from country boy to successful lawyer (her grandparents' farm appears in much Warner fiction) and her mother came from a good New York family. Married in 1817, this unfortunate woman bore five children in ten years, three of them dying in infancy, and died shortly after the birth of Susan's sister Anna in 1827. Mr. Warner brought his unmarried sister Fanny to live with them and raise the girls, and she became a permanent member of the household. In her early teens, when Anna was still a child—the sisters were eight years apart—Susan had private tutors for a variety of subjects and received lessons from her father and father's friends in music, Italian, French, painting and drawing, grammar, history, literature, geography, Greek, Latin, arithmetic, and botany. She was an intensely bookish girl, so much so that she was ordered into the country from time to time for her health. She developed a passion for riding horses, a characteristic of all her heroines.

Her father, who had speculated heavily and made several unwise investments in real estate as well, lost a great deal of money in the Panic of 1837, when Susan Warner was eighteen. The beautiful New York town house was sold along with its elegant furnishings, and the family—Susan, Anna, father, and Aunt Fanny—moved to their country property, Constitution Island, in the Hudson River opposite West Point. This land had been envisioned as the grounds of a sumptuous summer estate; now the old farmhouse that was to have been replaced by the Warner mansion became their permanent home. When they moved back to New York City in the wintertime, which they did when their means permitted, they went into lodgings. Not content to let well enough alone, or to behave like a distressed businessman in fiction by returning to his original profession and working himself back to financial comfort, Mr. Warner speculated further, engaged in litigation with his neighbors, and invested his increasingly limited funds in the construction of rental units from which—owing to unaccountable carelessness on his part in the deed of sale to the property on which these units were built—he never realized any money. Year after year, the Warners became poorer and poorer. The girls and their aunt learned to do all the work around the house and to practice all sorts of economies (lacking bonnets, they could not go to church). But such penny-pinching had little effect on Mr. Warner's massive disbursal of cash, and the women had neither the legal or the physical ability to restrain him. Anna Warner invented a natural history game, and the sisters were employed by its publisher to color the cards, twenty-four to each set. The cards arrived just after they had lost their furniture in a public sale, and the sisters sat down to their work on crates and boxes.

One evening in the kitchen, as Anna told the story years later in her biography of Susan, "Aunt Fanny spoke. 'Sue, I believe if you try, you could write a story.' Whether she added 'that would sell.' I am not sure; but of course that was what she meant." Begun in the winter of 1847, *The Wide, Wide World* took a little over a year to write. "It was written in closest reliance upon God," Anna commented. "In this sense, the book was written upon her knees." This remark has been misconstrued and mocked as evidence of Susan's sense of the divine mission behind her work. But Anna's telling makes clear that Susan was not praying for permission to become the divine mouthpiece; she was praying for success.

According to Anna, success came but did them little good. All the money that they made on *The Wide, Wide World* as well as Susan's next best seller, *Queechy,* and Anna's successful novel, *Dollars and Cents,* went to pay for Mr. Warner's lawsuits, debts, and bad investments. Their dream of making a quick fortune and living as ladies for the rest of their lives had evaporated by 1857, and the sisters resigned themselves, although with considerable bitterness at least on Susan's part, to a lifetime of hard labor and looking after father. Anna's claim that after 1856 Susan published at least one book each year until her death in 1885 is not supported by such bibliographies as the Library of Congress or Union Catalogs or Lyle H. Wright's *American Fiction* (although *Notable American Women* accepts it), but Susan and Anna together eventually published twenty-one novels, and they wrote religious books and books on gardening as well. Susan wrote thirteen novels (seven after 1875), Anna four, and jointly they wrote another four. Their later books did not have the same success as their first works, and often they sold their copyrights outright to obtain immediate cash and thus gave up their royalties. Thus, Anna says, they never knew financial ease. They supplemented their literary income by running a farm on Constitution Island, where Mr. Warner (who tried briefly to return to the law, but gave it up) issued orders and Susan countermanded them.

For both sisters, the lonely and toiling life they led acquired a certain dignity and meaning through their religious beliefs. Religion was both a compensation and a role. Anna quotes Susan in her diary for 1873, where she writes of her spinsterhood: "There came a vision of the great gladness . . . that has merely looked in at our windows and passed by! And then I thought afterwards, I was rather glad there was nobody between Christ and me." Susan derived immense pleasure from giving weekly Bible classes at West Point, and possibly she viewed some of her more pietistic novels as agents of conversion among her readers. *The Wide, Wide World* clearly has a profound though indirect relation to her life, referring to her loss of her mother and her immersion in a crude rural existence.

It opens in a New York City hotel room, where Mrs. Montgomery and her ten-year-old daughter Ellen are waiting out a cheerless November day. The mother, an invalid, dozes. The little girl, as she has been instructed to do, passes the time by looking out the window.

Rain was falling, and made the street and everything in it look dull and gloomy. The foot-passengers plashed through the water, and horses and carriages plashed through the mud; gaiety had forsaken the side-walks, and equipages were few, and the people that were out were plainly there only because they could not help it. . . . Daylight gradually faded away, and the street wore a more and more gloomy aspect. The rain poured, and now only an occasional carriage or footstep disturbed the sound of its steady pattering. . . . At length, in the distance, light after light began to appear; presently Ellen could see the dim figure of the lamplighter crossing the street, from side to side, with his ladder; then he drew near enough for her to watch him as he hooked his ladder on the lamp-irons, ran up and lit the lamp, then shouldered the ladder and marched off, the light glancing on his wet oil-skin hat, rough greatcoat, and lantern, and on the pavement and iron railings.

These well-turned sentences of *The Wide, Wide World,* with their direct prose, pictorial vividness, and rhythmical clauses, announce a literary talent unmarked by the alleged "feminine" excesses of overblown imagery and inflated diction. But Susan Warner's subject, and the angle from which she approaches it, are relentlessly and deliberately feminine. Turning away from the window, Ellen makes tea for herself and her mother, and the two contemplate their bleak future. Mr. Montgomery, after losing a law suit, has taken a position in Europe. Mrs. Montgomery, in failing health, has been advised to accompany him. She lacks the strength to care for Ellen, so the child must go to live with her father's sister, Miss Fortune Emerson, who lives on a farm in the country. Mother and daughter are devoted to each other and have never been separated before. Each knows, though neither expresses it except in tears, that the separation will be final. These tears, which flow throughout the novel, have exasperated male critics, who repeatedly satirize its lachrymosity; for Warner, her characters, and her readers, the freedom to express grief is one of the few freedoms permitted women, though it must generally be indulged in private.

Need we say something in defense of tears? Women do cry, and it is realism in our authors to show it. The nineteenth-century woman was not ashamed of her tears, and in woman's fiction, the heroines are encouraged to cry as therapy. It is recognized that grief may literally kill if it is not vented in tears. And other emotions—above all anger and frustration—may be safely expressed in tears when no other way can be indulged. One might theorize that the frequency of tears in a woman's fiction is proportional less to the amount of tenderness and sensibility that imbues it, than to the amount of rage and frustration that it carries. I speak of safe expression because rage and frustration may not be openly voiced by the powerless without unfortunate consequences for them. More than any of the other women, Susan Warner dealt with power and the lack of it.

At the beginning of *The Wide, Wide World,* two powerless

women are struggling to accept the apparent injustice of two
fathers, injustice from which they have no recourse. The earthly
father, a selfish, inconsiderate, and undependable man, is more
easily dealt with than the Heavenly father, for he does not need to
be defended. But as a pious woman Mrs. Montgomery feels that
she must justify God's ways to her daughter, even when those
ways include killing the mother. The decrees of God, she insists,
are invariably dictated by love even if the loving motive is not
apparent to mere human understanding. Many other devout
people in the novel take up this refrain, telling her that God's act
of depriving her of her mother was loving and gracious. Ellen
learns that the dispensation must be accepted and comes gradually to look ahead rather than back, but she never fully over-
comes her childish conviction that she lives in an unjust world.
Over the course of this long novel (690 pages in its first, two-
volume edition) Ellen learns to take pleasure where it is found
and to negotiate without being destroyed by the powerful unjust.
The story would have been different, of course, could she (or
her author) have broken through to gestures of defiance more
pleasing to the twentieth century or, better still, to an expression
of existential doubt or absurdity. But Ellen, who sees powerful
unjust people in the world—she cannot even make a minor pur-
chase for her mother without being badgered by a spiteful clerk—
sees no reason to conclude from metaphysical injustice that there
is no God. The reason for her struggle to believe that God is not
unjust follows from her certainty that he exists. One gets along
better with absolute power if one accepts it as beneficent.

Susan Warner's version of the orphan's story is different from
many other authors' in that she focuses so quickly and exclusively
on the issue of power and how to live without it. Although this is
not a purely feminine issue by any means (it concerned Melville,
for example; one might say that *Moby-Dick* is a masculine treatment of the same question) Warner handles it exclusively in a
feminine iconography. The loss of a mother is not traumatic to
female children alone, but only women will admit to the desola-

tion of this particular pain, and hence the primal injustice from which Ellen's story develops seems like an injustice suffered only by women. Since God is a paternal idea, it is an injustice perpetrated on women by man.

Beyond this terrible initiating event, however, Ellen's social trials—really much less severe than those endured by many heroines—are the sort that only women are supposed to suffer, whether they be fashionable people mocking her dowdy bonnet, or Aunt Fortune dyeing all her fine white stockings dun-colored (though White-Jacket and his sartorial anguish comes to mind here). In each case of humiliation or hardship, offenses are committed by those who have "charge" of Ellen, and the child cannot respond to them without damaging herself.

And then there is an offense beyond all special examples of provocation: the assumption by those who have guardianship of the child that they "own" her. How is one to endure such situations and yet remain a self? How can one submit to being owned and still be free? However much Warner's self-imposed restrictions to the feminine, to pious orthodoxy, and to a creed of superficial compliance have dated *The Wide, Wide World* for later generations, her questions and answers made sense for the time, and unquestionably for her own purposes she did right.

Ellen is taken on the journey to Aunt Fortune's by a fashionable Mrs. Dunscombe. Her final parting from her mother has been marked by violent grief, augmented by her "sense of wrong and feeling of indignation at her father's cruelty" in not revealing the day of parting until the very morning that they separate—a typical, selfish action on his part. "A child of very high spirit and violent passions," Ellen senses of how little account she is to all except the mother from whom she has been parted, and the feeling creates rage rather than fear. When Mrs. Dunscombe's fourteen-year-old daughter laughs at her unfashionable hat, "the lightning of passion shot through every vein . . . and hurt feeling and wounded pride." Unless she can better control her feelings and behavior, Ellen will find life intolerable.

Ellen's Aunt Fortune is a middle-aged spinster who lives with her aged mother and works a comfortable property; she is not poor but she displays a mean-spiritedness that a number of women authors discerned in country people who see no life beyond the arduous routines of farmwork. She is not vicious, but she is cold, narrow-minded, and bitter, with a rivulet of cruelty in her nature that finds an outlet in petty torments, like withholding her mother's letters from Ellen until she is "good." Except for denying Ellen a formal education (after teasingly implying she might go to school) she does the child no serious harm, but her coldness, coupled with her traditional belief that bringing up a child means breaking her will, leaves Ellen increasingly dissatisfied, restless, and resentful.

Matters do not come to a head, however, because Ellen finds a guide in Alice Humphreys, a young neighbor who lives with her father, a minister. (There is a brother in this family but he is away at school until later in the action.) Alice comforts Ellen and instructs her in religion; it is Alice's love rather than her doctrine that strengthens the girl, but Christianity gets the credit for Ellen's growth in control. Alice's religious teachings are actually quite pragmatic: "Return good for evil as fast as you can, and you will soon either have nothing to complain of or be very well able to bear it." She advises Ellen to be solicitous of her neglected grandmother—not to do her Christian duty, but to develop some affection in that loveless house. And as for Aunt Fortune, "see if you cannot win her over by untiring gentleness, obedience, and meekness." Actually, Ellen's new behavior does not win the aunt over, but it disarms her; unable to aggress against the child, she leaves her alone, and Ellen finds the freedom that she would never have enjoyed if she had remained defiant.

When Aunt Fortune marries the man who manages her farm, Ellen is allowed to go live with the Humphreys. There, surrounded by books and love, Ellen is gloriously happy. The return of brother John, a minister in training, completes an idyll of domestic felicity. Alice dies, but Ellen has grown into a noble young

woman under her guidance and can assume her place. The interlude is terminated by the death of Ellen's father (mother had died
some time before). Now she is sent to live in Edinburgh with
Scottish relatives named Elliott. Ellen does not want to go, but
has no choice. She does not belong to herself but to her parents,
even when they are dead, and must go wherever they decree. At
the Elliotts' she meets a new kind of struggle. These elegant, accomplished, sophisticated people make it clear that they expect
her submission in every detail, exactly as Aunt Fortune had, to
their way of life. Ellen is to do what they do, and never think to
pass judgment on them. They are deeply offended by her provin-
cial evangelical Christianity and her continually expressed long-
ings for the Humphreys.

"She was petted and fondled as a darling possession—a dear
plaything, . . . but John's was a higher style of kindness . . .
and his was a higher style of authority." Uncle Elliott takes away
a book that John had given her—taking things away from children is a common means by which adults manifest their ownership and authority. "But it is mine," Ellen protests. "And you are
mine," Uncle Elliott responds. From this situation there is no
escape other than a fairy-tale rescue, and John soon turns up in
Edinburgh to impress the Elliotts with his force of character and
to wrest concessions from them for Ellen that they would not
accede to when she asked for them herself. She may write to
John, for example, and be allowed more latitude in her religious
observances. Uncle Elliott goes so far as to accompany her to
church.

But John is constrained in what he can accomplish for Ellen by
a greater authority. "I have no power now to remove you from
your legal guardians," he tells her, "and you have no right to
choose for yourself." So Ellen must wait it out, with the promise
that she may return to America when she comes of age. Her
Christian-based discipline enables her to do this. "Three or
four more years of Scottish discipline wrought her no ill; they did
but serve to temper and beautify her Christian character; and

then, to her unspeakable joy, she went back to spend her life with the friends and guardians she best loved, and to be to them, still more than she had been to her Scottish relations, the 'light of the eyes.' "

The Edinburgh section serves as a coda and recapitulation of the theme that runs through the longer, rural section of the book. In their high-toned way the Elliotts aggress against Ellen no less than had Aunt Fortune. It is, however, far less realized; Warner had depicted the countryside that she knew so well with a scrupulous fidelity to detail, an ear for speech and an eye for custom, that makes *The Wide, Wide World* a thoroughly achieved work of local color. For this, at least, it deserves a place in American literary history.

Insofar as it does not follow Ellen past her adolescence, *The Wide, Wide World* might be typed as a juvenile; it does not deal with such adult issues as self-support, love, and marriage (although we assume that eventually Ellen and John will marry). The economic theme that dominates so much woman's fiction is absent here; but the terminology of ownership clearly implies a private perception of the economic theme as applied to human relations. The absence of romance, or the absorption of romance in the larger issues of family and guardianship, expresses overtly a concern that "romance" often masks in other woman's fictions. The heroine who marries happily at the end of most woman's fiction acquires a way of life, a home, a complex of human relations. Marriage is the means of establishing a family that is not a biological unit but a community of loving adults assembled under one roof. In this group the heroine plays both a child's and an adult's role. In fact, all the adults take different roles toward one another, rectifying, so to speak, the mistakes and curing the wounds that have been inflicted on them in their real family experiences. Such a surrogate family represents allegiance to the family ideal at the same time that it embodies a bitter criticism against families as the characters (and their authors) have really known them.

The ending of *The Wide, Wide World* is different from much woman's fiction in its vision of the heroine entering a domestic situation in which she is relieved from responsibility. Warner's vision of woman's restricted power allows no space in which their hegemony might be possible, and her sense of woman's needs does not include domination over others. What she wanted was relief and release from all obligation. Given the Warners' own lives, one might say that this ideal was false to any possibility of life as Susan knew it; but it is precisely such an unfulfilled life of unremitting responsibility that might generate the fantasy of complete freedom and protection. For Susan Warner, the memory of her adolescence when she was surrounded by luxury and refinement, tutored and made much of by her father and other accomplished gentlemen, became her vision of independence. She did not accept the argument that toiling away for money to get through a cold winter could constitute independence. Even the writing of fiction, a profession that might be imagined to yield satisfaction, she considered an arduous drudgery in comparison to her earlier life of self-indulgence and self-development. The cult of domesticity did not appeal to her because it centered woman's life on others. Her ideal of independence was intransigently self-centered. She cared neither to control others nor to serve them. Freedom for her meant being left alone, protected and comfortable, to pursue one's own interests. This is the situation to which Ellen is returned at the end of *The Wide, Wide World*. Once again, as in McIntosh's *Two Pictures,* we encounter a woman's version of the American unwillingness to grow up.

The heroine of Susan Warner's second novel, *Queechy* (1852), Fleda Ringgen, has a character much closer to perfection at the outset than does Ellen Montgomery. Selflessly, she takes the whole burden of her family's support on her inexperienced adolescent shoulders. *Queechy* shows that a woman can do this, and that she should if she must, but not that it is fun or good for her. If her character is already perfect, she does not need trials. Susan Warner depicts suffering in abundance in *Queechy,* but she is not a masochist, for she never calls it pleasure or claims that self-sacrificing drudgery enlarges the soul.

Fleda's ordeals are caused by defective men who shirk their duties and abuse their authority in a system that gives them all the economic power and responsibility. Men shrug off the responsibility on women while retaining the power, leaving women to struggle for bare survival with no hope of achieving financial comfort or security. A fairy-tale ending and continuous celebration of the heroine's perfections do not make up for *Queechy's* mood of hopelessness; Fleda's exceptional character makes her sufferings unmerited, and the improbable finale shows how little succor the author expects from mundane reality. As usual, Susan Warner fails to generalize from her particular situation to some vision of social injustice. The heroine is so clearly better than the rest of her sex that her story does not permit wide generalization and injustice is experienced as entirely personal. The reader who identifies with Fleda will think better of herself but not consequently of other women.

Fleda's world even more than Ellen's is structured so that she can be released from the unjust dominion of one man only by the intervention of another. She must be rescued. Her destiny is to exist and toil in obscurity until her perfections inspire a man to intercede for her. When *Queechy* opens, Fleda, an orphaned child of ten, is living in rural New York with her saintly grandfather. At this age she already possesses "that fine perfection of mental and moral constitution which in its own natural necessary acting leaves nothing to be desired, in every occasion or circumstance of life." She seems "a princess's child . . . dropped in some odd corner of the kingdom," or "a flower of the wood, raising its head above the frost and snow and the rugged soil where fortune has placed it, with an air of quiet, patient endurance;—a storm wind may bring it to the ground, easily—but if its gentle nature be not broken, it will look up again, unchanged, and bide its time in unrequited beauty and sweetness to the end." The compensatory force of this fantasy of the princess in disguise was probably a double-edged weapon to millions of women. It might have bolstered morale in circumstances that provided little external gratification, and thereby helped women to cope; it might have encouraged women to anticipate rescue and made their difficult lives even less bearable. Whatever its effect, Warner offered the fantasy in no spirit of condescension, not as an opiate for the masses. It strikes with the effect of a fantasy that has given its creator immense pleasure and perhaps has helped her to survive, and in this spirit it is submitted to the reader.

We see Fleda's effect on others at the outset of the story, when she and her grandfather are visited by two young men, her cousin Rossitur and his English friend Carleton, both about twenty years old. Rossitur has come with a proposal from his wealthy parents in Paris that Fleda join their family. Carleton is so "awed" by Fleda's purity that a religious conversion is initiated; this regeneration will, in the future, be Fleda's earthly salvation. Meantime, she has a long, devious path ahead. Rossitur's invitation proves most timely, for Grandfather dies suddenly, on the eve of foreclosure and dispossession from "Queechy," his farm. The grieving Fleda is taken by Carleton to Paris and on the ship she continues the work of conversion she has innocently begun. Uncle Rossitur proves to be a good-hearted, worldly, accomplished man, an esthete and hedonist. Later we will discover that his good heart is a function of his worldly success and comfort; he has no reserves for misfortune. Aunt Rossitur is a passive satellite, in her own way also unfit for tribulation. The older son is in the army, the daughter a social butterfly. Fleda finds a kindred spirit in her sickly cousin Hugh, who is about her own age. For several years she enjoys a luxurious cultivated life in Paris and New York. They are educated privately, by tutors, a system that works better for Fleda's innately disciplined nature than for Hugh's more wayward personality. Fleda develops the external graces of a lady; inherently of finer cloth than most, she now displays her quality to the world. So far as the author is concerned, when her mind has been enlarged, her manners polished, and her sensibilities educated, Fleda has become a woman without equal in all the world. What destiny has Warner in mind for this paragon? Uncle Rossitur fails in business and, totally ruined, permits a friend to set him up rent-free on a small farm where he is to try to live free of debt. This farm turns out to be Queechy; so, after a dream-interlude as a fine lady, Fleda is back where she began and worse off than before. She now has memories of a better life against which to measure her present lot, and her dear grandfather has been replaced by the increasingly sour-tempered Rossitur. Rossitur cannot accept his changed life. He cannot live as a poor man. He refuses to bother with the administrative details of farming or to undertake any physical labor himself. In his own eyes, he is far above the plain rural folk and he is offended by their bluff democratic ways. He quickly alienates all his neighbors and only Fleda's tact gets help in the fields and house. More and more he sits around the house wrapped in the airs of a gentleman, making demands on his dependents. Aunt Rossitur, inept at household work, expends her failing energies in soothing and flattering her husband. All labor and responsibility devolve on Fleda and Hugh.

So Warner draws a picture of two frail adolescents supporting two idle, healthy adults. Hugh, who is not only feeble but shy, struggles nobly with such chores as chopping wood and working the mill attached to the farm. Fleda runs the house with the help of a loyal, outspoken servant, Barby. ("I don't believe the world would go now, Fleda, if it wa'n't for women," says Barby. "I never see three men yet that didn't try me more than they were worth.") She tends the vegetable garden and hires the fieldhands. With an unflinching naturalism remarkably at variance with the narcissistic fantasy of the first part of the novel as well as its ending, Warner chronicles the wearying routines and penny-pinching strategies of the children. She also sketches a series of regional portraits. As the young people labor, Rossitur becomes ever more discontented and more shameless in his irresponsibility; he projects his guilt in the form of touchy pride and petty tyrannies. Hugh's health deteriorates; Mrs. Rossitur develops debilitating headaches.

When the older son comes home on furlough, he is appalled at his father's degeneration and scolds the family for craven submission to his whims. But when he undertakes to criticize his father, he sees by the older man's rage that the fawning flattery of the dependents is a strategy to contain his anger and control his potential for making their lives even more miserable. Though Rossitur has failed his dependents, they legally belong to him. After several years of inflicting misery on his family, Rossitur goes west to look after some land investments—so he says; the family knows that he is abandoning them and is relieved rather than saddened. But his ability to cause trouble for his dependents continues. His attempt to escape some debts by forging a note becomes known, and the family faces disgrace as well as poverty. It seems too high a price for six comfortable years and a lady's education, Fleda thinks. Her last efforts to save her uncle and his family, by going to New York and interceding with the young villain who threatens to expose her uncle, only enmesh her in further difficulty.

Carleton has been hovering in the wings for some time, sending Fleda flowers, and at this point he enters the action and settles everything. Male threats require male force to subdue them. On the train, taking Fleda back to Queechy, he wraps her in his fur cloak, and her troubles are over. "The comfort of the fur cloak was curiously mixed with the feeling of something else, of which that was an emblem—a surrounding of care and strength which could effectually be exerted for her protection,—somewhat that Fleda had not known for many a long day—the making up of the old want. Fleda had it in her to cry like a baby. . . . For years she had been taking care of others; and now there was something so strange in this being cared for, that her heart was full." Fleda's starved heart can barely accept its happiness. At the end, she is lifted out of her troubled world entirely and taken to England to live on a vast estate, in an elegant mansion full of servants. This is pure fantasy, of course, but *Queechy* carries it off because it has so thoroughly depicted that kind of straitened misery from which such a fantasy is created and the tremendous need to which it ministers.

Even more than in *The Wide, Wide World, Queechy* concludes with a vision of woman fulfilled within a protected domestic enclosure, although Carleton's estate is several orders of magnitude more grandiose than the unpretending Humphrey home. The novel exposes a vision that resembles Southworth's—far from being woman's sphere, home is still in reality the man's sphere. In rural New York, Uncle Rossitur behaves just like one of Southworth's planter patriarchs. But unlike Southworth, and much like McIntosh in her later works (in fact, McIntosh's later novels postdate *Queechy*), Warner does not look forward hopefully to a time when men will have been ejected from the home and it is run as woman's sphere of influence. She imagines a sphere that is policed by men but is internally free of power politics, of dominion exercised by either sex. Fleda is profoundly weary of other people. She does not want community but privacy. Removing to the fantasy world of the English gentry, Fleda withdraws altogether from the challenges and hardships of American life. Marriage is celebrated as an escape from adulthood. Warner's fiction is especially intransigent in its rejection of the conception of woman fulfilled through relations to others, whether she rules or serves them, and in its romantic assertion of the absolute primacy of self.

In American literature, such an assertion for men usually involves running away to "the wilderness," literal or figurative, and escaping involvement with the other sex either by celibacy or Don Juanism. Warner's Paradise requires one man. But although she does fantasize one perfect male in each novel, she allows the sex in general no superiority except in physical strength. Framed by its fantasy of Carleton the rescuer, *Queechy* is a bitter indictment of all other men (one is tempted to say of all real men) for their irresponsibility toward the women who are in their power. Beyond this it indicts a world that makes glowing promises to the young which it heartlessly breaks. Warner's romanticism thus looks forward and back: back to an idyll of woman protected and allowed to remain childlike, forward to a restless refusal to be content with crumbs from the table of the powerful.

The Hills of the Shatemuc (1856), Susan Warner's third novel, is said to have sold 10,000 copies on the first day of publication. It marks a return to the piety of *The Wide, Wide World* and a slide into a new ideology of resignation that persists in her later novels. If she chose to suppress her anger as a means of selling more books, she made a mistake, for none of her works after this sold to the extent of her first two. *Hills* is the story of how a young woman learns to be humble and unselfish and thereby gains an ideal husband. Winthrop Landholm is a poor farm boy who, encouraged by his deeply Christian mother, works his way through college to a successful law practice. Like the hero of a morality fiction, he never neglects a single family responsibility or refuses a call on his charity, and he is immune to diversions, amusements, or the manifold possibilities of self-gratification that beset attractive young men in a large city. In his self-control, diligence, morality, intelligence, and perfect serenity, he is an extraordinary (indeed, unbelievable) human being and very much unlike the heroine Elizabeth Haye. She is a spoiled rich girl, intelligent and sensitive but altogether self-absorbed. The difference between Elizabeth and Winthrop is greater than her wealth and his poverty, her selfishness and his magnanimity, her passion and his control. The greatest contrast between them lies in what is possible for them to achieve. However his attainments are accompanied by an ethos of service to others, Winthrop's is a life of self-aggrandisement and expansion of influence, while Elizabeth's is a steady contraction. The young girl imagines herself a princess or a queen. But when her father marries his flighty ward, a superficial heiress just Elizabeth's age, the daughter learns at once that she is a "nobody." Then, when he dies after squandering his young wife's fortune, Elizabeth is left to take care of this uncongenial stepmother.

Her dignity in tatters, her pretensions exposed as fatuous, Elizabeth accepts her lot as protector and servant to one she doesn't care for. Warner says it is good for her. And she proves it by making this same reluctantly supported stepmother maneuver Elizabeth and Winthrop into romantic relationship with one another. Winthrop, though he has long appreciated Elizabeth's good qualities, could never have loved her had she not transcended her early selfishness and accepted the steady contraction of her horizon with plausible grace. Like *What Is Gentility?* almost thirty years before, *The Hills of the Shatemuc* says that women should not expect to make something of themselves. They should find a good man who will make something of them, and in order to do this they must make themselves into a woman whom a good man will appreciate. This message, somewhat different in emphasis from that in *The Wide, Wide World* and *Queechy*, develops the idea of woman's being rather than acting with a new stress on self-abasement as a precondition for feminine reward. No humiliation is required for Winthrop, who is permitted to esteem himself and set his sights very high.

Susan Warner wrote her next novel in collaboration with Anna, who had enjoyed a certain literary success herself. Because she was eight years younger than her sister, Anna Warner (1827–1915) had a different experience from Susan's in the same family. She had lost her mother before she could remember her; Aunt Fanny was the only female parent she knew; she had not so clear an idea of what was involved in the loss of wealth. Consequently, perhaps, she was less angry and more flexible than her sister as well as less aggressive and less enterprising. She was apparently always willing to take second place to Susan, and her adoring biography of 1909 allots only a small role to the biographer. In her first two independently written novels, she assumes the stance of a child-sister observing the older sister who is the heroine. *Dollars and Cents* (1852) sold moderately well. Like *Queechy*, which appeared in the same year, it tells the story of a prosperous family fallen on hard times, of the incompetence of men, and the stoic struggle of women saddled not only with the results of men's incompetence but with the men as well. It appears to follow the family experience much more closely than do Susan's novels—in any event, Anna's account in her biography of Susan is very close to the narrative in *Dollars and Cents,* except that romance and marriage to an attractive young minister are provided for the fictional older sister.

The story opens as Stepmother is trying to dissuade Father (it is narrated in the first person, by the seven-year-old sister, in a style designed to create a child mind and perceptions) from making what she senses is a risky investment. Father is all manly condescension. "Pshaw my dear, you don't know anything about the matter—won't that content you? . . . Have you so little trust in my sense as to suppose that I shall take a flying leap off a precipice?" Such a leap, of course, is just what Father takes, but he is not one to learn from experience, and his self-esteem is unshakable.

Bundling his ladies off to a cottage in the country, he leaves all the heavy work to them while he sanguinely initiates lawsuits against his neighbors (villains all) and undertakes expensive improvements on his property. Father is not at all vicious, but he is totally unself-critical, and insensitive to the situation of his women. He takes their subservience to his wishes and their happy ministrations to his needs as matters of course. The women adjust as best they can. Lacking bonnets, they cannot go to church; still they sit up all night sewing Father's shirts and pantaloons so that he can make a good appearance at court. Father never sees what they so clearly see, that they are supporting him. To be sure, they are not income-producing, but their economies and sacrifices generate the little money that enables them to eat and him to continue his foolhardy course as imaginary landed proprietor.

As in *Queechy,* the situation is such that the superior women have no authority but all the responsibility. Their lives are mortgaged to the mistakes of the male, their energies fully engaged in salvaging something from his errors while keeping him in good spirits and affirming his unmerited assumption of superiority. Stepmother has the proper creed for all this: "There are few principles more important to a woman, my child, than that of patient submission to circumstances. They are very seldom brought about by her agency." But the girls, especially Grace, the older, express more rebellious feelings—although not to Father.

Rose, the narrator, comments that "the endless routine of meals and dishes, sweeping, dusting, bread and bed making,—the toil of mind to contrive and arrange it all,—the want of a pail of water when the clothes were to sprinkle, of *good* wood when they were to iron, of kindling when the fire went out,—the cold rooms and morning when and where we came down to get break-fast—it took women to understand or to get through it. But the spirit-machine, whether mental or physical, works not so briskly when it works in a circle." Yes, she says, women can survive, but what of that? Grace, who loved her New York life, deplores her situation. "How can one grow up unless one lives among other people?" she asks crossly. Father, dimly sensing their distress, announces cheerfully that "every true woman carries about with her a sort of india-rubber framework that fits itself to any niche where she may be placed; but at the same time one niche is better adapted to her than another. . . . [Men] are more angular and unmanageable, and not always content with their niche when they get it." Thus, he theorizes, though the girls are not in the best place for them, they are still flexible enough to adjust (if they are true women), and since they can adjust, they should not be complaining. Dissatisfaction, which is more characteristic of the "defective" male, turns out to be his prerogative. So Father tries to placate these women with the adage that they should be more content than men by nature. Therefore any discontent is a sign of their failure as women. More pragmatic, the women do not dispute his distinctions. They know what they feel, nevertheless.

The story reaches its climax when one of Father's improve-

ments—a mill—burns down and the sheriff comes to the house
to attach all their possessions. Of course Father is away in the city
pursuing some litigation. The three women must defend the house
and themselves. They live for a while barricaded within the house,
but at last are overrun. A public sale takes place, at which every
item of furniture is disposed of. They go into lodgings with a
friendly farmer-neighbor (like her sister's books, Anna Warner's
are rich in local characterization). All comes out well finally when
Grace marries and Father is saved from himself by an appoint-
ment to a professorship at a nearby college.

Dollars and Cents is unique in its realistic study of genteel
poverty and the series of adjustments made by the women to
continually shrinking means and for its exposure of an unpar-
alleled example of male fatuity. It lacks entirely Susan Warner's
tone of pique and self-pity. Indeed, it is rather bouncy, and the
bounce comes from two aspects: the heroine does not take herself
so seriously as a Susan Warner heroine does and consequently is
less personally offended by the injustice of the universe; and it
contains at its heart what it thinks is a good joke—the joke of
Father, so self-satisfied, and so foolish.

Anna's second novel, My Brother's Keeper (1855), is set in
New York back during the War of 1812; it tells how the heroine
(again an older sister viewed through the adoring eyes of the
younger) sacrifices love, health, and happiness to keep house for
her brother and by her womanly presence and patience to save
him from gambling and drinking. In view of the fact that New
York City is under siege, the sister's devotion is utmost heroism.
As is customary in this sort of story, the sister has virtually to die
before the brother sees the error of his ways. When her work is
accomplished, the sister is free to marry her beloved, a Quaker
of considerably greater moral firmness than the brother. Like
Fleda, the heroine has served her time taking care of others and
has earned the right to be taken care of for the rest of her life.

In 1860 the Warner sisters published the first of four jointly
written novels, Say and Seal. Each wrote alternate chapters, and

although their styles are quite different in their individual novels, they succeeded in producing a composite for *Say and Seal*. Later Anna referred to this as a "sweet" book, and it does represent a retreat from the stories of suffering and confrontation with which each sister had begun her literary career. It develops a small-town, intensely Christian love story between a local heroine of surpassing purity and delicacy and a magnanimous outsider who has come to teach in the boys' school. The romance is obstructed by a series of rival suitors and by inevitable separations, but the love felt between John Linden and Faith, the heroine, surmounts all obstacles.

Linden is an ideal Warner hero: devout, intellectual, firm, kind, gentle, and fair, a favorite mixture of the maternal and the manly. Faith is a new kind of Warner heroine, in many ways the antithesis of the proud, self-conscious, moody, willful types Susan had specialized in before. Faith's main qualities are simplicity, serenity, lack of self-consciousness, and reserve. The terms in which she is described—grave, sweet, deep, sober, quiet, delicate, pleasant, silent, graceful, gentle—invoke a mythic femininity, an unworldliness quite beyond the grasp of the Warners' character-istically modern heroines. In fact, Faith is a pastoral heroine in a pastoral myth. *Say and Seal* is a remarkable evocation of small-town New England life, in its complexity of social relationships, rituals, institutions, and its connection to time, history, landscape, and the seasons. The Warners should be recognized as pioneer local-colorists and naturalists; in *Say and Seal* they create a sense of time and place as dense as Sarah Orne Jewett's, just as in *Queechy* and *Dollars and Cents* they represent rural hardship in terms as unsparing as Hamlin Garland's. And like the best local-color writers, they simultaneously capture the essence of a place and time while mythicizing it as a timeless country, the pastoral country that exists as counterstatement to modern turmoil. Like pastoral figures, John and Faith have troubles that make a plea-surable escape from the turbulence of modern life. An old-fash-ioned woman, Faith lives in a world where old-fashioned virtues prevail, where woman has nothing to do but look up to her man, remain true to him, improve herself to be a fit companion for him—and man can be trusted to fulfill his responsibility to protect and guide this confiding creature.

In this atmosphere of trust, the love story is given a physical aspect that is unusual not only in the Warners' fiction but in all fiction of the time written by women. Faith, an incarnation of womanly modesty and decorum, is permitted to be erotically aggressive, and John is allowed to show a physical as well as a spiritual desire for Faith:

> She raised her head and pushing the hair back from his brow with her soft hurried fingers, she covered that and his face with kisses— with a kind of eager tenderness that could not say enough or put enough love and reverence into every touch. . . . Perhaps surprise made him passive; perhaps the soothing of her caresses was too sweet and too much needed to be interrupted, even be returned. He let her have her way, nor even raised his eyes. . . . One arm indeed was round her, but it left her free to do as she liked. . . . Only at last, with a sudden motion [he] brought her lips to his, and gave her back principal and interest.

In the safe world of the pastoral fantasy, and within the safe arms of a trusted beloved, a woman might freely express the sexuality that otherwise she had to hold in check. A passage like this offers support for the hypothesis that women held themselves back sexually not only because they thought sex to be evil or sinful, but because they found themselves greatly disadvantaged in sexual matters. Despite the myth of the sexually powerful female who brought men to her feet in droves, experience showed that sexual self-expressiveness was a dangerous strategy in the real world, the seduced woman more likely to be scorned than adored by her quondam lover. Earlier, I have alluded to the unremitting lesson of the seduction novels of the eighteenth century. Convinced that they could not possibly triumph over men, the nineteenth-century authors strove to define the field of heterosexual encounter as nonsexual. In novel after novel, heroines reject male characters who display predatory qualities, and look for a type that they consider to be more sensitive to their needs and claims. One would guess, on the basis of such rare passages as the one above, that among these was their concealed sexuality; they were looking for men who could be trusted not to take advantage of their sexual needs if they expressed them.

After their first works, the Warner sisters had turned from bitter comedy to romance. This evolution is in accord with the general change in woman's fiction later in the century. In appropriate comic fashion (I use Northrup Frye's terminology here), *The Wide, Wide World* and *Dollars and Cents* developed the ideal of a new society, centered on the heroine, wherein the major characters of the story would all find fulfillment. The marriages that conclude these novels celebrate a social as well as a personal renewal, the salvation, from the debris of human relationships, of a whole and healthy community. *Queechy* appeared to be following the same direction, but its ending shifted to the romantic mode, emphasizing a private exaltation of the heroine that fundamentally rejected any larger social unit. In *Say and Seal*, despite the exquisite representation of small-town New England life, the marriage of John and Faith signifies their withdrawal from society into privacy. Existing society, composed of rival suitors, defines itself as a threat to their relation, and their marriage means a new life for Faith as she leaves the community in which she has been raised, for one in which her husband is her only society.

This woman's version of the romance has given the term its popular meaning of "love story," for all the heroine's adventures are adventures in love, and her apotheosis, or exaltation, is accomplished through union, so to speak, with a God. Whatever its superficial resemblance to the woman's fiction so popular at mid-century, the romance is structurally unlike it and has almost the opposite tendency in its social implications. The romance rejects the controlling sense of social responsibility in woman's fiction, while conversely woman's fiction firmly locates marriage in an extensive social network.

The most successful imitation (in Harold Bloom's sense, mis-
reading) of *The Wide, Wide World, The Lamplighter* (1854)
was both more benign in its vision of society and more social in
its ideology. It would appear that the author, Maria Susanna
Cummins, had grasped the antisocial implications of Susan Warner's view of life and striven to rectify them. Author of four
novels all anonymously published (though their author's identity
was soon known), Cummins (1827–1866) lived an intensely
private life, unmarried, with her prosperous family in Dorchester
outside of Boston. She was educated at home and in the young
ladies' school run by Mrs. Charles Sedgwick, a sister-in-law of
Catharine Sedgwick. Her father was a judge, and she felt no
financial pressure to write; perhaps this accounts for her small
output. *The Lamplighter* is said to have sold 40,000 copies in the
first two months of publication, and 70,000 in its first year; it
inspired Hawthorne's ill-tempered outburst against "scribbling
women," under which blanket epithet all the mid-century women
authors are so often dismissed.

Although, like *The Wide, Wide World, The Lamplighter* depicts characters and scenes in various grades of society—it polar-
izes slum and mansion rather than town and city—its rendering
of locale is much less graphic. Susan Warner (and Anna as well)
had drawn representative local types in convincing concreteness;
Cummins creates representative moral types and costumes them
in localisms. Despite its pietistic orientation, *The Wide, Wide
World* educated its heroine pragmatically and piecemeal; *The
Lamplighter* has a more abstract design. *The Lamplighter*, too,
is far more melodramatic than *The Wide, Wide World*. Ellen's
father was truly drowned at sea. Gerty's father is assumed
drowned, but returns at the denouement to authenticate our early
intuition that Gerty was no true slum child (and thereby, though
perhaps inadvertently, to undercut the asserted democratic egali-
tarianism of the narrative). This same father is revealed to be the
long-lost love of Gerty's mentor, Emily Graham (*The Lamplighter's* equivalent of Alice Humphrey) and to have been the

cause of Emily's blindness. So, where Warner had been willing to leave her events disconnected and apparently random, Cummins felt that she needed to tie everything together; where Warner had been constrained to some degree by probability, Cummins was enticed by the melodramatic flourish. *The Lamplighter,* then, though a more tidy book than *The Wide, Wide World,* is also more absurd.

Yet much the most significant difference between *The Wide, Wide World* and *The Lamplighter* is that the guardians and caretakers in the latter book are kind and loving. Ellen is thrust from an original situation of protected happiness into a long bondage to insensitive, indifferent, and dictatorial overseers. Gerty is rescued from misery and neglect by Trueman Flint, the kindly old lamplighter, when she is eight years old and thereafter experiences only love and concern from her protectors. (The derivation of *The Lamplighter* from *The Wide, Wide World* is shown in Cummins' use of Warner's opening image of the lamplighter.) Flint shelters her. Next-door neighbors, Mrs. Sullivan and her son Willie, divide Gerty's education between them, Mrs. Sullivan teaching her housekeeping and Willie foreign languages. Emily Graham, a benevolent blind lady of indeterminate age for whose father Flint does odd jobs, provides money for good clothes so that Gerty can attend school; like Alice Humphrey she instructs the young girl in manners, morals, and religion. Together these people help her develop from a wild, passionate hooligan into a decorous young lady.

Cummins replaces the Warner world of human cruelty and exploitation with one of mutual support and guidance. But she shares Warner's sense of divine injustice. The characters league together for mutual aid in a world characterized by illness, poverty, accident, death, and separation of loved ones. The heroine says, "I begin to think everyone has trouble." Emily answers, "It is the lot of humanity, Gertrude, and we must not expect it to be otherwise." "Then, who can be happy?" "Those only, my child, who have learned submission; those who, in the severest afflictions, see the hand of a loving Father, and obedient to his will, kiss the chastening rod." "It is very hard, Miss Emily." "It is hard, my child, and therefore few in this world can rightly be called happy; but if, even in the midst of our distress, we can look to God in faith and love, we may, when the world is dark around, experience a peace that is a foretaste of heaven."

Emily's sentiments appear to embody a deeply orthodox and antiromantic position and imply a Victorian ideal of feminine submissiveness. But as feminine ideology it is not quite conventional. It denies that women are submissive by nature and asserts that submission is the means by which a woman can overcome or at least check her chief adversary, God. Try as they might, the Puritans reminded themselves, they could not force God's hand; it was his to dispense grace, that "peace that is a foretaste of heaven," as he chose. The dialogue above between Emily and Gertrude asserts that grace is self-achieved, not even granted according to a covenant that an honorable God will not refuse to honor, but attained through one's own effort, discipline, and toil. The goal of submission may now appear as acquiescence in an oppressive system, but Cummins' purpose is something different—to persuade woman that she is responsible for saving herself and equal to the demand. For the religious mind, this is as radical an appropriation of power as the franchise to the political.

Moreover, Cummins does not require such submission from Gerty in her human relations. When she is thirteen, her beloved lamplighter becomes fatally ill, and Gerty cheerfully nurses and sustains him in the last months of his life. Far from an instance of feminine self-sacrifice, Cummins shows this as a reversal of power relations: Trueman Flint has become Gerty's child. After his death, Gerty goes to live with Emily, alternating between Boston in the winter and the Graham's beautiful suburban home in the summer (The Lamplighter gives America one of its early fictional representations of the suburb). Emily's self-absorbed father acquiesces in his daughter's sponsorship of Gerty but has little to do with the girl himself. Her life is made painful at first by the malice of a jealous housekeeper (a much diminished version of Aunt Fortune), but her forebearance disarms the woman and greatly increases Emily's respect for her. In childhood Gerty was a passionate and embittered child, who, in a fit of rage, threw a stone through a window. Now she has achieved "the greatest of earth's victories, the victory over self" and become "at last a wonder to those who knew the temperament she had to contend with."

When Gertrude turns eighteen, she prepares to act on a long-nurtured plan of self-support through teaching. Mr. Graham, unexpectedly, asserts that Gertrude is beholden to him, and will not hear of her leaving. He feels that in exchange for her five years of residence beneath his roof Gerty owes him a lifetime's service. Technically perhaps Gertrude owes him exactly as she owed Trueman Flint, but she refuses to acknowledge a claim that rises from a love for power rather than a love for her. She thinks at first, "It is cruel in Mr. Graham to try to deprive me of my free will." "Sorry as I shall be to offend Mr. Graham," her reformulation runs, "I must not allow fear of his anger to turn me from my duty." Justifying inclination as duty, Gertrude is freed to do as she pleases. One can say "I must" where outer and inner constraints prohibit one from saying "I want." This strategy gives Gertrude a flexibility in dealing with life that the Warner heroine never achieves.

Thus justified, Gerty goes back to the city, helps Mrs. Sullivan nurse her dying father, and takes a daytime job as assistant in a school. Soon the old man dies and then Mrs. Sullivan; alone, Gerty now has the pleasure of refusing several friendly offers of a home by explaining that it is her duty to Mr. Graham not to appear to prefer any other friends to him. And, she explains, "I am anxious to be so situated, on Mr. Graham's return, that he will perceive that my assurance, or boast (if I must call it so), that I could earn my own living, was not without foundations." So Gerty gets a room of her own.

Gerty is now in a position to weigh all demands made on her

and reject or accept them as she sees fit. And she responds only to demands that allot her the dominant role in a relationship. Having established the terms of her independence she willingly returns to the Grahams when a call comes from Emily. Neglected by her father, who has remarried suddenly, and mistreated subtly by her fashionable stepmother, Emily turns to Gerty as a dependent to a benefactor. "It does seem a sacrifice for you to leave your beautiful room, and all your comforts, for such an uncertain sort of life," says Mrs. Jeremy, a friend, to Gertrude as they discuss her future. Dr. Jeremy adds, "It's the greatest sacrifice that ever I heard of! It is not merely giving up three hundred and fifty dollars a year of her own earning, and as pleasant a home as there is in Boston; it is relinquishing all the independence that she has been striving after." "No, doctor," says Gertrude ("warmly"). "Nothing that I do for Emily's sake can be called a sacrifice; it is my greatest pleasure."

Her route has been devious, but considering her limited resources, Gertrude has done remarkably well. She has a place. In the last section of the novel after she had returned to the Graham's, various women try to wrest it from her. Especially persistent are the new stepmother and her glamorous niece, Belle (Isabelle) Clinton. Except that Willie Sullivan, who has been rising in the world, appears to be in love with Belle, their malice and spite scarcely affect her. Willie's apparent defection deeply hurts her, and she sublimates her misery in a life-risking rescue of Belle from a steamship explosion. In fact, she has misread the evidence. Willie has always been hers. Just in time to give Gertrude away, her lost father returns. This last event subverts the story not only because it is so unlikely, but because Gertrude does not need her father. She is her own woman, and requires no parent to provide identity. In fact, the rationale for the father's return is to provide Emily, who would be left alone by Gertrude's marriage, with a new home. For Gertrude's father had been, before he inadvertently caused Emily's blindness and fled, Emily's fiancé. For all her goodness, Emily has not the force of character that Gertrude has; unlike the heroine, she needs a rescuer. The heroine has surpassed all her mentors.

I have generally been disregarding the subplots of these long novels, since my concern is with heroines; yet I cannot leave *The Lamplighter* without pausing at Mrs. Sullivan's dream vision. Mrs. Sullivan is resigned to her death except that she will never again see her son; she is reconciled even to this through the agency of a dream. Her soul, she dreams, leaves her body and flies to a gay, thronged city, where it discovers Willie in a gambling palace, on the brink of vice (capitalized in the text). Stationing itself at Willie's shoulder, the soul guides him safely through a sequence of temptations, culminating in the seductive snares of a fashionable beauty: "I seized the moment . . . and, clasping him in my arms, spread my wings and soared far, far away, bearing with me the prize I had toiled after and won. As we rose into the air, my manly son became in my encircling arms a child again, and there rested on my bosom the same little head, with its soft, silken curls, that had nestled there in infancy. Back we flew, over sea and land." Why has this vision prepared Mrs. Sullivan for her death? "I now believe that Willie's living mother might be powerless to turn him from temptation and evil; but the spirit of that mother will be mighty still."

A mother who has watched her soft little boy grow into an angular youth might respond to the nostalgia of this passage; a Fiedler-Freudian would see the clear wish of the mother to emasculate the male. Mrs. Sullivan, however, interprets the dream in terms of the social theory of woman's ability to deter the male from evil and stimulate his better nature. But observe how Mrs. Sullivan's original wish—the desire to gratify herself by seeing Willie again—has been sublimated into the desire to do him good; and this desire is further refined as death is required as the price of such influence. In Cummins' next novel, *Mabel Vaughan* (1857), she develops at length a story of woman's

influence and decides that after all women do not have to die to
wield power over others.

The Lamplighter tells one of the two favorite woman's stories:
the orphan's rise. Mabel Vaughan tells the other: the heiress's
fortunate fall. Both of these, in Cummins' handling, are stories
of spiritual as well as social regeneration. Gerty rises from poverty,
while Mabel rises by means of poverty, for her situation of
wealth and fashion is corrupt and hollow. Moreover, it is a situation in which women lack all power. In the fall of the family
from high station, woman finds her chance as organizer, admin-
istrator, counselor, and support. Perhaps fashionable life is corrupt
precisely because it is organized to exclude woman's influence.
Supremacy in the ballroom, one understands, is meaningless;
there woman is bought off by hypocritical flattery, offered
paste for jewels. Her merely decorative function gives her no true
power. The power base for a woman—the place from which her
influence can radiate and within which it is centralized—is of
course the home, which all the customs of fashionable city life
ignore or destroy.

As the novel opens, Mabel, third child of a wealthy family,
is about to leave the country home where she has been boarded
and educated since she was eight. Her widower father is looking
forward to her return and to her debut in fashionable society.
It is owing to the training she has received away from him with
her teacher and surrogate mother, Mrs. Herbert, that Mabel will
be able to triumph over the temptations that await her. For she
is beautiful, energetic, vivacious, and lovable, sure to become a
belle, likely to succumb to vanity and self-love despite her good
heart. In her father's elegant mansion, Mabel neglects her domestic opportunities, leaving her father to his money-making and
her brother Harry to idle dissipation, ignoring her rustic dependent aunt, Sebiah, and falling under the sway of her married
sister who lives in a hotel and has no interests beyond clothes and
parties. Mabel is thoughtlessly attracted, even entranced, by the
glitter and display and excited by the admiration and attention

she receives. She feels that her life is rich and full. She responds to the dallying advances of an older sophisticate, Lincoln Dudley, with an emotion that she mistakes for love.

Most of her first winter at home has worn away before she realizes that her brother is becoming an alcoholic. This discovery dramatically changes her opinion of fashionable life; yet she finds it difficult to sacrifice all social pleasures to stay home and lure her brother away from his bad habits, as she now realizes she ought to do. Support comes unexpectedly from a family of virtuous poor, consisting of the widowed Mrs. Hope and her three children: Lydia, Jack, and an invalid child, Rose. Rose, a representation of the divine child so beloved by the nineteenth century, provides Mabel with a model of patience, cheerfulness, and selflessness; bedridden, she is continually devising little amusements to keep her older brother Jack at her side and thereby out of trouble. Christian, domestic, and feminine coalesce in this image: Christian woman morally regenerates a man by keeping him in the house.

But Mabel must elect to do what Rose is constrained to do because she is an invalid. Is not Mabel being asked to cripple herself to save her brother? So it seems to her for a time. She cannot perceive her choices rightly until she fully appreciates the emptiness of social life and learns to draw satisfaction from doing good for others. She must have a change of heart that radically alters her sources of pleasure. Mabel's first lessons in the joy of helping others come when she performs small services for the Hope family. These lessons in gratifying others come not a moment too soon, for hardship strikes her and her family. Dudley begins a flirtation with another woman. Harry drinks increasingly and is badly hurt in a carriage accident occasioned by his intoxication. Her father and brother-in-law are in a train wreck in which the brother-in-law is killed. Like many men of presumed wealth in woman's fiction, he dies insolvent. His wife, Mabel's sister, goes into shock and dies too. Mabel's father loses all his money, and suddenly these rich, fortunate people are poor and beset by calamity.

Harry, nursed back to new life by Mabel, journeys west to join his father on their one remaining property, a tract of Illinois land. Mabel follows soon after with her two young orphaned nephews, her sister's boys. The reduced and reconstituted family begins life anew on the prairie. Vaughan hopes that the railroad will buy his land and make him rich once more; Mabel and Harry, now wisely conservative, see that they must become farmers. So Harry works the land and Mabel turns housekeeper, support to her father, counselor to her brother, teacher and surrogate mother to her nephews. We are asked to compare Mabel's happiness and power as queen of the ballroom and queen of the homestead. Cummins has constructed her story so that the answer is self-evident and convincing.

We see that woman cannot exert her influence or fulfill her nature in the city because the city is a realization of an acquisitive economic system where money shapes human relations. Getting is the man's job, and spending the woman's. Although such a system is degrading to both sexes it seems ultimately more harmful to woman, for it reduces her to a display mannequin. She accepts this self-limitation in exchange for gratified vanity. The cult of domesticity in *Mabel Vaughan* is thus an attack on American materialism. Regenerating the Vaughans in the West, Cummins prophesies that in the land of the future a domestic society will be founded to purify the corrupt urban East, just as in individual relationships women would purify men. Like Southworth, she puts her ideal community in the West.

Mabel's fall and rise had occurred within a year; she was eighteen when she left Mrs. Herbert and nineteen when she took her nephews west. Cummins now permits six years to pass before she arranges a marriage for Mabel, to a displaced easterner like herself, Bayard Percival, a fine young man who is both a prospering farmer and a rising politician. In these six years the territory around the Vaughans has become magically populated with the good people the Vaughans had known in New York. Aunt Sebiah comes out to live with them; the Hope family (except for Rose, who has died) relocates. To be sure, Cummins gives Mabel a splendid husband eventually, but the stress of her ending is on this loose, extended, quasi-kinship system of friends and neighbors. A larger version of the Vaughan family unit dominates the western territory and is ruled by a woman—Bayard's redoubtable widowed mother, Madam Percival. *Mabel Vaughan*'s ideal is the United States as a matriarchy.

After these two important novels, each a kind of generic epitome, Cummins turned her attention to other popular types. *El Fureidîs* (1860) is a romance of Palestine, which features—as do so many "exotic" romances—a fantasy of the "natural woman" as she develops in a nonwestern culture. These parochial romances often equated all nonwestern civilizations with a state of nature. Their fantasy represents a significant recoil from woman's fiction. The natural woman carries over her Protestant American sister's beauty, piety, innate purity, and delicacy; but she is much more expressive, athletic, passionate, poetic, brave, and physically daring. (The incredible success after the Civil War of Ouida's *Under Two Flags* is surely owing to the apotheosis of such a type in the camp-follower Cigarette, whose purity is spiced with suggestions of impropriety.) Cummins' example of the type, the heroine of *El Fureidîs,* is Havilah, daughter of a French-American father and a Greek mother, brought up in the mountains of present-day Lebanon. In her character, purity and passion exist in one person. The plot fantasizes a situation in which the free expression of passion by women is not dangerous or degrading. Importantly, it recognizes that passion in itself is not impure, but that the social context in which western woman lives makes the expression of passion strategically unsound.

The heroine of Cummins' last, historical novel, *Haunted Hearts* (1864), is at an opposite extreme—a woman whose one night of minor self-indulgence leads to a lifetime of social oppression and self-repression. She is a thoughtless flirt, and one evening's coquetry drives her disheartened lover—apparently—to murder and suicide. Thereafter she lives as a social pariah until her rehabilitated lover returns to vindicate himself and her. *Haunted Hearts* allows women no power except to injure, and no moral destiny other than silent suffering. Distanced by its setting in the past as *El Fureidîs* was by its exotic locale, *Haunted Hearts* is the polar opposite of that romance. Between romantic self-assertion and reactionary masochism, novels like *The Lamplighter* and *Mabel Vaughan* tried to find a way for women to negotiate in their cultural reality.

7

Ann Stephens, Mary Jane Holmes, and Marion Harland

In 1854 three women besides Maria Cummins began important careers as novelists. Ann Sophia Stephens, a veteran of the periodicals, brought out *Fashion and Famine,* her first novel in book form. Mary Jane Holmes inaugurated her literary career with *Tempest and Sunshine,* and Mary Virginia Hawes, later Terhune, published her first novel, *Alone,* under the pseudonym Marion Harland. All three works were best sellers. Fundamentally different in temperament and literary style—Stephens was a melodramatist, Holmes a comic writer, and Marion Harland (she continued to use the penname) a romantic moralist—they found common ground in their readers' apparently inexhaustible appetite for stories of feminine trials and triumph. Their three careers indicate the evolution, by the mid-fifties, of authorship into a profession open to women regardless of their life circumstances. Those whose careers we have considered to this point tend to fall into two overlapping groups—women in financial need and single women. Throughout the period begun by the works of Catharine Sedgwick, the claim of need for any woman or the rationale of a public service motive for the comfortable would sanction female authorship. But Stephens, Holmes, and Harland offered no excuses for their professionalism. They performed without trying to justify themselves.

Stephens (1810–1886), a native of Connecticut, had determined to be a writer in her girlhood. She had brief periods of formal schooling at the primary level, married in 1831, and between 1834 and 1837 contributed to the *Portland Magazine,* a literary monthly published by her husband. In 1837 the Stephenses moved to New York (uprooted, perhaps, by the Panic) and she turned to the popular magazines of that city. Her novella *Mary Derwent* about pioneers and Indians won a $200 prize and was serialized in the *Ladies Companion* from May through October 1838, and in this same year she joined their staff. Later her name was associated with *Graham's* and with *Peterson's* magazines. In the 1850s, conforming to popular taste, she began to bring out her novels in book form. Later in her career Peterson's published a uniform edition of her works (the publishing house did the same for Hentz and for Southworth) that contained twenty-four novels. In 1860 one of her early novellas, *Malaeska,* was republished as the first of Beadle's dime novels and she wrote several more works for that series. (Many other women wrote for Beadle's, although the dime novel is now assumed to be a masculine fiction.) Her literary income seems to have been, after 1837, the family support, and she put her career ahead of womanly responsibilities, traveling widely and leaving her husband at home with the children.

Mary Jane Holmes (1825–1907) was one of a large, poor, Massachusetts farm family. Self-educated, she taught school from age thirteen until her marriage to Daniel Holmes in 1848. Four years later, when the Holmeses remained childless and her husband took up, belatedly, the study of law, she began to write. *Tempest and Sunshine* was among the top sellers of the decade, and every novel that she wrote thereafter was also a success. Commentaries exaggerate her total output, but one con conservatively estimate her production at something over two dozen novels, with sales in the millions. Astute publishing arrangements helped her earn a fortune. She enjoyed her career and pursued its rewards well beyond the limits on money-making that feminine decorum might have imposed. Her husband raised no objections to her career; indeed, the whole arrangement seems to have pleased him highly.

Marion Harland (1830–1922) had published *Alone* and completed a second novel before she married Albert Payson Terhune, a Presbyterian minister. A well-educated girl, taught at home by her father and private tutors, from a well-off Richmond family, she had not written *Alone* out of financial need. And though even a successful minister does not earn a great deal of money, the Terhunes's circumstances did not require a second income. Her husband admired her talent and saw no threat to his own manhood in his wife's money-making abilities. In 1871 after she had written many novels, she published a cookbook called *Common Sense in the Household,* and in the last quarter of the nineteenth century achieved a national reputation as a domestic advisor much greater than her earlier reputation as a novelist. In the first decade of the twentieth century she extended her influence by initiating a nationally syndicated newspaper column of personal counseling. Her friends protested that such writing was not literature. No, she responded (according to her autobiography), "but it is *influence,* and of the best kind." Her professionalism existed together with her responsibilities as a minister's wife and her rearing of a large family. She bore six children; three survived to adulthood and all became writers, including Albert Payson Terhune, Jr., the well-known author of dog stories.

These three women seem to have been led to their careers by an attraction to writing, energetic dispositions, and the wish to control the shapes of their own lives. They wrote for autonomy and for satisfaction, asserting their right to gratifications traditionally reserved for men. They wrote for the pleasure of making money, rather than the need for it. Thus they violated, without apparent psychological damage, the middle-class convention that a woman does not work unless in financial distress, that unless needy she rests content with her husband's earning power.

Stephens, Holmes, and Harland, married women all, surmounted whatever difficulties they might have experienced in reconciling their feminine and professional roles.

The implications of their success may be obvious, but they are worth stressing. By the mid-fifties, it was apparently no longer the case that all the women professionals were writing out of economic hardship. Correlatively, their careers were not occasioned by the failure of their relationships with men; on the contrary, each of these three successful careers rose from the ground of a supportive and encouraging marriage. Moreover, it was no longer necessary for a woman to apologize for becoming a writer. Thus authorship appears to be the first profession in America that accepted women without special gender-imposed entrance requirements. Even teaching was unofficially understood to be a profession for the needy or the dedicated; moreover, its salaries were sex-discriminatory while the earnings of the women authors were not.

On the other hand, women were expected to write specifically for their own sex and within the tradition of their woman's culture rather than within the Great Tradition. They never presented themselves as followers in the footsteps of Milton or Spenser, seekers after literary immortality, or competitors with the male authors of their own time who were aiming for greatness. They probably would have experienced many more difficulties in their careers if they had. Pragmatically, they distinguished their work from High Literature, often in terms pejorative to the classics as remote from everyday human concerns.

This proscription on ambition and aspiration certainly seemed an intolerable limitation to many women authors whose careers began toward the end of the nineteenth century, and who wished to be regarded as artists rather than careerists, but it does not appear to have weighed heavily on the group of women active in the fifties. In fact, it seems to have suited their preparation and inclinations. They wanted to be professionals rather than artists, carrying out stipulated services for social and material rewards.

They wanted to have influence in the present rather than reputation in the future. The profession took them out into the world of their own day, whereas the artist, pursuing craft in seclusion, could not expect to attain the engagement in public life and the confirmation of personal power that the profession afforded. Consider the evident example of the true woman artist of the time, Emily Dickinson.

For women whose writing derived from and represented the motive of self-gratification beyond the domestic sphere, it seems legitimate to ask whether an espousal of domesticity in their work was hypocritical. Some recent criticism has argued that the women had to express domestic sentiments in order to find a publisher, while a few scholars have suggested that the women authors advocated domesticity in order to keep other women out of their own preserve. Such hypotheses would have to be supported by historical evidence that is lacking at the moment. There is no sign that there was some sort of informal quota system for women authors, enforced by male editors and publishers with the assistance of successful women writers. The success of an enormous number of women's books in the 1850s written by many different women suggests a virtually unlimited market open to any woman who could demonstrate drawing power with an audience. There is no evidence of censorship, formal or informal, applied exclusively to women authors by other men or women in the profession. Of course the women's literary production was analyzed by critics and reviewers, often in gender-specific terms, but adverse commentary subsequent to publication is not equivalent to censorship before it. Melville had more trouble with his publishers in this regard than the popular women. Indeed, the writers who suffered in the 1850s were not the women but the men who were aspiring to classic literary greatness.

When we concentrate on the content of the women's works rather than on their professional lives, we may pursue our inquiry in two directions. First, are there alternatives to domesticity presented in their novels; second, what precisely does the advocacy of domesticity entail? It must be granted that only a very small number of books show their heroines involved in lifelong professional or money-making activities. For most, self-support is an interlude. Most novels conclude with marriage for the heroine, and it is understood that she will terminate her involvement with the marketplace. There are exceptions to this generality, and of course a novel that ends with a happy marriage is not necessarily advocating the domestic life. In the structure of narrative, the ending wherein hero or heroine gets married and lives happily ever after signifies no more than that the issues raised in the narrative have been resolved. It is the basic ending of all fiction, including folk and fairy tale, regardless of the sex of the protagonist. On the other hand, marriage and domesticity were still the reality for the overwhelming majority of women of that time (it has been recently estimated by the historian Daniel Scott Smith that more than ninety percent of American women who lived to adulthood in the nineteenth century were married); one must not confuse realism with advocacy. Thus both the shape of fiction and the shape of reality conspired to suggest marriage as the appropriate ending to a novel.

As we have seen, a number of women authors provided a gallery of auxiliary, single, independent women characters in their novels, as though to remind their readers that married domesticity might well prove only an interval in their life histories. Women writers appear in many woman's novels, evidence that the authors did not wish to close off their profession to potential competitors. Finally, as we have repeatedly seen, domesticity when advocated was intended not to keep woman back but to advance her. The domestic woman was displayed not against a background of greater, forbidden opportunities, but against examples of such wasted feminine potential as the passive parasite and the self-destructive belle. Domesticity, too, had a variety of private meanings: it was one thing for Southworth, another for Hentz, or Warner, or Cummins. Neither Stephens nor Holmes comes across as a strong advocate of domesticity; Marion Harland maintained a clear domestic ideology, but with significant strains and ambivalences.

Stephens' greatest literary successes were two quasi-domestic fictions, *Fashion and Famine* and *The Old Homestead*. But to judge by the bulk of her output she was more comfortable with historical melodrama; most of her stories were historical romances that provided an extensive range of nondomestic characterizations of women (although these nondomestic characterizations followed, to some degree, literary stereotype: savage Indian maidens, female Byrons, and the like). Because these romances were set in a clear fantasy world, these undomestic women could not serve as models in the way that heroines of realistic fiction might. Moreover, Stephens stressed the sensational effects, the suspense and excitement generated by action, rather than any theoretical implications of her action for woman's status.

In 1858 she published a much-expanded revision of her story *Mary Derwent*, which had won the *Ladies Companion's* prize twenty years before. Its heroine is a white Englishwoman, Catharine Montour, who, after a series of domestic tragedies, journeyed to the American wilderness where she married an Indian and became ruler of his tribe. Her husband was himself only half-Indian; his mother was a white woman who, very much like Catharine, had fled to a primitive life in the forests of America. Stephens and her two women characters tell against the common assertion that only male authors and male characters envisioned the wilderness as their proper domain. These women are rejecting civilization exactly as the men did. In striking contrast to the male writers of the wilderness, however, Stephens (and other women as well) had no qualms about miscegenation. Interbreeding of white men and Indian women, of white women and Indian men, and of white men and black women are all common in fiction by women where the minority races figure in the story; and one novel by Mary Denison (*Old Hepsy*, 1859—see Chapter 9) breaches the greatest taboo of all, coupling a white woman and a black man.

In a subordinate pair of contrasting heroines in *Mary Derwent,* the titular character and her sister Jane, Stephens presents a different approach to feminine socialization. Jane, the epitome of normal womanhood, is beautiful and gregarious, but mentally slow and morally infirm. Her sister Mary, though beautiful of face, is hunchbacked; her deformity denies her the admiration continually received by her sister and turns her to spiritual concerns for satisfaction. Thus Stephens shows the female Byron— Catharine, a white Indian, a lofty soul soured by disappointment and driven to rebellion—and the spiritual, submissive woman as two deviant types from the social norm represented by Jane. Mary's adjustment is no less a defense and sublimation than Catharine's. Her spiritualized soul answers to her body's deformity. Since the kind of self-abnegation and heaven-seeking behavior manifested by Mary is so commonly extolled as feminine perfection, it is odd to say the least to find that type presented as a social pariah; but when one thinks further, one realizes that the many angelic female invalids are similarly, though less crudely, set off from normal social life.

But if Catharine in her way and Mary in another represent female deviants, the norm as represented by Jane is vapid and uninteresting. And Stephens shows that it has been molded by flattery, adulation, and courtship; finally the notion of any "natural" femininity disappears altogether. There are only social products and social outcasts. Unfortunately for the reader with an interest in the depiction of women, Stephens does not pursue the implications of this scheme once she has set it up. Her provocative formulations are lost in the elaboration of a gratuitous fantasy about secret identities, lost parents, separated spouses, carelessly imposed on the story that had been written for the *Ladies Companion.*

Countries called England and Spain, but in reality countries of the imagination, are the setting of *The Heiress of Greenhurst* (serialized in 1854 as *Zana, or the Gypsy's Legacy,* published 1857), an exotic novel about passionate gypsies triumphing over civilization. Its two heroines, mother and daughter, exemplify a melodramatic contrast between an abject slave-woman and a female Byronic hero; these are romantic exaggerations of the familiar contrast between eighteenth-century passivity and modern independence. Such polar absolutes in melodrama provide a happy escape from the continuous compromises of reality and realistic fiction. Gypsies, as well as Sicilians, Corsicans, and Arabs, were imagined to have formed societies based on passion rather than self-control, and novels in which these supposed races are featured contain a crude rebellion against Victorian values.

At the beginning of *The Heiress of Greenhurst* the mother, Aurore, falls in love with Lord Clare, and changes instantly from a fine free animal—a gazelle, a steed, a bird, a leopardess—into an abject, modest, shame-faced, passive, dreamy creature. Clare marries her secretly (for this she is cast out of her tribe) and takes her to England, where, ashamed of her because she is in no sense of the word an English lady—ashamed of her for the very reasons that attracted him to her—he hides her in a garden cottage on his enormous grounds. There she dreams her life away, living only for his favor. When Clare decides to take a new wife more suitable to his station, she exerts herself to the extent of returning to the gypsies, who stone her to death (in a very bloody scene) for marrying an outsider.

The mother's passively endured wrongs spur the rage of Zana, her daughter, who spends the larger part of the novel pursuing revenge. Accompanied by a colorful group of gypsy accomplices, she poisons the second wife and works fatal vengeance on others including her own father and her father's kin. At the end, with the legitimacy of her father's first marriage established, she inherits all his property. And this is really what *The Heiress* is about: power and ownership. Her willingness to act out the subordinate woman's role, or her inability to act any other, earns for Aurore only neglect and degradation. Zana refuses to be persuaded by the mystique of love that captured her mother. She wants what her father had and gets it. Like her father, she also gets the mate she desires; but this is secondary for her as it was for him. Stephens' vision, expressed in the spatial terms of ruling over a territory that is eventually the home writ large, a house and grounds, is a grandiose expansion of the domestic vision.

Fashion and Famine (1854) is a big-city melodrama, Stephens' ambitious elaboration of a genre that had been a leading popular form since the early 1840s. The influx of rural people to the city was so basic a feature of American life throughout the century that the genre found a ready audience long before the Civil War. No doubt the urban migration was stimulated by the massive rural foreclosures following the Panic of 1837. People entering the city from the country were naturally insecure and ambivalent about their experience. Country life had failed them; yet many clung to a rural ideology, rejecting the idea that anything in their new life could be better than what they had lost. Their uneasiness in the city found expression in the formula story of the attack on rural virtue by urban vice. Men were enticed, according to this formula, by drinking and gambling, into debts that drove them to embezzlement and forgery. Women were sexually seduced, through weakness or vanity, by heartless villains who ruined innocent maidens for sport. The settings alternated scenes of abject poverty with backgrounds of fabulous luxury. The story, written or dramatized, satisfied a naive sense of virtue and importance in the reader or viewer while depicting life in extreme and glamorous terms. Tragedy was averted in this melodrama, after many lurid episodes, by a rural hero whose good sense, forthrightness, and practical sagacity enabled him to withstand and outwit the villain.

Stephens, adept in all popular forms, used the conventions of this urban melodrama for her story of a heroine who combined female Byronism with abject passivity in love. Life transforms Ada, the betrayed innocent, into a wealthy widow, but she remains obsessed with her seducer. She returns to New York from England not to find her lost daughter or abandoned parents but to seek revenge. Passion, however, renders her powerless. Not she but Jacob Strong, her devoted manservant, routs the villain, even as his sister Mrs. Grey, a widow who runs a little truck farm just outside the city, takes care of Ada's parents and daughter. These two characters, rural in origins, have learned to survive in the city without sacrificing the domestic values that contrast with the exploitive structure of city relationships. After many sensational events and much description of extremes of city poverty and luxury, the villain dies and Ada turns to a life of good works. The magnificent mansion she had purchased to flaunt her power becomes a home for worthy poor women, and Ada presides here as a benign mother superior. Her model is the benevolent Mrs. Grey, another in the large group of single, independent, self-supporting minor heroines who figure so importantly in woman's fiction.

Beyond its melodramatic representation of urban life, *Fashion and Famine* shows that for women the so-called grand passion means abdication of all personal power. It exposes the idea of fulfillment through romantic love as a trap. With her wealth, her retinue, and her air of Byronic torment, Ada has the appearance of power but is really completely ineffective. Her self-indulgent histrionics make a good show but are nothing more than the thrashings of a caged animal. Lacking self-control, she has no lever to control others. The community of women at the end represents Ada's threefold rejection of her earlier mode of life. She has withdrawn from the city, from men, and from her own passions.

In her next and most popular novel, *The Old Homestead* (1855, successfully dramatized in 1856), Stephens achieved a smoother blend of urban melodrama and woman's fiction than in *Fashion and Famine* by focusing her story strongly on the destruction of the home and family by the city, and by substituting for the stagey villain some of the real destructive forces of city life—patronage, corruption, and such qualities of institutions as their inefficiency, inadequacy, and callousness. The novel is an important document—or should be—for students of nineteenth-century urban history. It opens on the eve of the final dissolution

of a family that has long been disintegrating. Starving little Mary
Fuller watches by her father's deathbed in a miserable top-floor
tenement room. Her drunkard mother hasn't been home for
months. Soon the father dies, and Mary runs into the street,
frantic. John Chester, a policeman making his rounds, takes the
girl to a nearby mansion—the mayor's, as it happens—for help,
but is rebuffed by the mayor, who is incensed to be told by the
public-spirited Chester that the city, or he as its deputy, ought to
take responsibility for the starving poor. Chester then takes the
girl to his own modest home—here Stephens depicts, with apparent realism, aspects of life in the tenements occupied by the
virtuous, hardworking poor.

This second family soon dissolves, because the unforgiving
mayor has Chester discharged from his job on a trumped-up
charge of dereliction of duty. Out of work and humiliated,
Chester seeks work for a time but his health and spirit are broken,
and one day he drowns himself. Mrs. Chester, looking for him,
collapses on the street and is taken to Bellevue Hospital, where
she dies amidst conditions, graphically described, whose horror
surpasses melodrama. Isabel (the Chester's daughter) and Mary
are put in the Children's Hospital (i.e. the city orphanage),
which Stephens also represents in circumstantial detail; and Mary
encounters her mother, in the woman's prison. After some time
the children are taken to live in the country by the mayor's wife,
now widow. (The widow's motives are obscure, and the mayor's
death from remorse unconvincing.) Isabel, the more beautiful,
becomes the widow's ward; Mary is lodged with a poor farming
couple, Nathan and Hannah, unmarried siblings.

The second part of *The Old Homestead* takes place in the
country, which has been devastated by the impact of the big
city on its life patterns, its population absorbed and its once productive farms turned into summer playgrounds. Mrs. Farnham,
the mayor's widow, wastes her fine property as a "resort," while
Hannah and Nathan, the fragments of a family most of whose
members have defected to the city, farm a stony property in stoic

bitterness. Ravaged as the country is, however, the residual strength, independence, and eccentric integrity of its people emerge as a hope for the future. Therefore Stephens plots elaborate kin and marriage connections to return all the attractive characters to "the old homestead" to begin a new life and reclaim the land.

In her preface to *The Old Homestead*, Stephens shows that she was aware that her novel, in its depiction of urban problems, broke new ground, and she links herself to the various new feminine reform movements:

I am not one of those who contend that women should ever become law-makers, save in the household and social life; but it is their peculiar duty to feel for the suffering, and every true woman inherits the feeling as an intuition which leaves the word duty far out of sight. It is her province to feel, to think, to act for the poor, and even beyond that, it is perfectly feminine to suggest. In this privilege of modest suggestion, if we could but understand it, lies an influence more beautiful and potent than the power we evoke. Men will cheerfully and respectfully act for us, when they would recoil from the incongruity of acting with us; but there is no reasonable project of benevolence that we can devise, which the men of America will not, in their own sphere, carry out.

Putting aside the obvious plaint that Stephens cannot imagine the poor as acting and thinking for themselves and glibly denies them political power or influence as a group, we may observe something of her attitude on the woman question. The vision of women acting together with men on political and social issues appears to strike her with the sense of incongruity that she attributes to men. But she does not acquiesce in the idea that women are to have no voice on such issues. On the contrary, the passage's early suggestion that women are more intuitive and feelingful than men, with the implication that they are therefore less intellectual, quickly modulates into a distinction between men and women as actors and thinkers. Women are the brains, men the brawn. Rightly handled, men can be made women's willing instruments, and it is right that they be so handled, since women have both a greater intuition of social evils and human need and the intellect to suggest reasonable remedies.

Stephens had no essential interest in woman's fiction as a type. After these two novels she returned to the more spacious and less precisely defined territories of the historical and melodramatic story. Woman's fiction necessarily develops as its chief organizing metaphor the closed and structured social space. Within that space is yet a smaller space, the room of her own that is the heroine's particular territory, identified with her self. Often, in an image that may be meant nostalgically, or as symbolic statement of the significance to the personality of its history, this space is represented by the childhood home. If the child has no home that she remembers, then her territory is one made meaningful at a later time in her development. The attachment to space is not by any means a gender-specific quality; but in the nineteenth century it seems that the major male writers were engaged in the process of trying to overcome the attachment to a particular space in favor of a looser commitment, while the women (belatedly, perhaps, or more realistically) were becoming increasingly insistent on their right to a defined space. Women like Stephens who opted in romances and historical novels for the same spatial detachment as the men were quite rare.

I have already spoken of the frequency with which heroines of this fiction run away from or otherwise leave home. However, when they do so it is to move into another, better structured space rather than to make a life in open territory. For most of the women writers the actual time of transit—the interval during which the heroine is outside of any social container and hence, from the authors' vantage point in a "no place"—is fraught with threat and danger. Some of them are more fearful than others but all are clearly more comfortable in a situation with rules and definitions. Woman's fiction reflects this preference and authors who did not share it tended to write historical melodrama instead.

The only writer of woman's fiction to see undefined space as opportunity is Mary Jane Holmes, whose writings are freer from middle-class conventions in general than the works of any of the other women authors. Perhaps she has this freedom because she did not come from the middle class; rising from the rural poor, she retained a certain outsider's humor in her handling of middle-class domestic embroilments. She is not only the freest, but the funniest of all the authors in the genre, and the only one whose sense of humor extended beyond the creation of comic characters and situations to the mocking of the literary genre in which she wrote as well.

Her characteristic gifts are least in evidence in her first success, *Tempest and Sunshine* (1854), which unfortunately is the most often cited of her works. To judge from her subsequent novels, *Tempest and Sunshine* might have been meant to parody certain psychological themes in woman's fiction, but if Holmes so intended she gave no unambiguous sign. Still her eccentric slant in this story of rivalry between good and evil sisters (the "sunshine" and "tempest" of the title) is evident to a reader who has learned to distinguish variations in the familiar pattern. Set in backwoods Kentucky, the novel develops its highly mannered story against an altogether inappropriate semicivilized background. One might attribute the ludicrous effects thereby achieved to the author's lack of skill were she not so clearly intending humor:

It was a large, old fashioned, stone building, with one chimney fallen down . . . and its companion looked likely to follow suit at the first high wind. The windows of the upper story were two thirds of them destitute of glass, but its place was supplied by *shingles,* which kept the cold out, if they did not let the light in. Scattered about the yard, which was very large, were corn cribs, hay racks, pig troughs, carts, wagons, old ploughs, horses, mules, cows, hens, chickens, turkeys, geese, negroes, and dogs.

In a setting that parodies the gracious manor houses of woman's fiction, Holmes develops a plot of exaggerated melodrama: is it to be taken seriously? Episodes of even the most anguished nature resolve, in Holmes's writing, into laughter.

Beyond her insouciant treatment of literary surface one discovers a canny analysis of motive and relationship. In *Tempest
and Sunshine* she makes clear that the perfect good of Fanny
(Sunshine) is a strategy for getting what she wants and putting
her sister Julia (Tempest) in the wrong. Fanny's ability to
manipulate her environment is established in the second chapter,
and in contrast Julia's diabolical machinations appear obvious
and inept. "The devil of a cent" Julia will get, the girls' father
thinks, "if she rides as high a horse as she generally does! I'll give
it all to 'Sunshine'; yes, she's more gentle-like and comes coaxing
round me."

In most woman's fiction the power of evil is shown to be
illusory or ultimately ineffective against the power of good;
Tempest and Sunshine is unusual, however, in its open avowal of
the exploitive possibilities of goodness, in its suggestion that one
might adopt goodness as a political strategy. The other woman's
authors ignored what Holmes pointed out: that goodness might
be calculated, and hence perhaps not really good, if goodness
must also be sincere. Such questioning of her genre's assumptions
is characteristic of Holmes.

Beneath the highly stylized rhetoric, Holmes touches on such
moral issues as the nature of virtue and such psychological questions as sibling rivalry. Her grasp of the origins of the competition
between sisters is acute, even though she achieves realistic
characterization in neither Fanny nor Julia. We quickly see that
Fanny, having preempted the sunny role, has left her sister no
part to play but the tempestuous, and that the prize for which
both sisters compete is the father's love. Julia, realizing that she
can never equal her sister in their father's affections, tries un-
successfully to content herself with stealing Fanny's suitors.
Neither sister is happy, for Fanny wants to be married, and Julia
cares less for marriage than for her father.

In the long run, Julia cannot even be successful in her plans to
deprive Fanny of possible husbands, and she knows it. "I'll see
whether 'Sunshine' as you and my old fool father call her, will

steal away everybody's love from me. I suppose I'm the dark shadow, for father calls me a spirit of darkness, and yet, perhaps, if he had been more gentle with me I might have been better; but now it's too late." When, in a scene of shameless melodrama, she is stopped at the altar from marrying Fanny's true love, the results are ultimately beneficial for her. Fanny marries and leaves home, and Julia—after a three-year disappearance during which she works under an alias in a millinery shop—assumes new value in her father's eyes. The book closes with an affirmation of devotion between the father and Julia, who is evidently never going to marry. "You are not alone, for I am left, and you love me a little, don't you?" asks the girl, returned from her exile. " 'Yes, yes!' said he, and drying his eyes, he drew her near to him, and added, 'thank God, who restored you to me, my Tempest, my Gale, my Julia.' "

It would be wrong to conclude from this analysis that Holmes intended a systematic critique of the genre she was using, or that her work achieved psychological and moral profundity. She had a shrewd, unorthodox intelligence that she made no effort to hide and an easy sense of the ridiculous that she shared with her readers. But her evident purpose was not to freight further a literary form that was already heavily burdened with moral earnestness. On the contrary, her purpose was to lighten the genre. The unexpected divergences from type made her stories less edifying and more purely entertaining. But for such stories to be experienced as entertaining, a reader would have to share at least for the duration Holmes's jaunty emancipation from convention. Hence if less instructive, her fiction might well have been no less liberating than more sober woman's fiction.

Holmes's second novel, *The English Orphans* (1855), did not have the same vogue as *Tempest and Sunshine*. The author's quirky toughness is more pronounced here than in *Tempest and Sunshine*, as though success had encouraged her individualism. *The English Orphans* has unique historical matter because it contains several chapters describing life in a country poorhouse, and several others describing life at Mt. Holyoke Seminary. The title refers to Mary and Ella Howard, two orphan sisters of an English immigrant family which we meet first on shipboard, approaching America. Mary is an unusually ugly little girl with a thin face, a sallow complexion, and two extra protruding teeth. Ella is a doll-faced beauty. But Mary is a strong and thoughtful person, Ella selfish and shallow.

The Howard family fares poorly in America and within a few years only Ella and Mary are left alive. The beautiful Ella is adopted by a wealthy widow while Mary is sent to the poorhouse. But she survives, even thrives there; in time she too is adopted and educated, becomes a schoolteacher, and ultimately goes on to Boston and a wealthy husband. Basically *The English Orphans* is a picaresque fiction of upward feminine mobility. The orphan begins at the lowest possible point, the poorhouse, and moves steadily up to wealth and high social position. She has a tough, easygoing relation to life, lacking both the paranoia and the egomania of those who fantasize a special destiny for themselves; she goes about the business of climbing the ladder one step at a time, without scorn for those below her or undue admiration for those above her. Holmes's special achievement here is to have made a heroine who has so few pretensions and is so apparently ordinary into someone clearly extraordinary. Mary is a true democratic heroine.

Holmes's third novel, *Lena Rivers* (1856), was her most successful, a characteristic blending of comedy and melodrama. The orphan Lena Rivers, child of a secret (and problematical) marriage, is raised in the Massachusetts mountains by her countrified grandparents. After the grandfather dies, Lena and her grandmother go south to live with Lena's uncle, a man who has married money and taken his snobbish wife's name. Mrs. Livingstone and Carrie, one of her two daughters, treat Lena and her grandmother most shabbily, because they are stingy, ashamed of grandmother's rustic ways, and jealous of Lena's great beauty. Grandmother, in her continual displays of rustic behavior and her inevitable though unintentional deflating of her daughter-in-law's pretensions and conceit, brings a running humorous democratic commentary to the novel, while in Lena's story Holmes combines several favorite fairy tales and fantasies. Ultimately this Cinderella gets not only the local prince but her father as well. When the story ends she has become in people's eyes the heroine that she really is. In a subplot she has helped Mrs. Livingstone's younger daughter elope with her tutor: she is not only Cinderella and the Ugly Duckling and Patient Griselda, but a nineteenth-century Wonder Woman as well. Carrie, much mortified, marries the aging military officer her sister had successfully evaded, and Mrs. Livingstone is left to the daily humiliations of Grandmother.

Holmes's next novel was *Meadow-brook* (1857), a picaresque first-person narrative. The heroine, Rosa Lee, comes from a large, poor rural family (most of the women authors came from large families, but a family with more than three children is rare in their fiction) and aspires from childhood to become a teacher, which she thinks of as conferring the "greatest amount of happiness earth can bestow." She fulfills her ambition early, getting her first teaching job at the age of thirteen (like Holmes herself). At this age she also suffers an unhappy love experience and considerable comic humiliation at the adept hands of a more sophisticated rival. When debonair Mr. Clayton abandons her to marry this woman, whom he imagines to be wealthier and better connected than Rosa, she is deeply hurt, but only briefly.

As nearly as I am able to judge, I was taking my first lesson in *love-sickness;* a kind of disease which is seldom dangerous, but, like the toothache, very disagreeable while it lasts. At least I found it so, and for weeks I pined away with a kind of sentimental melancholy, which now appears to me wholly foolish and ridiculous; for were I indeed the wife of Dr. Clayton, instead of Rosa Lee, this book would undoubtedly never have been written; while in place of bending over the inkstand this stormy morning, as I am doing, I should probably have been engaged in washing, scolding, and cuffing three or four little Claytons, or in the still more laudable employ-

ment of darning the *socks* and mending the *trousers* (a thing, by
the way, which I can't do) of said little Claytons' sire, who, by this
time, would, perhaps, have ceased to call me "his Rose," bestowing
upon me the less euphonious title of "she," or "my woman?"

As Rosa escapes an unfortunate early marriage, Clayton and
his bride move to Boston and undergo financial disappointments
and mutual disenchantment. Rosa's older sister Anna marries a
drunkard, convinced that she can reform him, and lives a harrow-
ing life until he dies in a drunken frenzy. Rosa, meantime, pursues
her own equable course. After a while she is taken to Boston by
a wealthy aunt and educated (Mr. Clayton is sorely distressed to
find her associating with wealthier and more prestigious company than he can claim); then she goes into the world as a governess to the children of a widow who lives in Kentucky and
eventually marries the widow's brother, a wealthy planter. At the
end of the novel, she is happily writing a novel that she con-
fidently predicts will be read by many thousands, married to a
man who surrounds her with "every luxury that taste can imagine
and money buy." And she has sacrificed nothing. The valuable
independence that is innate in her character cannot be lost in any
situation, not even conventional marriage. "No shadow, however
slight, has ever fallen between us, for though he has a fiery temper
and an indomitable will, they are both under perfect control, and
so much confidence have I in his love for me, that should I ever
in any way come in collision with his temper or his will, I have
faith to believe I could bend the one and subdue the other."

In *Dora Deane* (1859) Holmes worked up another variant on
the Cinderella story. Dora, orphaned and taken in by a cold-
hearted aunt, drudges in the kitchen while the aunt and her
calculating older daughter Eugenia systematically divert the income Dora gets from an uncle in India to their own comforts. But
when Dora goes to nurse the dying child-wife of Harold Hastings,
the village aristocrat, her luck changes. Harold sends Dora to his
sister in Boston, where education and kind treatment transform
her from Cinderella to the town belle, and then Harold, having

become a widower and fallen in love with Dora, goes off to India to find Uncle Nathaniel, report on the misappropriation of his funds, and bring him back to see that justice is done. At Harold Hasting's wedding, Dora's enemies are completely discomfited when the richly dressed unknown bride turns out to be their own spurned and swindled relation; Uncle Nathaniel makes himself known and their confounding is complete. Eugenia runs away with a fortune hunter who goes bad, and dies on the prairie.

In sentimental fiction derived from Richardson much is made of the details of dress; descriptions of clothing in woman's fiction are, like physical descriptions of the characters, part of the genre's familiar iconography as in the wedding scene in *Dora Deane*. Elaborate clothing is used as in fairy tales to reveal the hidden heroine beneath the previously tattered facade. More commonly, the heroine dresses in extreme simplicity, which sets off to her advantage the fashionable dress around her; this contrast shows her purity, grace, naturalness, and freedom from pretension and ostentation. Her obligatory white dress, lack of ornament, and severe hair style display a beauty that is independent of fashion and needs no artificial aids. Hence, the chief use of clothing in woman's fiction of this time is to reject rather than endorse the concept of fashion and to dissociate the feminine protagonist from an obsession with dress.

Holmes delighted, as we have seen, to use folk and fairy tale motifs in her novels, a trait which may partly explain both her facility and her popularity. Her special approach to these age-old motifs gave them a more contemporary, active, rendering: Cinderella takes a conscious part in calling the attention of others to her neglected virtues; Griselda demands contrition and restitution before she consents to return to her wifely duties; Euridice lives a full, busy life in the underworld. *Marian Grey* (1863) is based on the motif of the vanished woman, the theme of death and rebirth. The heroine, named in the title, has been raised in seclusion on a Kentucky estate by her guardian, Mr. Raymond, who has secretly diverted most of her money to his own estate.

On his deathbed, he extracts a promise from his son Frederic to marry Marian. Although Frederic is in love with a charmer named Isabel, he keeps his promise. But immediately after the ceremony, Marian learns his motives; though she is a timid, uncultured, self-abasing creature, her pride is roused, and she runs away.

While Frederic waits and pines, his guilt evolving into remorseful love, Marian gets all the way to New York City, where she finds protection in the home of kindly Mrs. Burt and her son Ben, a peddler. She lives with them for several years, during which time she goes to school—like every Holmes heroine—and is gradually transformed by education and experience into a self-dependent, cultured, ladylike adult. In this new character she returns to the plantation as a governess (Holmes had supplied the plantation with a dependent child). Marian is so changed that Frederic does not recognize her, and her presence involves him in a dilemma that he finds terrible but that Marian thoroughly enjoys: he begins to fall in love with her, while still mourning his lost bride. Either way, though he does not know it, it is Marian he loves, so for Marian his misery is a delight. Isabel is pushed out of the picture altogether. Marian draws out her husband's torment until she is pleased to reveal herself, whereupon he is beside himself with happiness and gratitude. In this story Holmes utilizes several obvious reversals of conventional male-female roles. The woman travels, the man stays home; the woman rises, the man does not; the woman controls the progress of the love affair, the man is passive and manipulated. Marian gets a chance to live her life over. She makes a new woman of herself, and in her new character gets everything she wants.

Thus, whatever folk pattern she uses, Holmes slants the story to give us the picture of a modern woman who rises in the world much as a man does, by self-betterment and looking to the main chance. Her heroines have little concern with perfecting or strengthening their inner character. They are already as strong as they need to be and feel no compulsion to be faultless. They are less agoraphobic, less threatened by the unknown, than the heroines of much woman's fiction, for whom the unfamiliar brings disaster. But if the heroine has little need for internal improvement, she readily acknowledges that she needs extensive finishing. Like a man, she requires education, experience, and sophistication. The Holmes character is, in effect, the rough diamond of rural ideology in the form of a woman. She is different from the two more conventional female protagonists: the rare jewel in a rough setting (like Fleda) or the brilliant with a hidden inner flaw.

From time to time Holmes's rhetoric reflects an obligatory piety, but her novels approach life and its problems in exclusively secular terms. Religious strategies play no part in the heroine's negotiations with her environment, and the derived ethic of self-sacrifice and womanly service is also absent. For the most part the heroine experiences the family as inhibiting and hostile, but as soon as she breaks out of the family enclave she encounters a social atmosphere that is not highly structured and whose fluidity suits her own flexible opportunistic nature. Thus, while some women writers were using fiction to define a sphere of special power for women in the reformed family, Holmes was suggesting that women were better off if they could operate according to the same rules as men. Beyond this, Holmes is unique in that she created heroines who were stimulated by anxiety rather than fearful of it and who settled comfortably into a wide-open world instead of using all their abilities to build some sort of refuge or fortress for themselves.

To move from the novels of Mary Jane Holmes to those of Marion Harland is to make a great leap, from a writer who does not fit any stereotype to one whose woman's fictions most closely correspond to a later age's idea of the sentimental. In her novels of the 1850s and early 1860s, the central concern is love thwarted by misunderstanding. The happy marriage and confounding of enemies that form the ritual conclusion to most woman's fiction are, in Marion Harland's work, a true resolution of the issues

raised. Her novels are about love and marriage in a way that
those of the other women are not. As I have suggested earlier
when considering the later novels of Susan Warner, the equation
of woman's fiction with "romance" in the sense of a love story is a
slightly later development in literary history and involves a certain narrowing of the broader social range of the first wave of
woman's fiction. The love story certainly grows out of this fiction,
but its limited focus creates a rather different view of woman
herself. By depicting her as a being wholly absorbed by romantic
love, it returned partly to the eighteenth-century idea of woman
living entirely in her emotions that the nineteenth-century women
authors had vigorously attacked in their fiction. Romantic novels
regard independence as an endurance test, a basically unnatural
and morbid condition, and they find nothing improving, fulfilling, or educational in the succession of trials to which they expose
their heroines. They stress the heroine's sufferings only to show
that no happiness was possible for her except in requited love.
Trials no longer have their uses. Compared to woman's fiction of
the 1850s, later romantic fiction is far less demanding of women;
it represents a retreat from moral earnestness. But later still, as the
nineteenth century came to an end, this fiction began to embody
a self-expressive ethic, a feminine claim to pleasure and a rebellion against the Victorian ethic of obligation. This anti-Victorian
idea of feminine freedom greatly complicated the literary picture,
for against it the demands of the woman's fiction of the 1850s
could seem oppressive rather than liberating. To sum it up,
woman's fiction was a counterstatement to the fiction of sensibility and seduction of the late eighteenth century; the fiction of
romantic love was a counterstatement to the moral earnestness of
woman's fiction and its ethic of responsibility to others.

But as I have said, the story of romantic love evolved from the
woman's fiction even as it rejected it, exactly as woman's fiction
had evolved from forms it rejected. Marion Harland's work is
transitional. Granting that men are stronger in mind and body
than women, she is more content to allow them a traditional

sovereignty. Marion Harland believes that woman's profound need for love makes her irredeemably dependent, so that she cannot possibly be satisfied by a life of independent self-support. On the other hand, Marion Harland has not elevated love into a religion or permitted love to take precedence over every other feeling in her heroine's makeup. Although she is more a champion of strong feeling than many of the other women, she believes that strong feelings invariably go with a strong mind and a capacity for self-discipline. She is fond of contrasting her heroines, women of depth and intelligence, outspoken and intense, to what she calls the "milk and sugar" or "bread and butter" boarding-school misses, bland concoctions quite unfit for any significant role in life. These women may be satisfied with a man who is traditionally patronizing, but the Harland heroine will not. She demands a relation of mutual respect and appreciation.

As we have seen, a good deal of woman's fiction isolates passion and emotionality as flaws in the feminine nature that must be corrected or controlled: *The Wide, Wide World* and *The Lamplighter* are clear cases in point. Other women authors, however—Hentz and Southworth among them—accepted passion as a virtue, sign of an intense involvement in the world. Although her morality more closely resembles the school of Warner and Cummins than that of Southworth and Hentz, Marion Harland appears to concur in their high estimate of passion. For her heroines it is not so much the curbing of passion that they must learn as the curbing of expectation. Their trials are not occasioned by inner defects; they are simply part of the structure of reality. It is a sign of the heroine's strength that in great tribulation she retains rather than relinquishes her intense responses to experience. Not even the loss of her beloved to a woman whose charm lies entirely in her blandness can tempt the Marion Harland heroine to put aside her cherished individuality. At the same time, however, circumstances are such that she cannot initiate a spectacular defiance.

The fact that the heroine's trials do not correspond to her

failings or to a providential intention does not make them any less real or painful. Perhaps it makes them more so. Long periods of suffering, deprivation, and loneliness come to everyone. They cannot be escaped, they cannot be transcended, they cannot be turned to profit. They must simply be endured, and rebellious clamor does not make them more bearable. Hence it is the fate of even the most intense and vibrant Harland heroine to subside, for a time at least, into mute anguish. This interlude has the effect of opening the heroine's eyes to the existential fact that she is alone in the world. A gregarious and loving person, she had moved in a circle of friends and protectors who now cannot help her. In her solitude she looks for a reason for her suffering, but finds none. Religion solaces her without providing explanation. Nor does it offer strategies of behavior; in fact, in the secular world of most Marion Harland novels, religion frequently intensifies the heroine's isolation by making her even more singular. Nor does religion compensate for its alienating effect by enabling her to transcend a need for human love. Suffering comes to an end at last, but through no act of human will. Like a cloud, it blows away in time. The weather clears, the landscape changes.

Marion Harland set her first several novels in the kind of Virginia life she knew, which had been largely neglected by other southern novelists—the upper-middle-class world of the small plantation, the summer residence, and Richmond. She is virtually the only southern antebellum urban novelist; most southern writers preferred the romantic rural extremes of fabulously wealthy planter and degraded poor white. As in all middle-class writing, money is important in her novels, but extremes of wealth and poverty, comfort and distress, do not often occur. The heroine's trials are more psychological than economic. When money is an issue, it is so only indirectly, in the way in which money shapes the relationships between the heroine and her associates. For example, she may be a petty heiress subjected to the designs of mercenary guardians or fortune-hunting suitors, and to the envy of less well-situated women. Sometimes a male and

female adversary league together to keep the heroine apart from
the man she loves, and when this happens, money is usually the
motive of at least one of the conspirators. Then the universe,
hitherto so friendly, assumes a hostile face and the heroine must
learn to live without the constant affirmations of herself that her
money, social position, beauty, and vivacity have always provided.

Harland's first novel, *Alone* (1854), was brought out by a
Richmond publisher and reissued in New York within the year.
Though not her best written work, it was her greatest success. It
tells the same sort of story that Hentz was telling, with a much
richer overlay of social detail, and with its melodrama subsumed
in a more intellectual scheme. At the age of fifteen the heroine,
Ida Ross, who has been brought up at Sunnybank plantation by
her saintly widowed mother, becomes an orphan. The emotional
girl is sent to live with a guardian, Mr. Reid (the text also spells
it Reed) and his daughter Josephine until she comes of age. Reid
is a worldly man with a cynical philosophy according to which
he has raised his daughter—as so many authors of woman's
fictions do, Harland contrasts here the virtue of a woman brought
up by women and the failings of a woman brought up by men.

He taught her deceit, under the name of self-control; heartlessness,
he called prudence; veiled distrust and misanthropy under clear-
sightedness and knowledge of human nature. All those holy and
beautiful feelings which evidence to man his kindred to his Divine
model and Creator, he tossed aside, with the sweeping condemnation—"romance and nonsense!" The crying sin was to be "wom-
anish;"—"woman" and "fool" were synonyms.

Although the untrained observer might see here the old heart-
head distinction, Harland is rather making the other familiar domestic contrast between the principle of gain and the principle
of love. As usual, the business mentality is a man's ethic, while
woman's is an ethic of community and love. Ida's uncongenial
life at the Reids is punctuated by a number of rhetorical encounters between Ida and her guardian, in which Ida freely vents her

scorn and dislike of him and his daughter. This is the sort of behavior that would have occasioned a lengthy chastening for Ellen
Montgomery or Gertrude Flint, but here it is offered for reader
approval as evidence of Ida's admirable spirit and a newly developed independence that had never been required of her in the
supportive atmosphere of her mother's plantation. For friendship
Ida must look outside the home, and happily she finds a circle of
warm companions and joins a group of free, gregarious, cultivated young men and women whose various social activities are
detailed, making *Alone* a kind of pioneer "college novel."

Ida meets and falls in love with a young minister, Morton
Lacy, who seems to reciprocate her feelings but suddenly announces his engagement to a beautiful and fashionable Miss
Smith. Ida's heartsickness creates a physical breakdown, and she
returns to her mother's plantation and the care of loving
servants—a regression to childhood, a temporary death of the
spirit. She discovers that her rich social life is beside the point.
"The love of those she esteemed most, had not strengthened her to
bear the trials incident to her position." When she returns to
Richmond she has adopted her mother's piety and becomes a professing Christian (a rather more serious and formal affair than
simply attending church and thinking of oneself as a believer).
She nurses her detested guardian through his final illness—a task
spurned by both his new, mercenary young wife and his embittered daughter who, true to her education, deserts him when he
ceases to minister to her acquisitive needs.

After Reid's death, Ida gets a more congenial guardian but insists on returning to Sunnybank. Alone, she makes the neglected
plantation flourish again, and takes up her mother's charitable
activities in the neighborhood. She is not happy, but she achieves
contentment. Eventually, she patches things up with Morton
Lacy, and they are married. Afterwards, they settle at Sunnybank.
More like Hentz than Southworth in this, Harland can fantasize
the southern plantation as a space in which home and the world,
women's and men's spheres, appear as one and the same. But

Harland imagines more of a partnership than a patriarchy and hence is more "modern" than Hentz.

Marion Harland's second novel, *The Hidden Path* (1855), was published in the north as were all her subsequent writings. Its two heroines are cousins named Isabel, distinguished in the text as Bella and Isabel. Bella is the country cousin, whose life turns to misery when her widowed mother remarries. The step-father is an oily villain who alienates the mother from her children and bilks the young people of money left in trust for them. Eventually Bella leaves her uncongenial home and works as a teacher in Richmond. This gesture lowers her social standing among those who are contemptuous of working women, and Bella's greatest trial is the disaffection of her childhood sweetheart, Willard, who turns his attention to a more fashionable woman.

When Bella leaves Richmond and takes up residence with her Philadelphia cousins, the focus shifts to Isabel, who has become a writer and rapidly achieved a reputation. Bella has stepped aside from the conventional woman's path by electing to support herself rather than live in an uncongenial dependency; Isabel has stepped aside by forging a career of intellectual independence, by speaking rather than listening as a true woman should. The author affirms both these unconventional choices and insists that Bella and Isabel are more truly womanly than those who interpret useless dependency as a privileged position and those who reject opportunities for independence and self-development. Harland is coming very close to a feminist position here, but she carefully defines the limits of her progressive ideas about women. It is given to Maurice (Isabel's brother) to clarify woman's boundaries:

We men—enlightened Anglo-Saxons of the nineteenth century, are as veritable tyrants to woman as were the feudal lords of the Middle Ages. We cultivate her mind, and forbid her to use it; unlock to her the store-houses of learning, and suggest that she secrete what she bears away; recommend to her to live a mean parasite, rather than brave patrician scorn by earning a livelihood by manual or intellectual labor. We are training up a generation of ornamental dunces—mentally and physically weak—to be the mothers and guides of the future guardians of our Republic and Religion. When I reflect upon this monstrous injustice, my condemnation is less harsh of those misguided traitors to their sex, who rush into an opposite, and as fatal an extreme, and batter at the doors of our churches, medical colleges, and court-houses.

Although Maurice says that the feminist extreme is as "fatal" as what we would today call the "male chauvinist" position, his rhetoric gives much more emphasis to the injustice of men than to the errors of the woman's rights movement. At the same time, his stance is clear: some professions are rightly denied to women, although their rights to work at suitable occupations and to the fullest possible education are firmly endorsed.

As Bella's great trial was to lose her man to a woman who represented feminine economic dependency against her self-supporting independence, so Isabel's is to see a childish, unintellectual, thoughtless woman—an ornamental dunce—replace her in the affections of Frank, her childhood sweetheart. Alma is an empty-headed beauty of the ingenue type, whose admiring receptivity to all Frank's opinions flatters and disarms him. She looks to him as a great mind to do all her thinking and make all her decisions, and he (amazingly to Isabel, who has imagined that her mental independence was one cause of his affection for her) sees Alma as his ideal woman. Isabel must accept this slighting of her abilities. She and her cousin are left alone with each other and their work, their writing and teaching. Neither is satisfied, yet both accept loneliness as their lot and, like Ida in *Alone,* attain a measure of acceptance. Bella returns to the plantation to nurse her ailing mother, and her stepfather's long history of villainy comes to light. Maurice proposes to Bella; Willard has married his fashionable parasite and suffers the consequences. Alma breaks her engagement to Frank as lightly as she had contracted it, and he, somewhat shamefacedly, goes back to Isabel. All ends happily for the heroines.

Harland's third novel, *Moss-Side* (1857), embodies her harshest vision of gratuitous suffering. It is narrated in the first person by the heroine, Grace Leigh, and tells of three kinds of feminine misery. Louise Wynne is manipulated by a cold-hearted, worldly mother into a fashionable mercenary marriage. Although her husband is a good-hearted fellow who truly loves her, he is also dull and foolish and Louise cannot love him. Her life is blighted. May Seaton, an old-fashioned home-loving woman, marries her idol Frederick, Grace's brother, but a month after the marriage he is drowned and she enters upon a lifelong widowhood. Grace herself is mysteriously forbidden by her father to marry the man she loves and doomed to pass the years of her life at Moss-Side, a small, poor plantation, serving her father and a spinster aunt and turning into a stereotyped old maid herself.

Many years later it turns out that Mr. Leigh had forbidden Grace's marriage because he once fought a duel with her lover's father and (so he thinks) killed him. But in fact the father had survived so Grace's suffering has been doubly unmerited: she has been innocently made to pay for her father's crime and then, after all, her father had not committed the crime for which he was making her pay. At the end of the story, when Grace is finally married—at the age of thirty-four!—she cannot but murmur, "These tedious years. . . . Why was I not spared them?" The novel gives no answer, nor does it provide even belated happiness for Louise or May.

Harland seems to argue here that there is no happiness for women except in love and that love almost never prospers. Thus woman's lot is unhappiness. It is important to observe that Harland's stress is on unhappiness rather than exploitation, oppression, victimization, or lack of self-respect; her center is psychological self-gratification rather than social or political effectiveness, evidence that her orientation is more privatist than that of many other women authors. This orientation leads Harland to interpret woman's rights as an issue grounded entirely in private misery and intended purely for personal self-satisfaction, and to attack it in

Moss-Side on this ground through the device of making discontented Louise become a most unattractive kind of woman's rights agitator. Failing to accept even the possibility that woman's rights might have its sources in larger social empathy, Harland at the same time holds a private ethic that leads to resignation and apathy rather than efforts for change and betterment. Resignation is certainly the final note of *Moss-Side,* despite Grace's marriage, for the novel permits woman no other fulfillment than love and denies such fulfillment to most of them.

Harland now turned to historical melodrama and short fiction. Passing over several novels in the historical mode, I conclude my survey of her work with a collection of short stories called *Husbands and Homes* (1864) which shows a new emphasis on bad marriage rather than no marriage as the source of the deepest feminine misery. All six of the stories in the group are chronicles of married misery, and, in view of the title, the book cannot be other than an ironic attack on the ideal of love-and-marriage that her earlier work had espoused. In "Nobody to Blame," a passive, inadequately supervised young girl gets trapped into marriage with a man who drinks, gambles, and swindles. After years of misery the villain dies just as the young woman, rescued by her brother-in-law, is ready to sue for divorce—a solution advocated by her family and friends as well as the author. "Leah Moore's Trial" tells of the agonies of jealousy endured by a self-distrustful but loving wife at the behavior of her husband with a flirtatious cousin, whom in fact he marries eighteen months after Leah dies of grief and neglect.

"Two Ways of Keeping a Wife" contrasts an indulgent and miserly husband. Two sisters marry two business partners. One, pampered and respected, carries out her domestic duties and enjoys her domestic role. The other, treated like a household drudge, is literally harried into her grave by censure, overwork, and denial. Dying, she holds her stillborn child and tells her mother, "I am very thankful . . . very thankful [author's ellipses]. The Father is good to it and to me, for you know, mother, *it was a girl,* and—it—is—best—so!" "How They Do It" mocks the idea of lifelong marriage, as one widower after another makes a second marriage after swearing lifelong fealty on his wife's grave. Frequently, the widower marries his wife's best friend. On a lighter note, "A Hasty Speech, and What Came of It" has a happy ending as its quarreling couple reunites, but its focus is on the strained relations between a hasty and harshly speaking husband and a sensitive, depression-prone wife. No one coming away from this book, in which women are abused, neglected, and die young, would think that the author conceived of marriage as the fulfillment of a woman's life.

Given this new skepticism, Marion Harland might well have found in the woman's rights movement an appeal that she had missed earlier, for one of the feminists' aims was to gain for women the legal and political power to check the oppressions of women that were possible, perhaps prevalent, within the marriage institution. However, Harland chose a different course from feminism: that of striving to alleviate woman's domestic situation with counsel and advice. She published *Common Sense in the Household* in 1871; in 1873 she published her last novel and thereafter devoted herself exclusively to a career as a domestic advisor. In this career she achieved a formidable national reputation, considerably greater than that she had attained as a novelist. Since she lived until 1922 and was active until the end of her life, she was influential in this form for close to a half-century.

8

Caroline Chesebro'

Caroline Chesebro' (1825–1873), who published about twenty volumes of fiction (short stories, juveniles, and novels) in a career that extended over twenty years, never attained a popular following, and today she is forgotten. Herbert Ross Brown, in *The Sentimental Novel in America* (1940), quoted a few passages from her novels, which a few subsequent critics have cited in turn, but that is the extent to which she is known. *Notable American Women* does not include her, and the *Dictionary of American Biography* has little to say of her life except that she was born in Canandaigua, New York, attended a local "female seminary," and was "a devoted daughter and in a period of family adversity showed herself not only unselfish but heroic," and that after 1865 she was a teacher of English composition at Packer Collegiate Institute. The entry takes a condescending tone toward her writing, describing it as stylistically stilted, old fashioned in sentiment, and tedious in its moralizing. This summary does not prepare one for the scope and originality of her work. She was one of the most unusual writers of the 1850s.

In all her novels woman's stereotypes and characters appear interestingly reshaped by the pressures of an imagination that found them inadequate to the stories she had to tell but that could not shape the narrative without them. Her characters emerge as complex beings with depth and unpredictability and give her novels a resonance not usually found in nineteenth-century woman's fiction, where the formula's requirements radically restrict character development. Had Chesebro' possessed the technical skill and sensitivity to language commensurate with her eccentric vision and her originality as a fabulator, she would have been an important American author. She knew that she was attempting something major, but she saw significance in her message rather than the form in which she conveyed it and fell therefore into several traps. Sadly, her work suffers as fiction precisely to the degree that she was committed to a moral vision, for she sacrifices both story and style to a naive conception of how to communicate intensity and seriousness. She represents earnestness by a ponderous, ornate, grandiloquent, inverted, repetitious, and archaic rhetoric. She stops the action for wearisome lecturing at the reader, and stops it again to permit her characters to lecture monotonously at one another. Her purpose was to portray a world populated by questing, troubled, serious, thinking, ethical people but she forgot that in real life people of this type would never put up with such harangues as she permits her characters to direct at each other. She reads therefore like an author for whom fiction is not a natural mode of expression; she distrusts the power of the fable. But each of her novels is an improvement on the previous one in this regard, and finally in her last, *Peter Carradine* (1863), she produced a minor masterpiece. Because her subject is woman, and because she deals so originally with it, she merits a prominent place in a study of woman's fiction.

As with many other authors of this period, Chesebro's first volume was a collection of previously published short stories provided with an introduction, designed to establish a reputation that later works might build from. The book, titled *Dream-Land by Daylight*, appeared in 1851 with a foreword by Mrs. E. F. Ellet, a well-known contributor to periodicals of the time and a member of Poe's circle. The foreword praises its author as one who "possessed powers of imagination unsurpassed by any female writer of this country." A casual reference to Chesebro's "interesting" personal history and her filial devotion seems designed to create curiosity and sympathy. To a present-day reader *Dream-Land* seems an apprentice collection, presenting the usual mix of touching, dramatic, and piquant matter to demonstrate its author's conventional expertise; the reviewer for *Harper's* (quoted by John Hart in the 1854 edition of his anthology) saw more:

> In "Dreamland" we find the unmistakable evidences of originality of mind, an almost superfluous depth of reflection for the department of composition to which it is devoted. . . . The writer has not yet attained the mastery of expression, corresponding to the liveliness of her fancy and the intensity of her thought. Her style suffers from the want of proportion, of harmony, of artistic modulation, and though frequently showing an almost masculine energy, is destitute of the sweet and graceful fluency which would finely attemper her bold and striking conceptions. We do not allude to this in a spirit of carping censure; but to account for the want of popular effect. . . . The products [of her genius] will obtain a more active currency when they come refined and brilliant from the mint, with a familiar legible stamp, which can be read by all without an effort.

The reviewer does not take Chesebro' to task for unladylike originality or energy (though he does call energy a masculine quality); these are qualities to praise in her work. He complains of her obscurity. Of course, all original writers have problems with language, which is a public medium and therefore requires them to compromise with their vision. Some strive to attain the highest degree of clarity compatible with an idiosyncratic perception, while others elect obscurity and others still flaunt it as a sign of genius. Chesebro's works show clearly that she wished to be understood; much of her repetitive rhetoric for example betrays an anxiety to get the point across unmistakably. Thus, in her case, obscurity is a defect. She does not seem fully to grasp the way in which her own vision intersected tangentially with the conventions she was using, and thus she failed to make those careful distinctions between the readers' expectations and her own representation, a task in which none of the popular writers ever failed. This is what the reviewer was pointing to when he spoke of works coming "refined . . . from the mint, with a familiar legible stamp."

Of her first novel, *Isa, a Pilgrimage* (1852), Hart comments that "it was a novel of highly original character, and one which gave rise to the greatest contrariety of opinions, both respecting its merits as a composition, and the revelations it was supposed to make of the social and religious views of its author." The *Harper's* reviewer found it too somber, but successful in its intentions. He praised its "power of reflection," its "intensity of passion," its "subtlety of discrimination," and the insight and originality of the leading characterizations. *Isa* is the story of an orphan who is also a rare spirit, greatly ahead of her time. Rescued from the poorhouse, she grows beyond all conventional opportunities for success and happiness and ultimately goes to Europe with her radical, freethinking lover, where the two pursue successful joint careers in teaching and writing. In a contrasting subplot centering on the lovely but conventional Mary Irving, Chesebro' shows that Isa's way is not for every woman, but at the same time that Isa's is the way of a woman of genius and perhaps all women of the future. Isa may not be a "role-model" but she is an augur. A few paragraphs at the novel's end, when Isa dies an infidel, present an equivocal condemnation of her apostasy, but the belated and tentative rhetoric cannot counteract the overwhelming consistency of the rest of the presentation, which, by forbearing to judge Isa's behavior and rewarding it with reputation and happiness, permits her to flourish in the reader's sight and judgment.

The story is narrated from a variety of angles: in the first person by Isa and others who know her, as well as in the third-person omniscient mode. It begins with Isa recounting how she came to awareness in the hideous surroundings of the poorhouse. Knowing nothing about herself, she still knows intuitively that she is not one with the vicious, idle people who surround her. When still a young child, she is adopted by the gracious Mrs. Dugganne and her son Weare (the strange names seem in part a reflection of Chesebro's reading of Poe, who also influences the philosophy of the novel), who have been attracted to the child on a charitable visit to the poorhouse.

The Duggannes live in retired domesticity, punctuated intermittently by the brief, violent visits of Mr. Dugganne, a drunkard who dies early in the story. Mrs. Dugganne, who answers his abuse with unfailing love and meek suffrance, is Isa's first ideal of womanhood. The peace, order, charm, prettiness, and quiet of the Dugganne house likewise represents the first and most traditional life-model that Isa comes to know. And Weare is her first masculine ideal, a man of solid intelligence and moral sensitivity, religiously orthodox and socially conservative.

Mrs. Dugganne raises Isa as a daughter, and soon she displays astonishing mental powers. She reads and thinks and learns as much or more than Weare, who is studying for the ministry and whose guidance she quickly outgrows, though she remains in love with him for many years after she has mentally surpassed him. As she reads more, her notions become more radical, and she is especially drawn to speculations on the supremacy of the human will, such as Poe's "Ligeia" and the (invented) writings of a fictional radical named Alanthus Stuart. She begins to write, and the editor of a journal that publishes her essays offers her a job and a home with him and his wife. Isa accepts, goes to the city, and quickly establishes herself in literary circles. During this interval she becomes a coworker of Alanthus Stuart and a close friend of Mary Irving, whose tragedy provides subplot and counterplot.

Mary had been a brilliant and talented young singer who, lacking the courage equal to her talent, made a mercenary marriage rather than suffer the demands and difficulties of a career. Her husband, though completely unintellectual, is wealthy, affable, sensual, kind, and indulgent, a man one might be content with. But Mary is miserable because she finds few points of sympathy with him, and she feels morally degraded by her free act of binding herself to him without loving or respecting him. As she accepts his gifts, his indulgences, and his caresses she is tormented by the sense that she has sold herself. She lives in an agony of self-depreciation and self-loathing.

At the time that Isa becomes her friend, Mary's life has been complicated by the reappearance in her life of an earlier suitor. This man, who had been a struggling artist when she rejected him, has become a successful society painter and worldling, and he reapproaches Mary in a vengeful, cynical mood. He plays on her lack of love for her husband and lack of respect for herself, trying to entice her into an adulterous relationship. Isa recommends that Mary simply dismiss the man, in outrage; Mary has not that degree of courage or hardihood. She can do nothing but pray and cling to the idea that, even though the passive struggle to withstand this man may kill her, "it is the mission and the glory of woman to endure, and to triumph only in endurance." Isa scoffs at all prayer as "the longing of weak hearts in the midst of self-desertion, to give vent, voice to that weakness." Mary, without disagreeing, can only respond, "I have no power to help myself." She turns to her religion, the cardinal tenet of which is that the "unfortunate and unhappy grow perfect through their suffering" and that therefore "our Father in heaven wisely ordains the great majority of his children to lives of sorrow." Her suffering thus rationalized, Mary submits to the ravages of psychological struggle. In death she escapes her would-be seducer.

There is some ambiguity in Chesebro's treatment of this episode, but she seems to mean us to see that although conventional feminine ideology is an ideology of weakness, weakness is not simply to be overcome as Isa imagines by an assertion of will. In her strength Isa is exceptional, as Mary realizes but Isa does not. Mary achieves such heroic resistance as is possible for her more limited character. The question that Chesebro' does not fully confront is whether an ideology of weakness actually contributes to that weakness, or whether it represents a realistic adjustment to actual limitations. However compassionate the author is toward Mary, and however she admires her for withstanding temptation as best she can, she clearly looks forward to a time when Isa's extraordinary heroism will be natural to the whole female sex.

Isa's sojourn in the city is interrupted when Mrs. Dugganne falls ill. She returns to nurse her adopted mother and realizes how little her values now correspond to the Duggannes'. When Mrs. Dugganne recovers, Isa bids her childhood home farewell forever. She returns to her city life only briefly, because her growing intimacy with Stuart makes a change in her life. Philosophically opposed to the present state of marriage, the two elect to live together unmarried and therefore find it necessary to go abroad. In Europe they live in happy seclusion; they have a child; their writings are widely read. After some years of this life, Isa dies, rejecting Christ and prepared to take her chances in the afterlife.

In this final section Chesebro' puts several related questions to the reader. Does it affect the meaning of Isa's "pilgrimage" that she has undergone no earthly punishments for her unconventional choices? Will she be saved even though she dies an infidel? Does radical behavior like hers inevitably culminate in religious infidelity? If so, is this culmination sufficient grounds for opposing all divergence from social orthodoxy? Clearly these questions pertain not to the "truth" of Isa's situation but to the construction we, as readers, wish to put on it. In effect, Chesebro' is using Isa's story to illuminate for each reader the assumptions brought to this fiction. Accordingly, she does not provide her own answers. Whatever her own views, it is clear that she means to suggest a likely if not invariable connection between all varieties of freethinking; first and foremost Isa is a religious rebel; her other unorthodoxies follow after, including her feminism. Thus, Chesebro' is the only author of the time to imply that the social upheaval around the issue of woman's place might be caused by strains in traditional religious thought rather than being a cause of such strains, as many antifeminists argued.

Isa is an important woman's book precisely because it makes the issue of gender subordinate to the issue of the heroine as a freethinker. The story matter-of-factly endows Isa with capacities and freedoms and influences beyond anything discoverable in contemporary fiction, probably in contemporary society. As a purely mental being largely free from the pressures of social conditioning and personal history, Isa is a psychologically unconvincing character; the corresponding lack of social impediment to her meteoric career brings into question the novel's social realism. Chesebro's accomplishment is not in these areas but in her assertion of the right to make a woman the central figure in a philosophical quest-fiction about the meaning of life, its punishments and rewards.

Her second novel, *The Children of Light* (1853), is as eccentric as *Isa,* though more narrowly focused on problems peculiar to women. The novel asserts its serious purpose in the dedicatory preface addressed to the author's sister: "The work that I have done has been wrought in no careless, thoughtless mood." *The Children of Light* is the story of two superior women who are disappointed in love because men prefer more ordinary partners. The novel concludes with their commitment to each other. The purpose is to show that exceptional spirits cannot hope for conventional destinies. Domestic and romantic fulfillment may be denied the superior woman, but in a community of such women each can find support and opportunity for her own work.

The two exceptional heroines, Asia Phillips and Vesta Maderon, are very different in their talents and circumstances. Asia is a poor girl, an orphan and gardener's niece (later we discover, as she does, that she is illegitimate), driven by a wish to make something of herself, to become somebody. She longs "to be struggling for some purpose—to be doing some great, some weighty deed—to be recording some individual achievement." Her class and even more her sex are against her ambition. "If I were only a man, no one should stand higher than I; but here I am—a housekeeper." Vesta lacks such personal ambition; all her considerable gifts of heart, mind, and spirit, find fulfillment in the concept of

WOMAN'S FICTION

service, of improving the lot of others. Appropriately, Asia's desires crystallize in the wish to become an actress, while Vesta finds her life goal in aiding a troubled clergyman to regain his faith.

But Vesta's clergyman accepts her love without returning it. He much prefers the childlike nature of one of his most pious parishioners. Vesta finds the offer of herself casually though respectfully rejected. Asia too experiences humiliation. Vesta's handsome city cousin Aaron learns of her ambitions and offers to launch her on a theatrical career. Soon the two are sexually entangled. In the first flush of erotic ecstasy Asia interprets her situation as further confirmation of her large, unconventional nature. But when Aaron abandons her to marry a woman of his own class Asia reacts by losing all self-respect. She sees herself as a slut, her wish to go on the stage as sublimated harlotry.

Asia and Vesta thus have both been set lightly aside by the men they had selected and, insofar as they had invested a portion of themselves in the expected response, have suffered in their own opinion. Yet they are both truly superior people, and to grovel in self-abasement because of this humiliation is more than destructive, it is immoral. It becomes Vesta's mission to draw Asia's thought away from despair and suicide and rekindle her self-esteem. In so doing, and reconciling Asia to her ambition, Vesta's own need for service is satisfied. At the end of the novel the two women are preparing to go to the city together, where Vesta intends to underwrite Asia's preparation for a career in the theater. Thus *The Children of Light* brings both the traditional and the new woman together in a feminine community. It suggests that greatly gifted women, whether traditional or not, cannot be fulfilled in traditional heterosexual relationships because the men will not allow it. It encourages all women to find their special vocations and pursue them. Finally and above all, it proposes in mutual support and aid—in "sisterhood" which is stated as such only in Chesebro's preface to her sister—the human relations that they do not find elsewhere. The odd women are the children of light.

In 1855, Chesebro' published a novel that is differently titled in two issues: *Getting Along: A Book of Illustrations* and *Susan, the Fisherman's Daughter; or, Getting Along.* Running to over six hundred pages, it is her most ambitious novel. It follows the lives of some twenty major characters loosely interconnected as friends and kin, encompassing a range of personalities, social ranks, and economic circumstances. It seems to have aimed at a total social canvas depicting an entire generation of young men and women at that point in their lives when they commit themselves to some kind of lifelong vocation or occupation. In each case the commitment—or the evasion thereof—mediates between the individual's dream of an open-ended future responsive to choice, talent, and effort, and the realities of social structure and personal history. Most of the characters are serious young people who long for useful as well as pleasurable lives and who grapple intensely with the conflicting claims of obligations to others and to self. Chesebro' shows that while nothing is more important than to resolve such claims, the synthesis must vary with individual talents and obligations. The question of vocation is raised with equal seriousness for both sexes, possibly with more seriousness for women, since it is more difficult for them to make good choices and since their choices tend to be permanently binding. Chesebro' shows a wide tolerance for her different characters' choices, but she demands moral earnestness from all. She judges most harshly those characters who avoid commitment by exploiting others, who live for a shallow self-gratification; and she is critical of those whose values are limited to money, material luxury or social status.

Neither for nor against marriage in itself, Chesebro' assesses each marriage according to the grounds on which it is contracted and the faithfulness with which its vows are fulfilled. She sees marriage as inevitable for most people, a variable institution cap-

able of either supporting or impeding personal and moral development. Of her many women characters, only two elect marriage
as their sole occupation in life, and for each of these two marriage means something different. One woman marries for money,
social position, and a life of ease; she marries not as her life-work,
but to avoid working. The other is a clinging, childlike woman
who marries as a vocation, but whose dependent nature makes
her unfit for the true work of marriage—that is, of being a companion to her intellectual husband. The limited personality that
can conceive of no work for woman but marriage is just the
personality that cannot fulfill the demands of true marriage.

With so large a cast of characters, *Getting Along* has no single
plot. As one of its subtitles announces, it is a book of illustrations.
We shall glance at its illustrations of women's lives. The woman
who marries for money is Isidore (Dora) Baldwin; the child-wife
is Violet Silsey. Violet learns that her simple silliness, which initially flattered her husband's vanity, soon irritates and embar-
rasses him. He never contemplates a sexual infidelity, but his
mind begins to stray as he seeks out the company of vivacious,
capable, and intellectual women. Too late, Violet realizes that
she has based her life on the false belief that a woman's happiness
follows from a deliberate election not to grow into an adult. The
lack of character that she has cultivated in herself, in accordance
with an ideal of the feminine as malleable and compliant, alienates her husband and makes her incapable of improving her own
life. Her marriage is saved only because her husband eventually
realizes that his intellectual flirtations are an evasion of his marital
responsibility. By marrying Violet as he saw her to be, he perceives, he incurred the obligation to educate her. He returns to
Violet and accepts what Chesebro' asserts to be his vocation.

Mr. Silsey does not undergo this change of heart without help.
He is guided by the woman he has most been attracted to, Miss
Watson, an eminent thinker and writer. Understanding Silsey's
motives, Miss Watson responds to his approaches by befriending
his wife. She invites Violet to her country home, which she has

bought with the income from her writing. She is an admirable character in Chesebro's eyes; later in the novel she also takes into her home the wife and child of a former lover now disgraced and in jail. When that man and his wife die, she becomes a mother to the orphan. Her work is a calling and a means of earning a living; she accepts further obligations to other human beings. Chesebro' rewards her with independence and a family without marriage.

At the opposite end of the scale of self-sufficiency we find Leah Chilton, a young woman living with her widowed mother and her brother, both of whom spend their days dreaming of the past when they were wealthy and socially prominent. Neither of them is willing to make the effort to regain financial comfort; Leah supports them, uncomplaining in her constant sacrifice. She teaches a school, manages the finances, does the shopping, crochets and embroiders in every spare moment for extra money—and dies early, of overwork and neglect of her health. When Mrs. Chilton and her son fortuitously reacquire something of their former status, they remember Leah with neither gratitude or remorse. She figures in their memories as something like a dowdy poor relation. To the author, Leah is a saint; a person to celebrate, but not to imitate.

Lucia True is another kind of woman working to support her family; for her these obligations are not inconsistent with self-assertion. Her unhappily married parents suffer financial ruin, her mother deserts the family, and Lucia and her brother rally to make a home for their father. Lucia obtains work as a colorist and illustrator and finds herself much happier than when she was the idle daughter of a rich man. Pursuing her profession tranquilly, she meets a talented young artist who is supporting himself as a housepainter, and the two make a good, mutually supportive marriage. Lucia likes helping her family; she likes earning money; and she likes her work. Work for Chesebro' is the means of simultaneously satisfying self-expressive needs and one's obligations to others.

Lucia's older sister Rose plays a brief role in *Getting Along*. At a time when the family was still wealthy she had married a swindling fortune hunter who has degenerated under stress into a drunkard and petty criminal. Totally demoralized and degraded, Rose lives in filth and poverty and will not see any of her family. One night, in a drunken rage, her husband beats her to death.

Stella Cammon is a Catholic whose wish to live a consecrated life naturally expresses itself in a plan to become a nun. For Chesebro' this is a terrible idea because it means a retreat from, hence evasion of, worldly responsibilities; but Stella, whose suitor is a handsome worldling, at first can see no life in the world but a worldly one. As she vacillates and hesitates, she meets a minister who is carrying out a combined religious and social mission among the poor, preaching and ministering in the slums. Aiding this man in his work, Stella finds a purpose; her marriage to him is inevitable and its fulfillment is more in the work than the romance.

The strangest story in this strange book is that of Susan, the fisherman's daughter. When the novel begins, she is living with her father in poverty and isolation in a cottage by the seashore. Like Isa, and Asia in *The Children of Light,* she is one of earth's rare spirits trapped in miserable surroundings. She wishes to grow and develop, and the story of her life is the story of this wish fostered and perverted by men who cannot help her without wishing also to dominate or use her. The first such man is a student, Mark Leighton, who lodges in the fisherman's cottage. The temptation of a pliant young mind is potent, and before long he is neglecting his own studies and spending most of his time in the gratifying roles of Susan's taskmaster and judge. He gives her books, but lays down elaborate laws to control her intellectual growth: he is at once encourager and oppressor. Susan, whose ignorance and need are equally great, accepts his intellectual authoritarianism as part of the educational relation, takes his wish to be master as a sign of the superiority which he too thinks it represents. And yet Chesebro' makes it clear that, in accepting Leighton's domination as part of her education, Susan has mistaken form for substance and submitted to a hostile control that undermines the value of her learning.

The theme of domination gets a stronger and stranger development in the next phase of Susan's life. A rich family named Baldwin, consisting of a widower father, his daughter Dora and two sons—David, a brilliant and handsome though selfish young fellow, and Clarence, who is mentally retarded—come out to the seashore to visit the old fisherman. Susan is perceived to have some special influence over Clarence. In her presence, he brightens up and seems more motivated to express himself and relate to the world. Clarence's tutor conceives the idea of bringing Susan to live with them as a means of curing Clarence. There is an experimental visit, and when Susan's father dies she is taken into the Baldwin mansion permanently. In return for an education, a good home, good clothes, and entry into the higher social circles of the small city in which the Baldwins live, Susan is asked to devote her life to Clarence. No character thinks the exchange unreasonable.

Even when it becomes clear that the tutor and the father expect her to marry Clarence, Susan finds nobody to protest for her. Clarence's status as a mental defective does not matter; it is assumed that Susan will be fulfilled as a woman by giving her life to his service. Only she feels something grossly wrong, but in the atmosphere of casual acceptance of the rightness of this marriage, she interprets her feelings as selfish, immoral, and, of course, unwomanly. Not until she realizes that she is in love with David, the other brother, does she acquire the moral courage to resist the family's plans for her future. At this point she makes no excuses. She asserts her primary obligation to herself, her right to follow her own judgment (and feelings) instead of the opinions of others. As a consequence of her refusal to marry him, Clarence regresses and dies. But despite this powerful appeal to her guilt, Susan is firm in her sense that she has done right; after a long hiatus, her inner moral strength takes control. David returns her love, and the author promises us that the pair will marry.

Running through all these women's stories is the theme of feminine self-sacrifice in conflict with the claims of the self; or, differently put, the question of whether or not self-sacrifice is truly fulfilling to the feminine nature. Chesebro' deplores Dora's mercenary marriage not because it is self-indulgent but because the idea of self that it indulges is so superficial, even degraded. Violet's marriage is undermined by a different but equally representative kind of feminine self-devaluation. Chesebro' insists that women who take life seriously must take themselves seriously too. Stella, Lucia, and Miss Watson all strike a balance because their work for others gratifies the self's better impulses while supporting a high estimate of self. Leah's self-sacrifice is saintly because she receives no reward from it, but is also futile. Susan's self-assertion and Stella's rejection of the convent are both instances of moral and emotional growth. From these many stories one formula emerges: providing that it is one's better nature that is asserted, it is morally admirable to assert the claims of self.

Getting Along does not realize its literary promise because Chesebro's techniques are too crude for the demands of her complex and subtle story. The style is cumbersome and repetitious, and she fails to make the many plots cohere in a single structure. Episodes too often become the occasion for the narrator's and characters' expatiations on the meaning of life, and the whole is stiffened by the author's total humorlessness. Paradoxically then this is one of the most interesting and one of the dullest woman's fictions of the decade.

One important strand in Susan's story is that of the perversion of her education, which should be a tool of liberation and self-development, into a means of maintaining her in a traditionally dependent, even victimized, role. Susan finds education used to force her mind away from some of its natural strengths, to suppress self-expression, to assert the dominance of a male instructor over her intellect. Thus there is an implicit clash between an ideal of education and its reality, between a sense of what education might do for individual development and what in fact the educational system does for the individual woman. Although men may be as much victimized as women by institutionalized teaching, they have grown accustomed to the system and learned to use it for self-assertion. And, of course, the system is a male creation, so it might be supposed to answer more closely to men's needs than women's. *Getting Along* raises the possibility that education, as it comes to woman through manmade institutions, may do her more harm than good.

This possibility becomes the dominant theme in Chesebro's astonishing novel of witchcraft delusion, *Victoria, or The World Overcome* (1856). This novel, set in 1650, is marred by an overlong and misleading introductory section, which gives the impression that the novel's heroine is Margaret Gladstone, a great English singer who has had a religious conversion and is going to America to join a Puritan community as a teacher. In fact, Margaret is a secondary character, but once the book finds its main story it achieves for the first time in Chesebro's fiction a strength and power commensurate with its theme. Margaret's role in the main story is to introduce the young Maud Saltonstall, a child of nature, into the Puritan world. She is shipwrecked and cast up on a remote shore where the Saltonstalls, social outcasts for no explained reason, live with their daughter Maud, who has had no contact with civilized life. Beautiful, brilliant, unpretentious, and highly talented, she is going to waste in isolation according to her mother, who persuades Margaret to take her into the world. Maud enters the household of the Reverend Mr. Rossitur as Margaret's ward.

Here she creates a tremendous upheaval in the household routine. Mrs. Rossitur, a loving and suppressed woman, responds to Maud's warmth; Mr. Rossitur, who sees in her the lineaments of a lost love, is also drawn; but their daughter Hope, who has been brought up like a man and is the most erudite young lady in the province, is troubled and alienated. Hope is fiercely proud of her preeminence, her learning, her self-control, her self-transcendence; she cannot accept the belittling view of her accomplishments that Maud unconsciously expresses. She wishes to put

Maud in her place as a follower and rejects Maud's longing for friendship. Says Maud, "If it was a friend you loved, you would be glad to have her in the same class, and you would like to talk it all over, and help each other." Hope answers, "It was better for me to be alone. . . . It always was . . . with some one leading the way." Hope's fantasy is of being a class of one, led by a teacher—a man, of course. (Her fantasy is likely to be realized through marriage to Jerome Stanton, formerly a pupil of her father's and now one of the most promising young ministers in Massachusetts.) She cannot tolerate a woman as an equal. Finally, she cannot understand Maud's metaphoric, impressionistic, intuitive language. She herself is inveterately literal and conventional in her speech.

Then Hope falls in love with Margaret's apprentice-teacher, Archibald Kinsett, an event outside her comprehension because of her engagement to Stanton. To make matters worse, Kinsett and Maud are in love, so Hope must deal not only with her guilty love but with her unacceptable jealousy. Chesebro's writing rises to the complexity of her perceptions here as she follows the struggles of a mind unprepared by the education it has received to assimilate emotions that are forbidden and hence that strike like the uncanny. Slowly Hope works through to the one interpretation that her philosophy will permit—she attributes her loss of self-control and her agitation of mind to an outside agency, and once she has done so it is an easy next step to identify the agent, the witch, as Maud. Like many a benighted person she interprets the relief she gets from this interpretation as a sign of its truth, and hence her belief becomes more fixed. Maud's poetic statements about communing with nature and hearing voices in the winds and clouds, her habit of breaking into spontaneous song, are now perceived by the deluded and literal Puritan minds as evidence of supernatural dalliances and possession.

"Within and without her," Hope thinks of herself, "was the same lurid, discoloring, distorting light. And whence did, whence could this light emanate. . . . From [Maud], from her alone it radiated, and fell like a blight on all things. The whole house was under a curse, she not excepted, who was appointed to the solitary watch." The love and jealousy she feels over Kinsett is translated into a certainty that he is in particular danger from Maud's enchantments. "A firm belief in her call to the work, prevented her from escaping it. She could but look into her own heart, and perceiving the havoc and anarchy there, resolutely set about its prevention in the souls of others. . . . Under the mastery of what she believed an irresistible religious impulse, which was not at liberty to choose its own paths of action, she was ready to fulfill the work she found to do."

Worn out by mental turmoil, Hope becomes very ill and blames Maud as instigator. Stanton is called in and proves no more capable than Hope of understanding his own motives. Because he loves Hope, he believes her and feels compassion for her suffering; yet he remains unaware of how these feelings create a bias against Maud. He cannot tolerate the possibility that Hope might be drawn, of herself to Kinsett; hence he eagerly seizes on the theory that her feelings have been induced by a malevolent agent. He approaches Maud in a hostile spirit that she is quick to sense and defy; unable to see himself as other than fair and equable in his questioning of her, he interprets her refusal to accept his authority as flippant disrespect and her refusal to confess as hardened Satanism. Her habits of language are as incomprehensible to him as they had been to Hope. Inevitably and horribly, Maud is put to death. A love of life does not prevent her from going to death willingly, because the world has been spoiled for her. Margaret and Kinsett see the wrong that is being done but have no power to stop it; Hope and Stanton never do recognize the enormity of their behavior, and they live happily ever after.

Like so many nineteenth-century attacks on residual Puritanism, *Victoria* is not entirely faithful to the Puritans themselves. But Chesebro' is talking about a timeless phenomenon, which transcends both the issues of religious morality and the treatment of women in a strongly hierarchical, codified society—the problem

of unconscious hypocrisy. At the same time, she has used the fact
that the witches and their original accusers in the Salem episode
tended to be women to point out how the accusers and accused
alike are product and victims of an unnatural system created by
men. Hope is ultimately a much more pathetic and pitiable character than Maud (who may have been intended as a tragic
heroine in the classic sense), because she is so little responsible
for the terrible things that she does and so little aware of them.
She has been brainwashed and recruited into a system that is
hostile to her. Although Chesebro' does not go so far as to say it,
she strongly implies in this story that women have inherent and
valuable qualities that are necessarily sacrificed if they live according to male standards and within male institutions. But the one
woman who resists is destroyed. From the point of view of the
woman's story, Chesebro' seems to be saying that a culture based
on Puritanism destroys women actually or psychologically; at the
same time, there are many ways in which *Victoria* goes beyond
a gender-linked theme.

In the same year that she published *Victoria,* Chesebro' also
brought out *Philly and Kit,* a volume consisting of two novellas
about poor women. The stories are mainly designed to create
middle-class appreciation for the virtues of the poor by showing them as essentially bourgeois in their values, anxious to
be decent, clean, thrifty, and industrious. Important from the
woman's vantage point is the fact that both heroines are working
women, though their occupations are humble enough, and praised
for this. There was a seven year lapse in Chesebro's publishing
between *Philly and Kit* and *Victoria,* and the novel that was to
be her last. *Peter Carradine, or The Martindale Pastoral* appeared
in 1863. This novel is much more congruent with the conventional patterns of woman's fiction than her earlier writings. Technically it is her best novel. The incidents are proportioned to one
another, the style austere, the tendency to harangue restrained.
One senses the literary influence of *Adam Bede* in its configura-
tions and dynamics of plot and a growing conservatism in Chese-

bro's vision. Perhaps *Peter Carradine* is more successful because it is less original and hence demands less from the author in the way of invention and from the reader in the way of interpretation. Yet Chesebro' at her most conventional is still idiosyncratic; we know we are in an untraditional fictional world from the opening pages when the heroine, Miranda Roy, loses her teaching position for striking a child. We have seen high-tempered, proud, and impetuous flawed heroines before; but in the usual woman's world only an out-and-out villainess would strike a child.

In *Isa, The Children of Light,* and *Victoria,* Chesebro' had used a two-heroine structure: Isa and Mary Irving, Asia and Vesta, Hope and Maud, supported by contrasting pairs of auxiliary characters. The many protagonists in *Getting Along* had been related to one another in a series of contrasts: Miss Watson versus Violet; Miss Watson versus Leah; Leah versus Lucia; Lucia versus Rose, and so on. *Peter Carradine* uses a triple-heroine structure: Miranda, the turbulent woman, is in the center of the design flanked by two kinds of serene characters. The serenity of depth is exemplified in Mercy Fuller, who comes to the town of Martindale to replace Miranda as schoolmistress; the serenity of shallowness is represented by Susan Green, a rich man's spoiled daughter. Mercy is cheerful, self-possessed, calm, and noble, incapable of emotional extremes because she has mastered her emotional depths. Susan is trivial and dissatisfied but lacking in the moral energy to suffer intensely; she lives in a continual state of passive fretfulness or of ennui that corresponds, not to the dullness of life in Martindale but to Susan's own emptiness.

The stories of these three women are not full of event. They are interesting because Chesebro' succeeds in evoking three unlike temperaments and their differing perceptions of the same world. *Peter Carradine* also creates a rich and complex study of rural society that is pertinent to her major theme. The subtitle "pastoral" is ironically employed because the author avowedly intends to show that rural life is no Arcadia and that the moral life is as

complex, human relations as intricate, and the opportunities for
moral choice as many as in an urban center. The opportunities
for complexity are created by the quality of the perception, the
stature of the actor.

This point is forcibly made in Mercy Fuller's story. She has
the opportunity to choose between two husbands—her cousin
Horatio, an elegant, cultivated, successful lawyer, who offers her
a luxurious life amidst brilliant surroundings, and Peter Carradine, a rough-hewn country man who has reclaimed himself
from drunkenness and turned his run-down farm into a local
showplace. Mercy chooses Peter for several reasons, all of which
are perceived by Chesebro' as evidence of her grasp of moral
realities. Horatio conceives of woman as a beautiful adornment,
and he offers a setting in which she can display herself. Peter
idealizes woman as his better nature and offers Mercy the role of
guide and inspiration. Because Peter's view of woman is so much
higher, Mercy accepts the challenge of being his wife. She will
have to do very little to satisfy Horatio; to live up to Peter's
expectations will require calling on her best energies constantly.
And through marriage to Peter she will be given an opportunity
to participate in the moral government of the world; and that,
she believes, is woman's mission on earth.

For the first time in her fiction Chesebro' enunciates the ideology of feminine influence, for she does not disagree with Mercy's
views. "A mother's work," says Mercy, "is the great work of this
world. Woman has never yet fulfilled her work. . . . Every man
has an ideal which woman was meant to make good. And so has
every woman a God to be incarnated in love. Her unbelief is
death. . . . I have heard women speak of their rights. If they
had made the men of the world what God had intended they
should make of them, there would have been no need of this
complaining." Mercy is only apparently speaking of biological
motherhood here, for the real function that she accepts is not the
bearing of Peter's children but the mothering of Peter himself.
Nor, when she speaks of the God that woman is to incarnate in
love, is she referring to the Miltonic idea that women worship

their men as gods. Rather, in her love toward a faulty man, woman incarnates a God of love in herself. Essentially, Mercy has no wish to marry. She is too self-contained to feel the need for completion. Her life as a teacher satisfies her. It is hinted that at an earlier stage she had desperately loved Horatio but that he had not returned her feeling; mastering this passion, she had overcome her need for love. She accepts Peter's offer as a call from God.

As all moral issues ultimately combine for Mercy in the one issue of her choice of mate, so do they for the other women in *Peter Carradine.* In this respect, the vision of the novel is far more restricted than any earlier Chesebro' story, accepting the idea that a woman shows her nature and completes it in her selection of a husband. Susan, empty-headed and weak-willed, falls in love with a handsome face. Her choice, a flashy, trashy local boy who comes from poor folks and whose ambition is contained in the longing for fancy clothes, cajoles her into a secret marriage. When he takes to petty financial crimes, Susan confesses the marriage to her father in order to get the rich man to pay off his debts. The father does so, but in return insists that Susan's husband go to Australia. Susan is now a sort of unmarried widow, and since she has no inner resources, she passes several years in a limbo of frustration and irritation. When her husband returns, surprisingly a wealthy man, he takes Susan away with him to a life of empty misery and selfish dissatisfactions. There is nothing to grieve over in this picture, Chesebro' comments sardonically, for each partner found a level in the other.

In contrast to the fixed characters of Susan and Mercy, Miranda's is a changing personality; her story is of the regeneration of a faulty soul. She is the daughter of a very poor man who is a widower and an invalid. Losing her teaching job, she loses the only decent opportunity for a woman to make a living in the village and returns to her father's house as housekeeper and nurse. To avoid a sterile future, she agrees to marry the local innkeeper, a man she respects but does not love, and who loves her without any insight into the capacities of her character. He does not perceive in her pride and violence the expression of a restless need

for meaning and dignity in her life, but interprets them as sign
of a naturally cantankerous disposition that will make her an
excellent innkeeper's wife. Miranda knows her engagement to be
a mistake even as she contracts it, and perhaps for this reason she
urges a promise of secrecy on her fiancé. But not until she becomes
converted at a camp meeting does she feel sure enough of her
ability to stand alone, to break it off. The spiritual growth consequent on her conversion enables her to accept an empty future
and the destiny of impoverished spinster dedicated to an aged
parent. Happily, the minister responsible for her conversion becomes interested in her spiritual welfare and later truly admiring
of her strength of character and her tremendous desire to improve
herself. Ultimately he marries her, giving her life a status and a
scope for action beyond her wildest dreams.

In contrast to Chesebro's novels of the fifties, *Peter Carradine*
is a work of compromises. The destiny of the individual is now
subsumed under the general destiny of the sex; and the destiny
of the sex is woman's work of carrying on the moral government
of the world. In contrast to the open-ended universe where Isa,
and Asia, and Susan the fisherman's daughter all struggled with
problems for which solutions could be found only by trial and
error, the right and wrong paths for the characters in *Peter Carradine* are clearly foreseen, because the universe is morally determined. Chesebro's idea of woman's mission implies an ordered,
lawful universe wherein such individual odysseys as those of her
earlier heroines could not occur. Her repertory of life-styles for
women has narrowed exceedingly; nothing is left for them but
lives of service or of dissipation. The theory that by her domestic
influence woman furthered God's government of the world was
an old one by 1863; that Chesebro' espoused it for the first time
so late in her career as well as in the reign of woman's fiction
argues for her contracting sense of female possibility. Once the
most radical of the authors of woman's fiction she turned in *Peter
Carradine* to the mainstream. And belatedly she crafted one of
the rare, fully realized, Victorian American novels.

9

Other Novelists of the Fifties

The story of feminine trials and triumph dominated woman's writing in the 1850s. In many cases women writers with somewhat different interests attempted to fit other issues into the shape of a woman's fiction. Lessons in domestic management, old-fashioned melodrama, as well as abolitionist, temperance, anti-Catholic, antimarriage, and evangelical fiction all appeared under its guise. Relatively few of these tangential works were popular successes, possibly because they aroused expectations that they did not satisfy. The most popular authors worked very close to the formula, giving it an individual temperamental stamp and enlivening it by their enthusiastic endorsement of its message. With its predictable configuration of characters and sequence of events, the formula was at once simple, representative, and immediate. The less successful novels were more specialized, their heroine too clearly a minority type, her world too narrow or unfamiliar, for the broad reference that permitted a popular success. Chesebro's example is a case in point. In the discussion that follows I shall treat other "deviant" works in three categories: first, conventional fictions by women who wrote chiefly in forms other than the novel; second, fictions with aberrant heroines; third, fictions in which the woman's story is subsidiary to a nonfeminine propagandist purpose.

Before considering these groups, however, it is probably well to consider the novels of Harriet Beecher Stowe (1811–1896) in relation to the type of fiction that absorbed the energies of the other women authors of the time. Because she did not write woman's fiction, a full discussion of her work is not appropriate to this study. Even so, she was the most important American woman novelist of her day, and her depiction of women and their problems cannot be entirely without relevance. It is widely recognized that she idealized both a maternal state and a maternal deity in opposition to the patriarchal systems she perceived as dominant. In the case of religion she frequently distinguished between harsh male-made doctrine (especially the doctrines of Election and Predestination) and a loving, motherly God. When it came to life's nondoctrinal harshness, she was disposed to split the Godhead, making a masculine Jehovah the cause of suffering and a feminine Christ the source of comfort. These ideals existed in her writing irrespective of persons, however, so that men and women characters possess "masculine" or "feminine" qualities with little regard to their gender.

There are, however, two qualifications to this general truth about her writing. First, the present-day institutions of church and state being, as she saw, the creation of white males whom the system put in positions of power and dominance, it followed that white men would more likely than not be inclined to defend these institutions. Again, an education in the niceties of Calvinist doctrine being generally the male prerogative, it followed that the less educated—women and slaves—would be less likely to espouse a patriarchal religious world view. In a sense this is to say no more than that those who are protected and exalted by a system will protect it in turn, while those whom the system bypasses or oppresses will seek an alternative. To some extent, then, Stowe calls on women who are placed so that they can see the system's evils, to bear witness to an opposing truth. Insofar as she does so, she is of course demanding of women something quite different from the allegedly traditional passive femininity and domesticity.

She is calling for self-determined action and for responses by women to institutions beyond the family. In *Uncle Tom's Cabin* and in *Dred* (the antislavery novel that followed in 1856), all the good women are engaged in various acts of civil disobedience and subversion of the law.

Stowe's is not woman's fiction, however, because the good women are not engaged in their own cause, either as individuals or in the interest of their sex, but in a cause where their own welfare is not directly involved or may even be endangered. When juxtaposed with woman's fiction, we see Stowe's work as pursuing a course that sometimes appears to go against the secular and self-fulfilling current of the popular genre, especially in its emphasis on self-sacrifice. This appearance is particularly marked in her three religious novels: *The Minister's Wooing* (1859), *The Pearl of Orr's Island* (1862), and *Agnes of Sorrento* (1862). In each of these novels Stowe develops a heroine who is an embodiment of Grace, an illuminated state of entire and loving trust in God. She knew through training and by bitter experience that such a state, though it may be wished and striven for, is never to be achieved by any effort of the individual, and she was profoundly aware of the bitter paradox of the deeply religious person whose very longing and self-awareness destroyed the unconscious receptivity that made an experience of Grace more likely. Thus each of her three heroines is carefully set apart from the normal human world—populated by men and women both—where doubt, anxiety, despondency, and unremitting effort are the religious norm. They possess a kind of childish simplicity coupled with spiritual sensitivity that separates them from ordinary people, as the author and her characters frequently remind the reader and each other. Perfected beings, they have no functions to perform vis-a-vis themselves; their purpose is to validate religious belief and the spiritual world for others, including the audience.

All three of these novels are plotted as love stories, two ending in a happy marriage and one (*The Pearl of Orr's Island*) in the heroine's death. But these outcomes are not important for the woman herself, who exists largely as a living lesson for others. One might be inclined to characterize these heroines as representing an illiberal ideal of womanhood, but to do so would be to employ the wrong frame of reference. Stowe is not talking about womanhood, but about sainthood, and since the condition cannot be achieved by imitation, these characters are not models of what every woman should try to achieve or become. They exist on another plane, in humanity but not of it, and their Christlike function is not limited by or directed to gender.

There are immense technical problems involved in portraying an unearthly character in an earthly form within the confines of a realistic novel, and in my view Stowe did not surmount them. The line between the real and the unearthly is indeed difficult to distinguish. Apparently Stowe believed that a saintly young girl was a more probable character than a saintly young boy, largely because of the real differences in male and female education. A boy with spiritual tendencies would be quickly immersed in physical or mental activity; a girl would be left to herself. As one character puts it of Mara, the "pearl" of Orr's Island,

"That child thinks too much, and feels too much, and knows too much for her years! . . . If she were a boy, and you would take her away cod-fishing . . . the sea-winds would blow away some of the thinking, and her little body would grow stout, and her mind less delicate and sensitive. But she's a woman . . . and they are all alike. We can't do much for them, but let them come up as they will and make the best of it."

This curious passage cuts two ways, for of course one *can* do much for women, and the discourse suggests the remedy: take them cod-fishing like boys. And the tone of the passage encourages us to doubt whether Mara will finally be better off for not being sent cod-fishing. Her gracious condition is presented here in the language of deprivation.

Oldtown Folks (1869) has been incorrectly identified as the first work of New England local color, but though it is not a pioneer it is certainly a striking recreation of small-town New

England life, and the New England mindset in the years of the early republic. Its most interesting characters are older people: the men and women of a stern, austere, narrow, profoundly religious earlier day. The young people whose education and love affairs occupy the foreground of the novel are much less engaging, but the chief young woman is of note for being unlike earlier Stowe heroines as well as conventional woman's heroines. She is a vivacious, glittering, brilliant, good hearted exhibitionist, neither deep nor spiritual but thoroughly lovable, and beloved by all. After a sobering marriage to an unprincipled man who dies an alcoholic, she is permitted to marry the narrator (in her later fiction Stowe frequently used a male first-person narration) without any fundamental alteration in her character. This relaxed heroine operates in a fictional world free from the religious tensions that occupy most of the other characters in *Oldtown Folks*, and free also from the didactic pressures of woman's fiction.

In 1871, however, Stowe published two novels that address themselves directly to the condition of women, and they place her firmly in the liberal if not the radical camp where feminist issues are concerned. *Pink and White Tyranny* is the story of a disastrous marriage between a noble but somewhat naive New England man of a good old family, and a beautiful, social-climbing flirt; in many ways this is a novel of manners, as parvenus clash with tradition. The hero is betrayed into this marriage by the coincidence of his ideal of womanhood with the childlike, innocent demeanor of his bride; he imagines her to be all that he wants in woman—a being at once to be instructed and worshipped. His cruel awakening serves a double satirical purpose. There is a familiar satire on the conventional upbringing of women as attractive and mindless playthings. At the same time there is a satire on the masculine idealizing of helpless, infantine dependency as the epitome of femininity. In the hero's sister and in the girl he did not marry are seen counterexamples of good women, and these are characters very much like the strong-minded, strong-willed, autonomous beings we have seen in woman's fiction.

The point is made more directly, and with references to contemporary woman's issues, in *My Wife and I*. This novel upholds the centrality and sanctity of marriage for men and women alike, and argues that in order to make marriage what it should be, women must be educated like men to earn their own livings and thus be free not to marry if they do not want to. One of its three heroines has refused to marry; she works in her father's business handling his foreign correspondence and is paid like any other clerk. A second has also declined to hunt for a husband and goes to France at the novel's conclusion to study medicine. The novel attacks the radical fringe of the feminist movement as charlatanism, and excoriates the doctrine of free love and women who adopt men's clothes and male manners, but it does so largely out of a conviction that such behavior will discredit the really important and right aims of the woman's movement. These, as articulated by several sympathetic characters, are an education identical to men's (including professional education), employment in a wider range of occupations and at fair wages, nondiscriminatory legislation, and—after perhaps a generation of preparation and education—the ballot and participation in the political process. Clearly, then, Stowe's ideology of womanhood was not constrained within notions of childlike, dependent domesticity. Although she did not share the chief concerns of the authors of woman's fiction—the self-realization and self-improvement of the individual—she appears to have shared their conviction of woman's capability and potential.

Even the fictions of Stowe's that consider woman's issues, however, are not woman's fiction, because they do not utilize the basic woman's story. I turn now to the kinds of tangential fiction outlined at the beginning of this chapter, fiction that, unlike hers, implied the woman's genre without actually fulfilling its expectations. In 1850, a novel published under the pseudonym "Olivia" called *Ellen Parry, or Trials of the Heart*, signalled the literary debut of Emily Edson Briggs (1831–1910). Marriage in 1854 diverted her from novel-writing, and when she moved to Washington, D.C., at the beginning of the Civil War she became a newspaper columnist and acquired a national reputation. A collection entitled *The Olivia Letters* (she retained her early pseudonym) and subtitled "Being Some History of Washington City for Forty Years as Told by the Letters of a Newspaper Correspondent" appeared in 1906. *Ellen Parry* has an English setting and thereby defines itself as a romance, but like McIntosh's *Woman an Enigma* it is concerned with the inculcation of strength and character in the heroine through trials. Its protagonist, a spoiled, willful heiress, must rise to circumstances when her father dies bankrupt. After years of spinsterhood and governessing she finally marries a wealthy, middle-aged widower. As a wedding present he offers to buy her father's house and restore her to her former life, but she refuses. She has no wish to go back to the protected past. Although the author has praised Ellen's decision to break an early engagement to a cad, she believed that marriage is more fulfilling to a woman than single life because it permits greater independence:

A married woman is, unless under very unfortunate circumstances, more favorably situated for the development of her character than if unmarried. She has more and weightier responsibilities; she has more to call forth and nourish her affections; she is removed from dependence into power; no longer an orb borrowing its domestic sunshine from a superior source, she becomes herself the sun from which attendant planets must derive the moral light and warmth which makes the genial and healthful atmosphere of home.

Julia Caroline Ripley Dorr (1825–1913) was known in her own time for her poetry, which was published at first without her knowledge by her husband and eventually totalled many volumes. A South Carolinian by birth, she had moved to Vermont with her family as a small child and was raised by her widower father. *Farmingdale* (1854)—a later edition was called *The Mother's Rule*—was published under the pseudonym "Caroline Thomas," her mother's name; in *Lanmere* (1856) she resumed her own name. Both novels are set in small-town Vermont. For its depiction of real life *Farmingdale* was compared with *The Wide, Wide World,* which it strongly resembles in other respects as well. Even more than Warner's novel, it showed that the country was not a reservoir of domestic virtues and values. The chief adversary in the story is a hard-driving, mean spirited aunt, who provides a "home" for the heroine, Mary Lester, and her little brother Tommy when they are orphaned. In return for shelter, Aunt Betsy feels justified in working the children to the limits of their strength. She works herself, her husband, and her son in the same relentless way, for her only value in life is acquisition. *Farming-dale* approaches a Hamlin Garland kind of naturalism in its unsparing depiction of the mind- and body-numbing labor of a farm, the narrow values of country people, and the casually callous mistreatment of rural children.

When son John reaches twenty-one he chooses to leave the farm. Partly through Mary's influence, he has recognized the spiritual and mental poverty of his life and determined to make something more of himself than his mother's vision encompasses. (Leave-takings like this, bitter on both sides, have become a convention of fiction in our own day; it is interesting to find one chronicled as an ordinary nineteenth-century event.) Aunt Betsy holds Mary responsible for the loss of her son, whom she valued (devoid of imagination and love as she is) as a good field hand; her dour temper grows yet harsher, her abuse of the children more deliberate. Mary sticks it out until Tommy's failing health requires defiance.

A neighbor family takes the fugitive children in, and Mary earns her keep there for a time by spinning and weaving. Then she moves on to an education and a teaching job. Her teaching life begins auspiciously but is soon clouded by scandalous rumors circulated by her aunt, alleging an improper relationship between Mary and her cousin John. Although these rumors are quickly squelched, Mary has learned a hard lesson about the vulnerability of single women.

The novel concludes when Tommy, supported by Mary's

earnings, enters college and Mary accepts a position as principal of a Female Seminary. No romance is foreseen in her life. "I have no wish to be particularly independent, or anything of that kind," Mary tells friends, "but while I have strength to labor, either with my head or hands, I shall feel better and happier to do it." Two of these friends, wondering if Mary will ever marry, conclude that it makes no difference. "I do wish she could marry; she is so eminently fitted to adorn a home," says one. "I don't much care whether she marries or not," says the other. "Mary will adorn her station, wherever it may be. She will make an admirable wife; or if not—" "What then?" "Why, then, she will be the dearest old maid in the world, and do credit to the sisterhood." In conventional terms, Mary's character is an interesting blend of the womanly and the unwomanly. She is "womanly" in her lack of interest in independence and her wish to live for others, especially her brother, but "unwomanly" in the means by which she serves and in her strong drive to work. The superstructure of *Farmingdale* is unusual in that it shows a world governed by women from the beginning. The matriarch Aunt Betsy has acquisitive values more usually associated with men, and instead of seeing the supplanting of male values by female, we see a young woman redeem a world suffering from a matriarch's rule.

The theme of the damage inflicted on a household and the loving heart of a child by an unnatural woman dominates *Lanmere*. Little Bessie Allison is an active, hearty, natural child. Her normal behavior elicits more or less continuous punishment from her cold-hearted mother, a religious formalist who has succeeded in making a schemer and hypocrite of her older daughter Margaret, and long since driven a son, Reuben, from home by her censorious, inquisitorial, and domineering manner. Bessie is saved from apathy and despair by her own buoyant temperament and by the large circle of friends and allies she attracts. She is vindicated at the end of the story when the new minister, whom both Mrs. Allison and Margaret expect to propose to Margaret, asks for the hand of Bessie. Dorr's two novels are both interesting in that they criticize the closed rural family during the same period when many writers were looking to the reestablishment of that family as the national salvation and woman's opportunity. Moreover, in both novels the dominant force in the morbid home is a woman. Dorr looks not to a replacement of patriarchy by matriarchy, but to a reformation of the matriarchy.

Virginia Townsend (1836–1920) was an active literary professional. She published extensively in magazines, was associate editor of T. S. Arthur's *Lady's Home Magazine* from 1856 to 1872, and remained a contributor to it until 1882. She wrote two series of novels for girls in the 1860s and 1870s. A selection of her magazine pieces was published in 1857 as *Living and Loving;* her single contribution to woman's fiction in the period, *While It Was Morning,* appeared in 1858. It is narrated in the first person by the heroine, Ethel Lindsay, a woman of genius who rises from oppression and obscurity to independence and recognition. Left a destitute orphan in childhood, she is taken in by "Aunt" Keziah Strong, a mean-minded and ignorant woman who is no blood relation and expects fulltime labor from the child in exchange for the roof over her head. At age fifteen, Ethel, driven to make something more of her life, appeals to rich neighbors who immediately become her patrons. Through them she finds a supportive home with a widowed minister and his unmarried sister. We find again the conventional stress on self-elected "families."

Ethel's engagement to a cousin of her patrons is terminated by the machinations of a duplicitous friend. For a while she succumbs to grief and shock, but finally recovers and devotes herself seriously to authorship. *Lanmere* has a happy ending when Ethel, who has outgrown first love, is rewarded with marriage to a far superior man. She continues as an author after marriage, for the "very faculty in her which made the book, may warm, and deepen, and enrich her affections." Townsend makes no apologies for Ethel's failure to remain true all her life to a green infatuation.

Margaret Junkin Preston (1820–1897), a Southern poet, published a domestic novel called *Silverwood, A Book of Memories* anonymously in 1856. She was not a skillful storyteller and failed to fit theme to fable. Her avowed intention is to extoll home life, but home is shown instead to be the focus of unremitting catastrophe. From its opening sequence with the Irvine family gathered together—widowed mother, oldest son, and four daughters— to the end, it tells nothing but bad news. There is a bank failure, a house burned down, injury and sickness and death, a villain absconding with savings entrusted to him, a plantation auctioned. The putative heroine of the novel, alone toward its close, has learned nothing about trouble other than that it must be endured. Facing life with dread, she is rescued at last by marriage. *Silverwood's* praise of home rings false and is irrelevant to woman's fiction, for its trials have no uses.

Another Southerner, Eliza Ann Dupuy (1814–1880), wrote some two dozen serialized gothic thrillers between the late 1840s and the 1870s. She achieved fame with *The Conspirator* (1850), a historical fantasy loosely based on Aaron Burr's alleged plot to make himself king of Mexico. In her favorite situation, exploited in *The Conspirator,* a villain gains possession of the heroine by blackmailing her father. This story leads to a set scene wherein the girl's scornful rejection inflames the villain's lust and rage to the point that these two emotions become a single passion. As is so often the case in melodrama, unrealistic characters are the vehicles for real human feelings generally considered to be outside the realm of polite discourse. Given the virtual elimination of sexual motivation from conventional woman's fiction, it is only in the crude extremes of melodrama that we find this material handled. The villains of melodrama, whose wish to possess a woman is identical with the wish to degrade her, represent the antithesis to the ideal men of woman's fiction.

I have found only one novel by Eliza Dupuy that follows the form of woman's fiction, *The Planter's Daughter* (1857). In this novel, Dupuy's melodramatic motifs have been toned down and reinterpreted in a domestic context. The opening situation shows a Virginia family consisting of Mr. Harrington, a widower; his two daughters—Adele, who is as beautiful as an angel, and Pauline, an intelligent, high-minded woman whose unassuming loveliness is overshadowed by her sister's flamboyant attractions— Mr. Harrington's sister, a maiden lady who has raised the girls, and Victor, a wastrel son. Mr. Harrington, a planter, lives in the old, opulent, Virginia style that he deems appropriate to his status—a style which, unfortunately, he cannot afford. Through his extravagances he falls victim to a northern speculator, Reginald Malcolm, who covets Adele. Intuitively, Adele dislikes him; therefore, Malcolm conceals his designs by paying court to Pauline, who falls in love with him. His better nature responds to Pauline's virtues, but he lusts for Adele. When he makes his intentions clear, he is rejected by the whole family, which unites against him and accepts financial ruin rather than permit him doubly to insult the women: Pauline, by abandoning her, and Adele, by marrying her.

Having made this gesture, the Harrington men are unable to live up to it. Neither can triumph over poverty. Victor goes bad almost immediately; like so many other young males in southern fiction, he cannot work at a steady job or defer any sensual gratification. Ultimately he makes a bizarre attempt to shoot his former fiancée who has abandoned him for a wealthier man and then kills himself. The father simply gives up and dies of shame and a broken spirit. Without the appurtenances of the Virginia gentleman, he is nobody. But the three women survive; they set up an exclusive school for young ladies, and in due time Adele gets married. Pauline, recovering from the conventional long illness brought on by grief, buries her love for Malcolm and becomes a contented woman. Dupuy has merged the power struggle of melodrama with the domestic conflict between exploitation and affection. The community of three women becomes the redeeming unit of social love. Dupuy shows that women must know how to survive economically and emotionally without men and promises that they will be able to do so. In the father's sacrifice of security for show, Victor's childish weakness, and Malcolm's predatory intellectuality, Dupuy creates a composite picture of the male that gives women little to respect and nothing to lean on. (But then, inconsistently, she brings back a reformed Malcolm to marry Pauline as her "reward" at the novel's conclusion.) Although her meshing of domesticity and melodrama worked well in *The Planter's Daughter,* and considered—albeit briefly and elliptically—some aspects of heterosexual relations that woman's fiction usually ignored, Dupuy's basic orientation was not congenial to this genre. Woman's fiction develops the good woman as a powerful, effective character, the bad woman as a weak failure. By the 1850s, it is generally only in melodrama that one finds the old-style villainess flourishing. Dupuy was much drawn to these old-style villainesses, with their powerful passions, scheming intellects and blatant lust for power. Given the fact that such characters were effective only in melodrama, it was melodrama that she chose mostly to write. Perhaps, in fact, her fiction in the main was a reaction against the remorselessly high standards applied to women and their behavior in woman's fiction.

When a schoolgirl at a seminary at New Hampton, New Hampshire, Emily Bradley (1827–1863) submitted a story to Joseph C. Neal of Philadelphia, who edited *Neal's Saturday Gazette and Lady's Literary Emporium.* Neal printed this and Bradley's other contributions under her pseudonym "Alice B. Lee." She married him in 1846 (he was twenty years older than she) and was widowed a year later at the age of nineteen. For several years she carried on his editorial activities while pursuing an active authorial career. Marrying Samuel G. Haven in 1853, she had five children but kept on writing. She wrote as "Alice B. Neal," "Alice B. Haven," and, for her many juvenile works, as "Cousin Alice."

Her first book-length fiction was a series of linked sketches called *The Gossips of Rivertown* (1850). In a mode later to be immortalized in *Winesburg, Ohio,* the work moves from one small-town household to the next, exposing various private miseries and triumphs. The connecting theme is the misery cre-

ated by gossip; hence the title. Among the various sketches, the
most interesting is the story of Mrs. Jackson, wife of the town's
mill owner, who is suddenly widowed when her husband drowns
in a flooded river. Though she is desolated by her loss, she thinks
of others affected by his death; anxious to keep the mill hands
employed, she determines (with the concurrence of her brother-
in-law, who is executor of her husband's estate) to continue the
mill operation rather than shut down the plant and sell it. Mrs.
Jackson thus becomes the first woman factory owner and manager
in American fiction. She becomes so, however, from charitable—
that is, womanly—motives. The gossips slander her as a greedy,
acquisitive woman, and Alice Neal makes it clear that, had Mrs.
Jackson's motives been personal gain, her conduct would have
been reprehensible. As was so often the real case during this
historical period, women tried to claim a larger sphere of activity
for themselves without disturbing the accepted notions of the
feminine.

The Gossips of Rivertown is technically accomplished, for it
blends a variety of literary modes—comedy, pathos, tragedy, and
so on—into a connected structure; and it is a beautifully written
piece of local color. Like many of the women who specialized in
children's books, Alice Neal had perfected a clear, simple style; to
this she added a vivid descriptive ability and a gift for understated
evocation:

There is nothing more desolate than the streets of a small country
town, in a northern latitude, at the close of the fall. The sidewalks
are carpeted with withered leaves that rustle to the footsteps of the
few passers-by; a cloud of dust obscures the vision, while the slowly
creaking signs and flapping shutters are in melancholy and dis-
cordant union. . . . The mellow radiance of the Indian summer
has departed, the morning sun has scarcely power to dissolve the last
night's frost, and the wayside pools are skirted with a brittle coating
of ice. Now and then a large farm wagon creaks slowly down the
street; once or twice through the day the wheels of a light vehicle
tells you that the physician is speeding on his errand of mercy; but

otherwise the silence is rarely disturbed. The sky grows dark as evening draws on, not with heaped and threatening clouds, but a leaden, heavy, impenetrable pall sweeps slowly over the horizon.

Except for the "errand of mercy," the passage is impeccable, and demonstrates that some of these women had mastered the esthetic resources of understated language.

In her second long adult fiction, *The Coopers, or Getting Under Way* (1858), Neal, drawing on her experiences as housewife and mother, plotted the course of a middle-class marriage from its early days in a boarding house through to the successful managing of home and business life. She makes it clear that the woman's work in running her home is exactly analogous to, and no less risky or strenuous than, man's running a business. Like Gilman's *Recollections of a New-England Housekeeper* and Hale's *Keeping House and Housekeeping* (See Chapter 3), on which it may be modeled, *The Coopers* presents housekeeping as a career, requiring preparation and businesslike capacities including managerial skills, financial acumen, decisiveness, and authority. For all that she is a cheerful, energetic, and perceptive soul, Martha Cooper finds herself completely unequipped for running a house, ironically in part because her upbringing has been so conventionally feminine. Feminine charm may manage a husband, but it will not do for servants. After a few years of married life, the vivacious bride is brought to the verge of nervous collapse by a combination of overwork, frustration, and a growing sense of worthlessness that makes all tasks seem beyond her abilities. "I am so weary, so very weary of myself, and everything! I have been this long, long time!" she laments, taking to her bed after the birth of a child and lacking the will to get up again.

Neal does not blame housework for the wife's unhappiness any more than she blames business for the husband's. The American middle-class wife has a job, which is to manage her household; she has only the choice of doing this job poorly or doing it well. If she runs her house well she will enjoy the satisfaction that comes to anyone who masters a task, and she can do this if she takes a professional approach to her responsibilities. The novel ends cheerfully when, with the help of an older friend, Martha succeeds in ordering her surroundings and hence rising above them. Her success is paralleled by her husband's in business; the Coopers are well "under way" as the subtitle has it, when their story comes to a close. This example of moral Biedermeier is rich in detail, from washtub to andiron; it is an unpretentious and sociologically valuable re-creation of daily middle-class life in mid-nineteenth-century America.

Similar bourgeois realism defines the texture of two extremely popular little novels by Elizabeth Stuart Phelps (1815–1852), *Sunny Side* (1851) and *A Peep at Number Five* (1852). Phelps was the daughter of a Congregational minister who taught at Andover. At age sixteen she attended the Mt. Vernon School in Boston, under the direction of the Reverend Jacob Abbott, for whose religious magazine she began to write stories published under the acronym "H. Trusta." At age twenty-seven she married Austin Phelps, a minister who followed his father-in-law's example and became a professor at Andover in 1848. *Sunny Side,* though rejected by four publishers, sold 100,000 copies in its first year in print; *A Peep at Number Five* had a similar sale, though, understandably, the author did not experience the same difficulty in getting it published. Long susceptible to nervous crises, Elizabeth Phelps died of "cerebral disease" after the deaths of her father and infant son in the same year. Her promising career was terminated before it was fairly launched. (Her daughter, writing under the same name, became a popular author in the next generation; she published *The Gates Ajar,* a hugely successful book, in 1869.)

Sunny Side and *A Peep at Number Five* are companion pieces; the first chronicles the domestic life and trials of a country minister and his wife while the second repeats this procedure for a city minister. Neither is a work of piety; the theme of both is money—the lack of it in a minister's life, and the consequent strains in the domestic fabric. Time is a minor motif—also the lack of it, as the minister is called on endlessly and thoughtlessly while his wife is subject to similar unthinking demands. Abundant in detail and simple in style, these two works are first-rate examples of domestic realism, and strong testimony to the preeminence of money motifs in middle-class fiction.

In both novels, Phelps develops idealized pictures of the minister's wife, who requires virtually superhuman powers to cope with her responsibilities. She must run a household, participate in numerous parish functions, be on call for frequent unexpected visits by women of the congregation, and absorb the tensions generated by a husband who is much in the house but so absorbed in his work that he hardly notices his wife from one day to the next. At one point, when Mrs. Holbrook, the city minister's wife, has been ill in bed for a week ("her busy life wore on her, and she was often ill") she tells her husband that she wishes she were one of his parishoners, for then she might look forward to a visit from him. He contritely moves his desk into her room for the afternoon, silently writing away until the scratching of his pen thoroughly unnerves her. In a sardonic scene, a group of minister's wives discuss the sterling qualities of one of their group—a woman who manages to carry out all her responsibilities to family, husband, pocketbook, and parish. Where is she now? asks one. Dead, answers another. Everyone understands that her perfections have killed her. The minister's wife, perhaps, is an early example of the "two-career woman," the full-time housekeeper and full-time minister's assistant.

The last work Phelps brought out in her lifetime (a collection called *The Last Leaf from Sunny Side* was posthumously issued), *The Angel Over the Right Shoulder* (1852), is a short story published as a Christmas book, about a young housewife's conflict between domestic duties and the wish to develop herself as an individual. (Its separate publication has caused some hasty critics to assume that it is a novel.) She longs for study, intellectual stimulation, a more earnest life; her round of days absorbed in one petty household crisis after another seems frivolous and use-

less. With her husband's well-intentioned support, she sets aside
an hour a day for private study. But no one in her home respects
the hour—in fact her husband, needing a button sewed on, is the
first to violate it. In the end, she is reconciled to what appears to
be the inevitable by a dream-vision that shows her the dignity
and value of service to her family. Compared to the significance
of her wifely and motherly duties, self-development is frivolous
and superficial. Although *Angel* rapidly retreats from the issue it
has broached, it is one of the rare woman's fictions of this time
to recognize the phenomenon of domestic schizophrenia.

I turn now to a varied group of women's novels in which the
pattern of the trials-and-triumph story is varied by the focus on
heroines with unusual life experiences, works that would be read
more in a spirit of curiosity than with empathy and identification.
Therese Louise Albertine Robinson (1797–1870) was a German
woman, daughter of a professor and an accomplished linguist and
philologist herself. After her marriage to Professor Charles Robinson she immigrated to the United States. She continued research
in Slavic languages and folklore, and wrote extensively about her
new country for the German press, using the pseudonym "Talvi."
In addition she wrote three novels in German, which her daughter
translated into English. One of these, entitled *The Exiles* (1853),
may well be the earliest immigrant novel. It cleverly adapts immigrant experience to the form of a woman's fiction.

The heroine, Clotilde Osten, gives up the comfort and security
of her wealth and high social station in Germany to follow her
lover Hubert, a political refugee, to America. Their ship is
wrecked and the lovers are separated. Clotilde is washed ashore on
the Florida coast, as destitute and unprotected as a young woman
setting out on her life trials can possibly be. She is cared for by a
young Florida planter and his mother, a devout Catholic; these
people find a governessing position for her in a southern city.
After a while she rediscovers Hubert: freedom-lover that he is,
he has become an abolitionist and is languishing in a southern
jail. The lovers escape to the North, where they marry and try

to run a farm. By this point in the story, *The Exiles* has become a kind of commentary on America as perceived by the educated foreigner; it is more intellectual and abstract than the typical woman's fiction. In a final flourish of plot, Robinson has Hubert killed in a duel and Clotilde, who cannot endure another separation, collapses and dies of grief. It is in this death, more than her foreignness, that the heroine deviates from formula. No other heroine of American woman's fiction fails to recover from a romantic tragedy.

The life of Anna Cora Mowatt Ritchie (1819–1870) is a more poignant example of trials, triumph, and tragedy than anything in a woman's fiction. One of several daughters in a well-to-do family, she had eloped at the age of fifteen with James Mowatt, a rich and handsome lawyer some thirteen years older than she. In his comfortable house she read extensively and indulged a taste for amateur theatricals that had been encouraged in her father's home. When her husband lost his money and his health in 1841, she improvised a series of bold careers: she gave public poetry readings (her biographer, Eric Barnes, calls her the first "lady elocutionist"), did a great deal of hack writing, composed a novel of manners (*The Fortune Hunter,* 1844) and an epistolary novel (*Evelyn,* 1845), both of which were adaptations of European models to a New York setting, and wrote an extremely successful play, *Fashion* (1845), considered by some to be the first truly native drama. Following the success of her play, she went on the stage herself, making her theatrical debut in a star role. For eight years she was America's leading actress. Mr. Mowatt died in 1851, and in 1854 Anna married again, unhappily as it turned out, to a southern newspaperman, William Ritchie. She is said to have been a major force in changing general moral attitudes toward the theater. Because she was impeccably virtuous and of high social standing, she made attendance at the theater respectable.

She never returned to the stage after her second marriage, but she wrote several works designed to create sympathy for the life of the theater. Her autobiography of 1854 was a popular success; less so were some works of fiction about actresses, *Mimic Life* (1856), a collection of one long and two shorter narratives, and *Twin Roses* (1857), a novel. These works present the actress as a domestic heroine, who feels no desire for personal fame and lacks vanity or assertiveness; she simply needs to make a living, to support herself and often a family as well. She is deeply virtuous, committed to her work, and attached to her home. Her life alternates between the stage and her home; it is neither glamorous nor unconventional. Because acting is exacting, fatiguing, and dangerous—stage accidents abound in Mowatt's fiction—the actress makes a personal sacrifice far greater than any possible personal reward. Around the actress cluster a variety of other sympathetic feminine types: bit players, seamstresses, wardrobe keepers, all working for need. Mowatt emphasizes the ultimate selflessness of her heroines by giving most a tragic death from accident or overwork. As in *The Exiles,* such well-intentioned endings remove the fiction from the main tradition of woman's novels, because woman's fiction was designed to show its readers how to live, not how to die. The novels remain interesting for their presentation of backstage life, and for the long, careful descriptions of the staging and interpreting of well-known dramatic roles.

Ruth Hall (1855) and *Rose Clark* (1856), the two novels of Sara Payson Willis Parton (1811–1872), who wrote under the pen name "Fanny Fern," are stories of the trials of heroines who deviate from convention. The circumstances of the author's life had forced her into defiance of respectability, and her novels are exercises in self-vindication. Educated at Catharine Beecher's seminary in Hartford, Connecticut, she had made a happy marriage at the age of twenty-six. The sudden death of her husband in 1846, eight years later, left her penniless, with two daughters and no preparation for their support. Neither her father, a publisher and editor of religious newspapers and children's magazines (to which she had occasionally contributed), nor her well-off in-laws would help her. In 1849 she made a disastrous second marriage that ended three years later in divorce. Teaching and sewing did not bring in enough to keep her family together, and she reluctantly sent her elder daughter to the in-laws. Her brother, the literary lion Nathaniel Parker Willis, patron of several women authors, would not aid his sister in establishing a literary career. But she began to publish short essays and sprightly paragraphs in the newspapers and by 1852 was among the most popular newspaper writers in America. A collection of her work, *Fern Leaves from Fanny's Portfolio* (1853), and a second series in 1854 were immediate best sellers. In 1855, Robert Bonner of the New York *Ledger* put her under contract for a column at a hundred dollars a week; she is said never to have missed an issue. At the height of her success she retained a weight of anger against all those who had failed to help her, and her novels contain the fiercest repudiation of kin and blood ties in women's writing of the time.

Nathaniel Hawthorne sensed this anger and therefore excepted *Ruth Hall* from his contemptuous dismissal of women's novels (but his praise, like his blame, should be taken with reservations since there is no evidence that he understood the intentions of woman's fiction). Other commentators have been led astray by her flowery pen name and classed her with a mythical sisterhood of rhapsodic rhetoricians. In fact, Fanny Fern's newspaper pieces are jaunty, irreverent, and colloquial, written in a style highly responsive to the rhythms and vocabulary of ordinary speech. She deserves restudy as an accomplished practitioner of a vernacular prose style. She was direct, wry, witty, and incisive, more often satirical than sentimental. Here is a characteristic extract, from a piece in *Fern Leaves* called "The Tear of a Wife:"

Smile! It flatters your husband. He wants to be considered the source of your happiness, whether he was baptized Nero or Moses. Your mind never being supposed to be occupied with any other subject than himself, of course a tear is a tacit reproach. Besides, you miserable little whimperer! what have you to cry for? A-i-n-t y-o-u m-a-r-

r-i-e-d? Isn't that the *summun bonum*—the height of feminine
ambition? You can't get beyond that! It is the jumping-off place!
You've arriv!—got to the end of your journey! Stage puts up here!
You have nothing to do but retire on your laurels, and spend the
rest of your life endeavoring to be thankful that you are Mrs. John
Smith! "Smile," you simpleton!

Insofar as the popularity of *Fern Leaves* shows something about
American taste, it reflects the public's attraction to the humorous,
skeptical, active, practical perceptions and style of the common
person, and not the imputed tearful sentimentality of the Victorian woman. Fanny Fern's brother, in these stereotypical terms,
was far more feminine than she.

The theme of *Ruth Hall* is the gifted, virtuous heroine mistreated by her family—hardly something new. Nor is the anger
expressed in it something new; the question of how to deal with
anger gets a different answer in works like *The Lamplighter* or
The Wide, Wide World, but the presence of anger is understood
as a basic fact of the heroine's emotional makeup. The novels of
Southworth, Hentz, Holmes, and Marion Harland all permitted
their heroines to triumph in satisfying ways over their enemies,
thereby indulging the readers' wish for revenge. The unconventional aspect of *Ruth Hall* is that it generalizes from the heroine's
unfortunate experiences, not to the formation of a superior family
structure centered on the heroine, but to a repudiation of the kin
and marriage structure entirely. At the end of the novel the autobiographical heroine, who has taken the pen name "Floy," is
satisfied with an independent career and has no wish to enter any
domestic situation.

Like the author, Ruth Hall has made a first happy marriage,
but in the light of her experiences as a widow, happy marriage
comes to seem a fool's paradise. Where woman's fictions generally
show that woman may have to live alone and make a living, they
place her ultimate happiness in loving human relationships including one with a good husband. Conventional novels permit
women to enter professions in which they may acquire fame and

wealth, but carefully indicate that fame is desirable only as the opportunity to extend a good influence, and that in itself it can never provide satisfaction to a woman. In contrast *Ruth Hall* shows how very happy her fame and money made the heroine, and how pleased she is—now that she had been enlightened as to the truth of human nature—to be free from the swindle of love. Of course she accepts the obligation to support her children and loves them. But this is the love of a benefactor toward dependents; Fanny Fern has rejected entirely the idea that women need a love they must lean on. She does not even accept the ideal of a love between peers. Living in a man's world, Ruth realizes that success is possible to her only if she plays the man's game; more than this, she decides that the rules of the man's world are not an artificial structure, but express the realities of human nature.

The villains of *Ruth Hall* are Fanny Fern's father, brother, and her in-laws; the villain of *Rose Clark* is her second husband. (*Ruth Hall* did not include a second marriage for the heroine.) *Rose Clark* contains two heroines. The titular heroine, a naive character, had been orphaned and raised by a vicious aunt, who first overworked her and later sent her off to school—not out of concern for Rose's welfare but because she had married and wanted the child out of the way. At school the lonely girl is persuaded into a secret marriage. Her "husband" disappears and leaves Rose pregnant; the aunt repudiates her. Desperate, Rose sets out with her baby boy to find her husband, in whose fidelity she continues to believe. She settles in New Orleans, where she becomes friends with a woman artist, Gertrude, who lives alone and supports herself by her painting. Gertrude's solitude is the result of a disastrous marriage to a man named Stahle, which Gertrude had contracted, like Rose, to find the love she had been denied in her family.

But Stahle was a "sensualist," for whom "marriage was only the steppingstone to an else impossible gratification." His attitudes quickly disgust his wife, and when he realizes how she feels about him he begins to hate her. He leaves her and hires detectives to catch her in some immoral act. Ultimately he divorces her on the grounds of desertion (she had refused to rejoin him). Although it is Gertrude's contempt that has occasioned the emotional separation of the couple Stahle is held to account for the formal breakdown of the marriage. He could not live with her scorn. Rather than attempt to live up to her idea of a good husband, he tried to lower Gertrude to his idea of a "good" wife.

The point at issue between Gertrude and Stahle—his sensualism and his consequent attitudes toward his wife—is especially pertinent to nineteenth-century American woman's attempt to improve her situation. I have touched before on the way in which women believed that, in the sexual domain, they were invariably victims. Because of this belief they tried to define encounters between men and women in such a way as to exclude sexuality altogether. This was a radical step, meant to force men to approach women as human beings with minds and hearts rather than as objects of lust. Within the marriage relation, women appear historically to have exercised control over sex by inhibiting its expression. Some social historians feel that their primary purpose here was to free themselves from the dangers and difficulties of childbearing and childrearing and thus make their lives safer and more free. But the psychological purpose, expressed in so much woman's fiction, of controlling men's attitudes toward women also remains relevant within marriage. Far from being flattered by her husband's sexual appetite for her, Gertrude was deeply offended by it. She took it as a sign that he could not perceive, or had no interest in, her mental and spiritual gifts. She believed that lust was accompanied by contempt for its object, and that her husband's approach to her was therefore inherently degrading.

Despite her situation as a divorced and emancipated woman, Gertrude shows no sign of a sexual appetite of her own. Obviously her strategy required inhibiting her own sexual responsiveness; under the circumstances, such responsiveness would have appeared a dangerous weakness, an admision that her husband's low view of her was warranted. Sexual appetite was one among many feminine frailties that the nineteenth-century woman was trying to overcome as she prepared herself for full participation in the world. By the end of Fanny Fern's novel, Rose Clark has been reunited to her husband, who was as faithful as she believed him to be, but Gertrude has remained free and romantically unattached. Thus for Fanny Fern—and she spoke for many feminists of her time here—the liberated woman was sexually liberated, not in the modern sense but in the sense of being liberated from sex.

Values like Fanny Fern's are at work in the autobiographical novel *Mary Lyndon* (1855) by Mary Sargeant Nichols. Nichols (1810–1884) was the victim of an emotionally and financially impoverished childhood and a ghastly first marriage to a Mr. Gove, who, in the words of *Notable American Women,* "did poorly in business and relied on Mary's desperate needlework for support. Ignorant, tyrannical, and mean, he wanted an obedient servant for a wife." In *Mary Lyndon* the author portrays herself as carrying out much of this needlework lying flat in bed, to which she is generally confined because of the sufferings caused by one terrible episode of childbirth and four equally terrible experiences of stillbirth and aborted pregnancies. In 1842, after eleven years of marriage during which her husband appropriated her earnings, thwarted her attempts to read and study, and forced his unwelcome sexual attentions on her, Mary Nichols ran away with their daughter. Her husband harassed her for five more years—he kidnaped the daughter for a time, for example—until he found another woman and divorced his first wife. Mary Nichols' main interests were in health reform, and she later achieved reputation and success in that field; but in her early days of independence she turned to novel-writing because authorship was an established occupation for literate women.

Two of the three novels she published in the 1840s were eccentric woman's stories. In *Agnes Morris* (1849) the heroine proves herself in a sequence of domestic trials, including the unconventional burden of a hypochondriacal mother who becomes a morphine addict. Her noblest act is to take under her wing a seduced, abandoned innocent and to support her and her baby despite considerable moral disapproval from others. As a schoolteacher, Agnes cannot afford moral disapproval, but she perseveres and is finally vindicated by the love of an estimable young man. In *Two Loves* (also 1849), Nichols contrasts a flighty social belle and a serious, moral woman; she pushes the belle's progress further than usual by ultimately involving her in adultery, prostitution, and disgrace. Both of these novels show a taste for artifice and the lurid, and a relatively weak narrative gift.

Mary Lyndon is quite different. Nichols had clearly seen how apt the form of woman's fiction was to her own life, and made convincing use of the pattern to shape her autobiography. The heroine is a sensitive, questing, intelligent person born into a world that is at best unresponsive to and at worst destructive of her identity and integrity. Her mother is a typical hard-working New England woman who wastes all her strength in the material cares of her household and has neither time nor sympathy for her daughter's emotional needs. Mary's father considers himself an intellectual and an enlightened man but his views of woman are medieval. He forbids Mary to learn to write, although he allows her to learn to read so that she can read to him. Health conditions, diet, and medical care are appallingly inadequate in rural New England, and such fashions as tight lacing, gauzy low-cut dresses, and thin evening slippers are suicidally inappropriate to the climate and mode of life. Consequently, women pass the greater part of their lives in illness and pain.

In adolescence Mary converts to Quakerism, on the strength of a book she has read, and finds a temporary outlet for her emotionalism and sense of difference from her neighbors. She marries a man she does not love, because she knows no alternative to marriage for a woman and cannot think of a reason to refuse him. She experiences marriage as an institution designed to make a slave of the wife: she must keep her husband's house, support him, and serve all his physical appetites, but she may not demand anything from him in return. He may work or not as he chooses, and neither helps around the house or responds to any expressed need of hers. Although many women authors had criticized marriage, Nichols' attack is the most extreme.

Like her author, the character Mary runs away from her husband. Before she is freed to remarry by divorce, she experiences two romantic attachments. Although Nichols asserts that these extramarital romances were chaste, she is clearly working toward an idea of free love, because for a married nineteenth-century woman to acknowledge love for another man was considered moral adultery by many even if there was no physical consummation. On the other hand, the ideal of free love is intentionally freed from sexuality as well as from legal marriage. In Nichols' experience, legal marriage was legalized prostitution, and she idealizes a tie that is spiritual rather than legal or sexual. Her second "lover" shares these views and, hence, Mary makes a happy second marriage.

On the subject of the second marriage, *Mary Lyndon* is more radical than it had been on the subject of free love. In *Rose Clark,* Fanny Fern had shown Gertrude's virtue by making her refuse to consider remarriage after her divorce. This was evidence that she had not jettisoned her first husband for self-gratifying purposes. Indeed events had been arranged to make her husband the deserter. In contrast, Nichols permits Mary Lyndon to run away from her husband and enter into a second marriage without guilt when she meets a compatible mate. Women are given the right to initiate a marital breakup and to marry again if they want. They are permitted to assert their own emotional needs, in defiance of a conventional view of feminine virtue as inevitably self-controlled. Since Mary's second marriage is based on a spiritual affinity where the first had been the result of psychological coercion, we are meant to perceive that the second marriage is more virtuous by far than the first. Several women authors had endowed their heroines with second loves superior to the first, but few of them allowed for a second marriage unless they eliminated the first husband by outside agency. Nichols permitted her heroine to do for herself what other authors had done for their heroines.

Mary Nichols is often placed on the fringe of the woman's rights movement in histories of feminism, and so is another unconventional author, Elizabeth Oakes Smith (1806–1893). Smith confessed to her traditionalist mother that she longed for an education and to become a teacher; horrified, her mother married her off at sixteen to Seba Smith, who was then almost twice her age. Oakes Smith, as she later designated herself, describes this travesty and its aftermath poignantly in her autobiography:

I was well, but not fully developed, for I grew nearly two inches afterwards. Mr. Smith was almost twice my age, wore spectacles, and was very bald. . . . I was so foreign to all this, so unfit for the occasion—I, a dreamy, imaginative, undeveloped child, whose head was not furnished with a fibre of the actual. . . . Most conscientiously did I bend my young faculties to redeem the obligations involved in my new position. My husband was most exacting, and greatly disinclined to the responsibilities of a family man. He was essentiallly a bachelor, yet, having a wife, he was not disposed to allow her to let up on any point of duty. Happily, perhaps, a sense of duty was my weak point. . . . Thousands of young housekeepers could sympathize with my short-comings, and those of a poetic turn will see how carefully I folded my wings that I might not be remiss in any one home duty. The folly and sorrow was that I felt myself to be a poor, weak creature, unfit for the place occupied. I had lost my girlhood, and found nothing better to take its place.

In fulfillment of her duties, she eventually bore six sons. "I felt painfully that had I been a boy, time and space would have been given to me to fill up this arrested beautiful development, while marriage, which a girl must not refuse, was the annihilation of her. I saw no reason for this, but the fact remained, and I was secretly glad not to add to the number of human beings who must be from necessity curtailed of so much that was desirable in life; who must be arrested, abridged, engulfed in the tasteless actual." In the 1830s, Seba Smith was a newspaper editor and publisher who achieved brief literary fame for his humorous "down-East" *Jack Downing* letters. Oakes Smith helped him to put out his journals and sometimes contributed to them, using on occasion the pen name Ernest Helfenstein. In the Panic of 1837, Smith lost a good deal of money invested in land speculations, and the family moved from Portland, Maine, to New York City.

In the city, Oakes Smith quickly became the dominant member of the family, her literary success eclipsing her husband's. In the 1840s she published in all the leading periodicals; her 1843 volume of poetry was a critical success. Singled out for special note was a long narrative poem, "The Sinless Child." Its philosophy of nature and childhood was likened to Wordsworth's but in fact it was less concerned with childhood than womanhood. In the image of Eva, the sinless child who enjoys a secret and direct communion with the spirits of nature, and dies after kissing a man (the kiss redeems him from a career of drunkenness and other dissipations), Smith was projecting a favorite vision of the women poets—it is found much less often if at all among the novelists, since it is not suited to an active heroine—of the vestal spirit free of the least taint of "the actual." The thrust of the poem for Oakes Smith and her women readers would be the assurance that they had once been such pure beings themselves, and that, insofar as their imaginations still enshrined such an ideal, they retained a virginal core that sex, conventions, children, and housework had not corrupted. "The Sinless Child" expresses woman's hope that she has not been brought down to the level of her own degrading experiences, that she is better than she seems. It is a fastidious view of human experience that is not easily shaped to the form of a woman's fiction, as the genre flourished in the 1850s.

Toward the end of the 1840s Smith became interested in the woman's rights movement. She wrote a series of feminist articles for Greeley's *New York Tribune,* collected in 1851 as *Woman and Her Needs.* This work sets forth a strong though inconsistent feminist position. In the fallen, male-dominated world of today, women must be given the same opportunities that men have, she wrote. They must be permitted to make money and achieve reputations. Women who are trained only to marry can do nothing else. Women who are trained for occupations would be fully developed human beings and could then marry or not as they chose. If woman could freely elect it, marriage might become the sacrament it is hypocritically alleged to be.

Simultaneously Oakes Smith projects the vision of a utopian world in which woman's freely expressed nature would be something quite different from man's. Man is more material, woman more ethereal. He is appropriately designated "Lord of the Material Universe" since he is better at science and at "those protracted labors needful to the harder development of the understanding." As for woman, her mind when "unstinted and unadulterated, has in it more of aspiration, more of the subtle and intuitive character, that links it to the spiritual; she is impatient of labor . . . she cares less for the deductions of reason. . . . The angels recognize her as of nearer affinity." These two visions are incompatible, for if woman's inherent capacities are so unsuited for the world's work, if she is impatient of labor and so on, she cannot hope to attain professional parity with men in the fallen world.

It is her utopian rather than realistic vision of woman that Oakes Smith embodies in her feminist novel, *Bertha and Lily* (1854). The chief motive in the design of this work seems to be to show, in a series of repetitious scenes, the incredible superiority of Bertha to everybody around her, and especially to the young minister Ernest Helfenstein (an in-joke) who, limited and plodding in understanding, always stands back and gapes at her powers of reason and of virtue. Bertha, who has endured and recovered from a great (unspecified) tragedy, has settled peacefully in a small town, where her influence radiates around her as naturally and irresistibly as sunlight. Some in the town perceive her as an officious meddler, but this view is a function of their own narrowness. (A reader today will probably find Bertha's self-congratulatory tone alternately arrogant and pathetic.)

But there is a twist to this story. Bertha's tragedy, we learn, was to have been seduced and borne a child who was taken away from her during an interlude of madness. By society's standards she is a fallen woman. Yet no one dares patronize her. Midway through the narrative, her seducer arrives, chastened and with no other wish in life than to marry his victim. But Bertha rejects him and he dies of grief on the spot. At the conclusion she is reunited with her child and married to Helfenstein. The vision of feminine superiority that Oakes Smith embodies in Bertha is not radical, but she is certainly radical to embody it in a fallen woman.

Oakes Smith published her second novel, *The Newsboy,* anonymously in the same year as *Bertha and Lily,* 1854. This work was produced in connection with her charitable involvement in the condition of these street waifs. Since its central character is a young boy, the novel has only a tangential relation to woman's fiction, but one that is not without interest. Trying to master the new urban reality, it brings together in one structure descriptions of poverty and degradation, sentimental vignettes of life among the poor as they try to achieve bourgeois values in miserable circumstances, and an exotic plot wherein the newsboy becomes rescuer of his patron's daughter and hence a hero and a son-in-law. Perhaps Horatio Alger found a model in *The Newsboy.* American literature is in need of a study that will point out the large number of male-centered stories of the 1850s and after, written by men, that amalgamated the hero's adventures with a home emphasis. Certainly Alger's heroes established "homes" for themselves, domestic spaces wherein, after they had succeeded, they acted as "parent" to other homeless boys. Such domestic behavior is often the first or the key ritual act of many a supposedly rebellious hero of American masculine fiction, whether the home is a raft in a river or a camp in the Michigan woods. This needed study might result in a reclassification of many of our male authors and show the extent to which women and men alike in America have introjected the culture's insistence on home as the center of human value. Psychologically, such stories show—what

is more readily admitted for women's fictions than for men's—the
man's desire to take the place, not of his father, but of his mother.
Since our culture does not permit men to take on the psychological attributes of mothers, the wish expressed in these men's
stories has been denied (above all, perhaps, by the father-centered
Freudians).

In the 1850s, Oakes Smith began to travel and lecture on the
rights of women. The feminists welcomed her, and she gave up
literature for woman's rights agitation. I have found only two
authors besides Oakes Smith and Chesebro' who used fallen
women as heroines (although scores of heroines suffer from the
ambiguous status of a "secret" marriage). One of these was the
poet Alice Cary (1820–1871), an Ohioan who moved to New
York with two sisters after her first successful volume of poems
was published. A collection of sketches, *Clovernook* (1852), was
highly successful, but two novels were not: *Hagar* (1852) and
Married Not Mated (1856) are so badly written as to read like
parody. In *Hagar* the heroine is seduced in a scene that might
have been written a hundred years earlier; after many years as a
social outcast she is courted by an idealistic young minister (who
must be many years her junior) but refuses him and disappears,
leaving a fifty-page explanation of her past life. *Married Not
Mated* has some vigorous low-life characters and funny episodes
but its tone is wildly uneven and the narrative does not cohere.
Like Oakes Smith, Cary was a feminist, a poet, and an adherent
to outdated images of women.

The second author who used the fallen woman is Harriet
Marion Stephens (1823–1858), who had a brief career as an
actress and then turned to authorship. She published in and
edited journals; a collection of stories appeared in book form, and
she published one novel. *Hagar, A Story of Today* (1858)—
Hagar was of course the generic name, biblically derived, for
outcast women—features a tempestuous Southern heroine who
runs away from home and is seduced. After an obscure interval
in her history she surfaces in Boston society, which is represented

as seething with illicit affairs. In such a context Hagar differs from other women only in not concealing her past. For her forthrightness she receives respect, not contempt, from her acquaintances, except those who have something to hide. "There's *too* much of you—that's your only fault. . . . There ought to have been a dozen children by when you was born, to have shared your individuality. You are independent, and can't help it." At the end of the novel she has become a famous author and is going to marry Boston's most sought-after bachelor. She comes closer than most heroines of woman's fiction to a twentieth-century idea of an emancipated woman.

It is hardly surprising that there were so few fallen women in nineteenth-century woman's fiction. As I have suggested from the first, this genre evolved to counteract the pernicious vogue of seduction stories. The women writers did not hold the type of the fallen woman in contempt, but they did see evidence in her story of traditional feminine weaknesses that they wished modern women to overcome. They wanted to show that good women were not necessarily weak, that the loving heart could coexist with moral strength and intellectual fortitude.

After the Civil War, Louise Chandler Moulton (1835–1908) became a well known poet and reviewer as well as a notable literary hostess. She had begun to write at an early age; two volumes of her sketches were collected in the 1850s, and she wrote a novel, *Juno Clifford* (1856), when she was twenty. It is a juvenile performance, projecting an image of the wicked stepmother as rival for the affections of the heroine's beloved. Juno Clifford is a beautiful, dark, passionate woman married to a man much older than she. She adopts an attractive young lad from the slums, Warren Hereford, and falls madly in love with him. Warren reveres Juno as his mother; he is in love with Grace Atherton and fails to perceive how Juno successfully comes between him and Grace, just as she has come between Warren and his blood family. But Juno's situation is ultimately self-defeating, for she can control Warren only in her maternal role, and when, after her husband's death, she reveals the true nature of her feeling for him, her power is ended. Warren returns to his family and resumes his courtship of Grace, now a widow with young children. To his surprise, Grace rejects his suit; later, after she has written a successful book, she accepts him.

If *Juno Clifford* had followed the formula of a woman's fiction it would have centered on Grace, showing how she rose from the ashes of a disappointed love to self-renewal and autonomy. First she marries a kind protector, emancipating herself from futile romance. When his death leaves her with children to support, she succeeds as a writer and thus emancipates herself from marriage. Moulton's choice of Juno as her central character gives the impression of reverting to the stereotypes of an earlier day. Less interested in her triumphant nineteenth-century heroine than her dark lady, she creates in Juno a stock figure of feminine villainy, the woman whose power over others rises from the passion within her that eventually goes out of control. Warren is less stereotyped than featureless, and the quasi-incestuous situation is routine eighteenth-century gothicism.

A number of novels written during these years defined themselves as woman's fiction but were in fact propaganda novels for a variety of causes supposed to be of special interest to women. Occasionally one finds a simple, sensationalist melodrama posing as domestic fiction—for example, Dupuy's *The Country Neighborhood* (1855), whose local color goes no further than its title; or Mary Andrews Denison's *Gracie Amber* (1857), a trite story of working-class virtue assailed by fashionable vice. More often, one finds thesis novels on such issues as temperance, abolition, and evangelical conversion.

Caroline Hayden's *Carrie Emerson, or Life at Cliftonville* (1855) is an exemplary story about the terrible results of gossip. Sarah Marshall Hayden's two linked novellas, *Early Engagements and Florence* (1854), published under the pseudonym "Mary Frazaer," showed how a girl who married one man while loving another inevitably destroyed the health and happiness of her husband and children.

Mrs. H. J. Moore's first novel, *Anna Clayton, the Mother's Trial,* anonymously published in 1855, is bitterly anti-Catholic. Anna's sufferings follow from marriage to an English Catholic controlled by his evil priest; the mother's trial of the subtitle is the kidnaping of her two children by designing Jesuits. Two later novels, *The Golden Legacy, A Story of Life's Phases* (1857) and *Wild Nell, The White Mountain Girl* (1860), attack class pretensions in American life. In *The Golden Legacy* an English heiress visiting America changes places with her companion to observe the degree to which "democratic" Americans are infatuated with social status. In *Wild Nell,* the mountain girl is educated on a whim by Walter, a rich young man who had taken shelter in her mother's cottage during a storm. Later Nell appears in society and wins Walter's love. But he takes her for an orphaned heiress, and when she announces her true identity he repudiates her. She is vindicated by marriage to a wealthy British aristocrat while Walter, realizing too late that his love was true, dies of remorse. In both novels the heroines are self-dependent and morally courageous beings; these qualities impel the action but do not form the thematic center.

Harriette Newell Baker and Jane Elizabeth Hornblower wrote evangelical tracts in the form of woman's fiction. Baker (1815–1893) was a minister's wife and a prolific author of pious juveniles, including such series as "Bertie and the Carpenters/Gardeners/Masons/Plumbers," "Little Frankie and His Cousin/Father/Mother/at His Plays/at School/on a Journey," and "Little Robins in the Nest/in Trouble/Learning to Fly." She used the pseudonyms "Aunt Hattie" and "Madeline Leslie." In 1855, 1856, 1857, and 1869 she published four novels in a "Home Life Series" about the beauties of Christian character and the difficulties encountered by true Christians in a secular world.

Cora and the Doctor (1855) is a first-person epistolary and journal account by Cora to her English mother of her experiences as the wife of a doctor in a small Massachusetts town. Her husband is as much minister as doctor, using his influence and access to sufferers as a means of weaning them from alcohol (which appears as the great destroyer) and bringing them to Christ. *The First and Second Marriages* (1856), has a nominal center in a protagonist who is married successively to a country and a city clergyman, and the contrast between her happiness and the widespread marital disharmony, personal misery, and violence-ridden lives of those who lack faith. *The Household Angel in Disguise* (1857) is the least proselytizing of the series; its theme is meekness and forbearance in contrast to worldly arrogance. The influence of two good women—a scorned stepmother and a snubbed servant's daughter—reforms an unchristian household.

Baker's tractlike works espouse a simpler—I would say crasser —view of the relation between Christian and worldly success than did novels by such as Cummins and Warner. These latter assumed that the Christian was neither perfect nor happy but only striving to become so; they did not claim that faith brought good fortune but only that it helped one to bear ill. By contrast Baker makes a facile equivalence of secular rewards and religious faith. *Juliette* (1869), the last in the series, has somewhat more depth to it. The devout heroine is forbidden by her worldly father to profess her faith; she runs away and makes a life for herself as a worker in the Lowell mills, where her piety influences others. In effect Juliette's Christianity makes her life not easier but harder. The novel fits the mold of woman's fiction in that Juliette goes out into the world, takes care of herself, and succeeds on her own terms.

Hornblower dealt with more immediate issues. In *Vara, or The Child of Adoption* (1854), the adopted child is the daughter of missionaries and Hornblower's aim is not to show the child's development in unfriendly surroundings (although this situation exists in the novel) but to help readers understand the missionary life and to advise missionaries on the proper conduct of their profession. Like *Vara, Nellie of Truro* (1856) is just barely a novel, and only by title a woman's fiction. It shows how, despite the benign neglect of her large, wealthy family, Nellie becomes a Christian. Again digressing from the focus of its action, it devotes itself to contrasting two clerical styles: that of the informal and sympathetic clergyman as against the unimaginative formalist. Obviously for Hornblower the novel is a pretext for expository writing.

The efficacy of religion in curing alcoholism is argued in Baker's novels and many other contemporary works. The temperance novel is a genre in itself, and becomes intertwined with woman's fiction only when it centers on the feminine victims of the drunkard's disease. (Incidentally, temperance writers see alcoholism as a disease and generally do not hold the drunk himself culpable; because he could not help himself, they agitate for legislation.) Metta Victor (1831–1885), an Ohioan and a poet who broke into prose in 1852 with a collection of highly wrought exotic stories called, most inappropriately, *Fresh Leaves from Western Woods,* turned out two temperance novels that center on such suffering women. *The Senator's Son* (1853) chronicles the long decline of Parke Madison from his first glass of wine at his father's table at age four to his suicide in mid-manhood during a bout of *delerium tremens.* Along the way he has caused the death of his mother, the martyrdom of his sister Alice (who has married a villain to keep him from blackmailing her brother), the victimization of his wife Lucy, whom he beats, harries, and brings into poverty, and the abuse of his daughter Carrie, whom he scalds with a kettle of boiling water in a drunken stupor.

In striking contrast to woman's fiction, which frequently uses the motif of the drunkard, the temperance novel stresses, as it must, the failure or inadequacy of feminine moral influence to solve this problem. Many women sacrifice themselves and exert influence to no avail. A temperance novel must show woman's power as insufficient because its purpose is to get temperance legislation passed. Were feminine power all that was needed, the "Maine laws" would not be required. Such influence as women have should be used where it may have an effect—on the voters and the legislature. Here one comes very close to the question of the suffrage for women. If women had the vote, might not prohibition legislation be more rapidly enacted? A novel by a Mrs. Henrietta Rose, entitled *Nora Wilmot, A Tale of Temperance and Woman's Rights* (1858), addresses itself with a minimum of plot to this question and decides that women already have more than enough influence to see that temperance legislation is passed, although they are not yet using their influence in a systematic and concerted way.

Metta Victor's second temperance novel, *Fashionable Dissipation* (1854), follows the decline of Charles Lennard, who takes to drink from a guilty conscience when his fiancée, Rosa, is badly crippled in a train accident and he finds himself losing interest in her. He breaks his engagement, goes off to the city, falls into the snares of an adventuress whom he marries, and lives a miserable life while Rosa, encouraged by the devotion of a second suitor who has abjured liquor, slowly recovers and becomes even more beautiful than she had been before her accident. The tone of this work is much lighter than *The Senator's Son,* and in general, Victor was less comfortable in earnest fiction than that for which she later gained a reputation, dime novels in the sixties (she wrote more than a hundred of them) and satire in the late sixties and seventies.

The great antislavery novel was *Uncle Tom's Cabin,* and Stowe rightly saw that there was no way to mesh the slaves' story and the story of feminine trials-and-triumph. The slave was not a woman, and the slave woman's problems were of another order of magnitude than the bourgeois heroine's. Nevertheless, Mary Hayden Pike (1824–1908) did make the yoking, and her novels, while ideologically appalling, enjoyed a wide though brief popularity. *Ida May* (1854) and *Caste* (1856) were both best sellers. *Ida May* is in two parts. In the first, a beautiful little white girl is kidnaped for the slave market. Her beauty appears to doom her to the New Orleans "fancy trade" but fate—or the author's timidity—decrees differently. Sold to a benevolent master, Ida May lives a charmed life until midadolescence when her whiteness is finally revealed and she becomes an adopted daughter instead of a slave. In the novel's second part Ida May has inherited southern property, and her intention to free her slaves causes severe conflict with the rest of her adoptive family. She barely escapes a lynch mob but in the end has set out for the West with her (rediscovered) father and husband-to-be in order to establish a center for training former slaves in the habits of freedom. This "antislavery" novel contains all the trappings of a woman's fiction— an apparent orphan, uncongenial surroundings, a decision that requires defiance of one's guardians, moral influence exerted on a weak male (her husband-to-be), a malicious female rival, a cruel patriarch, and finally the formation of a utopian family centering on the heroine.

Helen Dupre, the heroine of *Caste,* discovers that she and her brother Charles, who has recently married a beautiful white girl, are quadroons. Charles informs his white in-laws of this fact, and his wife is taken away from him; soon after she dies of grief. Their jealous stepmother does everything she can to prevent the reunion of their father, Colonel Bell, with his children, although he is most anxious for it. Helen's fiancé, an aristocratic planter, breaks their engagement. But even at the story's lowest ebb, Helen and Charles have white friends in both the North and the South. Ultimately, their father disposes of his wife in an insane asylum and takes Helen to live with him; they are joined in time by the fiancé, who has had a change of heart, and the trio make a home in Italy. Charles, in the meantime, becomes deeply engaged in the condition of Black people in the north; the only aspect of *Caste* that does not insult its subject are its sections depicting northern prejudices. It is obvious from the long vogue of this kind of fiction—one thinks of Sinclair Lewis's *Kingsblood Royal*—that Pike's device of putting white characters in blackface is a simple and effective propaganda device. Still there remains a wide disparity between the form of woman's fiction and the content of the antislavery novel; neither serves the other.

Mary Pike's last novel was a historical fiction titled *Agnes* (1858). Set in the Revolutionary period, it features noble rebels, evil Tories, and lurking Indian tribes. Its chief interest lies in a contrast of women in love. On the one hand is Agnes, abjectly in love with an unworthy object; on the other Evelyn, whose love for a deserving man does not compromise her dignity or independence. Agnes has been secretly married to the villain, Colonel Stanley, who quickly deserted her. Now he wants to marry Evelyn, whom he "wins" when he threatens to publicize her father's secret rebel sympathies. Evelyn loves someone else, but acquiesces in his blackmail; she makes no secret of her loathing for Stanley and her expressions of scorn inflame the villain's lust even more. She is saved by the arrival on the scene of Agnes, to whom Stanley is still married; but Agnes herself cannot be saved. Willfully blind, she reattaches herself to a man who clearly despises her. " 'You are very kind,' " she tells Evelyn, who offers her protection from Stanley, " 'but I must not leave my husband.' . . . The words were in a whisper, but there was a certain pride in them which did not escape Evelyn's notice. . . . [Her] proud heart revolted at such humility of affection. It seemed to make a bond-slave, crushed and trampled, of that divine sentiment which should be throned as queen."

Agnes considers her forgiving love to be Christ-like and superior to Evelyn's judging love; Evelyn rejoins that since she could never love an unworthy man she has no need either to judge or to forgive. The story supports Evelyn's position, for soon after Agnes rejoins her husband he abandons her once more. Agnes feels now that she has nothing left but to die. In the iconography of woman's fiction, she is an old-fashioned, submissive feminine type contrasting to Evelyn's modern self-dependency.

The last of the propagandists I shall consider is Mary Andrews Denison (1826–1911), author, according to *Notable American*

Women, of some eighty popular novels. (Wright, in contrast, lists a total of thirty-five works, of which twenty-five were published after 1860; but Wright's bibliography does not include any of the dime series novels.) She directed her work at an audience a good deal less sophisticated and educated than the woman's authors we have considered, for her stories are shorter, simpler, and cruder. Her works treated a variety of issues, sometimes several in a single story; her characters are broadly sketched and her stories unsubtle. Obviously she was conveying, to an audience that had little fiction reading experience, the sense of reading an exciting and worthwhile work, replete both with event and morality.

In *Opposite the Jail* (1859) the heroine is caused to be thrown into jail by her wicked aunt and jealous cousin. While waiting for vindication, which comes in a dramatic courtroom scene, she has a religious conversion, and the story digresses to show the effects of religion on the various prisoners. *Old Hepsy* (1858) is an antislavery novel that features as its heroine the supposed white girl, Lucina, who is in fact the daughter of a white woman and a black man. Fresh from a northern boarding-school education she is taken into the home of Mr. Kenneth, a drunkard and profligate who owns a large plantation, and informed that she is a slave. The efforts of Mrs. Kenneth to shield her from her master's unexplained hostility toward her only make him more vindictive. Later we learn that she is Mrs. Kenneth's daughter by a slave who was also Mrs. Kenneth's half-brother. Given the dispersal of white blood through the slave population, Denison shows, any act of miscegenation is likely to be an act of incest. The attraction of white women for black men is repeated in the Kenneths' legitimate daughter, who falls in love with a slave by whom, in a kind of Romeo-and-Juliet scene, she is poisoned. At the end the Sodom and Gomorrah of the Kenneth household has been reduced to ashes, but Lucina escapes to the North with her father, where they work for abolition and civil rights. *Gracie Amber* deals with class antagonisms and chronicles the heroic resistance of a poor working girl to the approaches of an aristocratic villain. *The Mill*

Agent (1864) reverses the pattern of *Ten Nights in a Barroom,* showing how a teetotaling Christian mill manager reforms a dissipated factory town. "The place that boasted that once it knew no church, has now more than five spires pointing heavenward, five assemblies of worshipping Christians who walk humbly before the Lord."

The crudeness of fiction like Denison's and the other propagandists may be partly explained by their purpose but even more by the audience for which they wrote. A contrast with the woman's fiction we have been studying illuminates the greater literary sophistication of the latter. Woman's fiction may look inartistic when put alongside the work of Hawthorne or Henry James, but it reflects a more subtle sense of life and a more complex use of the capabilities of fiction, than the great mass of published narrative. Although woman's fiction too is in a sense propaganda, the nature of its propaganda—advocacy of self-respect, self-reliance, independent thinking, depth of feeling in the sex—prevented the authors from reaching for the too ready response. They could not *talk* about making their readers more thoughtful without *trying* to make them so, and they did this through the agency of a fiction that was meant to give them something to think about. In contrast to the propaganda fiction that closes the reader's mind, woman's fiction was meant to open it. It worked through the intrinsically fictional experience of absorbing the reader into an imaginary world. Hence, such fiction was, for a growing population of first-generation literate women, an education in fiction as well as in life. Undoubtedly, it is from the training ground of this fiction that there emerged, after the Civil War, the first group of women literary artists, and the feminine audience to appreciate them.

The period before the Civil War had seen a remarkable confluence of feminine literary energies into one form. After the Civil War, for a number of reasons, this unity began to fragment. The serious women authors retained the earlier generation's interest in local color and manners but rejected the basic trials-and-triumph plot. That plot, where it appeared in post-bellum woman's literature, began to take on a different significance. The moral energy that had animated the antebellum writers found other channels than fiction, and the characteristic woman's fiction began to modulate into escapist romance.

A novel that signified this modulation was published in 1860. Called *Rutledge*, it was the first of ten popular novels by Miriam Coles Harris (1834–1925), the last of which appeared in 1891. *Rutledge* is a disarmed *Jane Eyre*, using the plot elements of that popular novel of 1847 for the values of entertainment, romance, and suspense. It is the first fully developed American example that I have found of a genre that continues to attract large numbers of readers today, the so-called "gothic romance." *Rutledge* is narrated by its unnamed orphan heroine. It begins when she leaves boarding school, escorted by a middle-aged family friend, Mr. Rutledge, to join her guardian aunt. Injured in a train wreck, she and Rutledge pass a few months recuperating in his family mansion, a fine, decaying old building in an indeterminate, unregionalized location. The heroine perceives that Rutledge has a weighty secret, connected to the scandalous disappearance of a beloved older sister many years before; she discovers that the house too has a secret, a locked room that nobody may enter. The mysterious house and the mysterious man are equivalent; the heroine has taken up residence in the hero's psyche.

Alienated at first by Rutledge's brusque manner, the heroine soon finds herself attracted to his careworn, sophisticated personality; he in turn is aroused by her fresh, honest spirit. Their developing romance is arrested by the heroine's departure to the city and her aunt. Rutledge is sure that she will forget him in the dissipations of city life and, self-protective, he begins to ignore her. Piqued, she responds in kind. Mrs. Churchill, her aunt, is a young widow with three daughters, the oldest just entering society. A slave to fashion and ambitious for her children, the aunt keeps the beautiful young heroine out of sight so as not to spoil her daughter Josephine's chances. The heroine spends

much time in the nursery with Mrs. Churchill's neglected youngest child, Esther, a nervous and poorly disciplined little girl. We
recognize the familiar motif of the household destroyed by worldly
values.

A variety of persecutions and the traumatic death of Esther on
an evening when everybody but the heroine is attending a ball, as
well as Rutledge's apparent indifference, lead the heroine to
accept the attentions of a handsome foreigner, Victor Viennet.
At a houseparty at Rutledge's manor, one year after the story
opens, she becomes engaged to him, and is naturally assumed by
the other characters to be in love with him. Then follow many
gothic events. Victor kills a sinister person who has been blackmailing him, and is hidden by the heroine and her maid in the
secret room. Some days later Rutledge and the heroine enter the
room to find that Victor has killed himself; his suicide note explains that he was the illegitimate son of the long-lost sister.
Overcome with remorse and terror, the heroine has a nervous
breakdown (which is misinterpreted by all as grief over the loss
of her beloved). She ruptures relations with her aunt, and goes to
live in the home of Rutledge's minister. Rutledge goes abroad for
several years. He returns on the eve of the minister's death, mis-
understandings are cleared away, and the novel closes on the
couple's tight embrace.

Although *Rutledge* is a story of the heroine's sufferings, it
cannot be called a story of her triumph because the happy ending
does not represent a victory over inner or outer adversaries. The
novel is not concerned to demonstrate the heroine's moral and
intellectual growth, her capacity for independence (she never has
to live alone or support herself; she has no dependents with claims
on her), her dignity and worth as a human being. It is obsessed
with the emotion of love. Two subordinate motifs run through the
story—the wish to eliminate all competition, and the desire to
possess the forbidden. We can observe these motifs in the woman's
fiction we have analyzed, but there they are modified by the moral
themes that control the action. Some might wish to argue that

woman's fiction merely disguises such motifs beneath a moral veneer, and that in comparison to *Rutledge* it is simply hypocritical. But obviously, the form and effect of the fiction change when the primitive motifs are merged with moral and intellectual concerns. In contrast to the gothic romance that capitalizes on them, woman's fiction urges that various childish impulses be merged into an adult life-scheme. The gothic romance permits these impulses to be represented without guilt in their pristine force. Above all, the genre is meant to stimulate and release erotic and romantic emotion.

The women authors of the 1850s were trying to urge their sex beyond childishness and beyond a bondage to sex. They believed that in the past women had been perceived as, and conditioned to behave like, childish sexual animals. Support for this belief came from the seduction novels that formed the staple of feminine reading in the earliest period of our national history. Seduction novels were written by men as well as women, for it was a form that argued, not simply that woman "should" keep her place, but that her inherent weaknesses gave her no choice in the matter. The authors of woman's fiction had invented a formula that denied this contention. In a book like *Rutledge,* their image of the new woman is in turn denied. Depending on our vantage point, we may see this denial as a regression to earlier ideas of the woman as weak and controlled by her erotic impulses; or as a radical revolt against Victorian repression and inhibition, an assertion of woman's right to her feelings and to their expression. However we interpret it, we must note that the gothic romance continues to be a flourishing fictional form into our own time, while woman's fiction as it was written in the fifties has long since disappeared.

10

Augusta Evans and the
Waning of Woman's Fiction

A literary type does not disappear in an instant; at any historical moment, the old-fashioned, the current, and the advanced exist together. Seven years after Harris' *Rutledge,* the novel of feminine trials and triumph reached its most complex and most popular expression in *St. Elmo* (1867), by Augusta Evans, later Wilson (1835–1909). This novel was not her first book or her first best seller. *Beulah* (1859) had been a best seller and *Macaria* (1864), smuggled through the southern blockade to the North, eventually reached a wide audience. But *St. Elmo* sold more copies than either of these; in fact it is believed to have sold more widely than any other single woman's fiction, and is ranked among the most successful works published in the nineteenth century.

Like some of the other works considered in this study, *St. Elmo* has been approached by critics reluctantly, if at all, with a contempt proportioned to its success. Its reputation has been all but buried under a scorn it would probably have escaped if it only had the grace to fail. Understandably but naively, its critics seem to think that if Wilson had not written *St. Elmo,* her enormous audience would have made a best seller out of *Moby-Dick* or *The Marble Faun* instead. Within the genre of woman's fiction there appears always to have been room for another success. These novels did not hurt the sales of Melville or Hawthorne. Our serious writers have always known themselves a select group writing for a special and limited audience but this knowledge has coexisted with the fantasy of writing a best seller nonetheless. Such a contradiction is inherent in an economic system where the self-supporting writer must sell widely.

The elite group of authors has always been understood in terms of greater intelligence and literary cultivation than the mass of readers; less often have the problems of our serious writers been recognized as sex-related, in that the writers have mostly been men and the readers mostly women. While these writers and the critics enlisted in their cause have suffered, hundreds of women authors (I do not exaggerate here) and millions of women readers have enjoyed a mutually profitable relationship. It is widely agreed that since the middle of the nineteenth century, no book can hope for popular success if it does not attract large numbers of women readers, because women were and are the majority of readers in America. To the extent that the writer (or his critic-defender) is a misogynist, or contemptuous of women, or indifferent to them, or uninterested in their concerns (and these categories may well encompass most of our serious male authors), his dilemma with an audience is acute.

In the kind of fiction that first cemented the bond between the woman author and her feminine audience, the subject of the transaction was woman—her life, her strengths, her trials, her possibilities. It took the form, as we have repeatedly seen, of a story in which the heroine is thrust into life deprived of all the supports on which she might have expected to depend, and for which her upbringing might have prepared her. Instead of a petted and pampered existence suited to her conditioned dependency and compliance, she finds herself in an insecure, undependable, difficult, and often hostile environment. The world makes demands instead of gratifying them. Happily, our authors said, the world's hardships provide just the right situation for the development of individual character. The disillusionment, inevitable in any case, is an opportunity. If women rise to the opportunity they can master not only themselves but the world.

Augusta Evans' heroines are the strongest, most brilliant, and most accomplished in the long line of woman's heroines. They make their way in the world not because someone has deprived them of their props, but because they scorn to lean. Generally, the heroine is offered all manner of support and refuses all. Thus she triumphs not as a matter of facing necessity, and turning misfortune into challenge, but as a matter of choice. She is a heroine by election rather than a heroine in spite of herself. Beulah, in the novel that bears her name, and Edna Earl of *St. Elmo,* are offered every advantage—are begged, indeed, to accept wealth, love, protection, position. But both remain true to their own vision of what their lives should be and resist. Edna, as we shall see, resists the greatest of all temptations, the temptation to reform a handsome scoundrel who loves her (so he says) as no man ever loved woman before.

This heroine represents the innate heroism of all women, which generally (given woman's training in dependence) must wait until circumstances call it out. She also represents something that the plots of necessity had largely concealed: that a woman might *wish* to struggle and strive, that she might find the protected and pampered ideal life (assuming it were attainable) frustrating and dull.

To choose the heroic path as a matter of principle means that the Evans heroine is more aggressive and self-determining than other protagonists in woman's fiction. Consequently, the author herself is operating at the limits of what is seemly in women and consistent with their innate femininity; her work accordingly reflects a greater degree of tension and conflict than other woman's fiction. Perhaps this is one reason for her success, for this problem is real. Precisely because she is ambivalent and self-contradictory, Evans' books appeal to the doubts and vacillations experienced by many women who were learning to conceive of themselves, for the first time, as no less human than men. Where were the boundaries of feminine self-assertion to be drawn? On what grounds could one say, so far and no further? At what point did the new woman violate her own nature? Did she have a special feminine nature?

No heroines are more willful, proud, and stubborn than Augusta Evans'; traits that Cummins or Warner would have excoriated constitute her heroines' best qualities. On the other hand, no author is more proscriptive than she about what activities are not suitable for women. Her books are more fiercely antisuffrage, for example, than any other of the leading authors of woman's fiction. *St. Elmo* exists at the point of highest tension in a balance that cannot be maintained. In her next novel, *Vashti* (1869), Evans had altered from expansionist to admonitory, and this change in her is symbolic of a major change in all woman's fiction after the Civil War. The woman's fiction which had been so importantly limit-breaking, became with a slight shift of balance a limit-enforcing genre.

In style, plotting, and attitudes Evans brought together the two divergent schools of woman's fiction: the prudent, cautious, measured writing of the northerners Warner and Cummins, with its correlative sense of limiting circumstances, its emphasis on self-control, calculation, and safety; and the open-ended, flamboyant, colorful work of southern writers like Southworth and Holmes, who emphasized experiment, risk, and adventure. Evans' heroines are careless, even reckless in the short run; they take and express umbrage at the slightest provocation. Yet they know their goals and never lose sight of them; in the long run everything is calculated, reality properly assessed, and nothing left to chance. In another amalgamation of tendencies widely separated in other woman's fiction, Evans endows her heroines with Byronic qualities usually reserved for the lady villains of melodrama and romance: alienation, tempestuousness, pride, vengefulness. Yet at the same time her heroines are moral, virtuous, and pious. These yokings create a kind of unquietness of tone which makes Evans' novels intense, turbulent, and exciting even when the action is relatively restrained. Finally, Evans takes a profoundly ambivalent stance toward pleasure and self-sacrifice; she distrusts the easy and soft so thoroughly that she creates heroines who are acutely uncomfortable with pleasure. Pleasure is not pleasurable to them; they are at ease in the strenuous, martial atmosphere of deprivation and combat. Yet this quality cannot be labelled as masochism. It is, rather, a "masculine" preference for the rigors of battle over the bower of bliss. Here Evans violates one of the deepest held of feminine stereotypes, dear to women as well as men—the conviction that women are the peaceful members of the species.

One of the strategies Evans employs to convey her heroines' great abilities is a patina of erudite allusion. Her learned protagonists cannot speak two sentences without dropping a dozen references, and dialogue often seems to consist of contests in pedantry. Like the *nouveau-riche* that in this respect she was, Evans is tremendously proud of her learning and anxious to show it off. Her method is unfortunately crude, and has turned the experience of reading *St. Elmo* for many into unintended comedy. The means are inept but we should not lose sight of her purpose. Throughout the period between 1820 and 1870 woman's fiction had strenuously advocated an education for women that went far beyond "finishing" and included the same subjects as were taught to men and fostered the same mental habits. Warner and Cummins showed their heroines mastering such subjects as arithmetic, astronomy, European history, geography, and modern languages. Evans goes much further. Her heroines learn ancient history, theology, Greek, Latin, Hebrew, and take their place as scholars, discoverers of new knowledge as well as absorbers of what is already known. The author wants to show woman's intellect as in every way the equal of man's: not only the flight of fancy, but arduous reasoning, thorough retention, careful documentation, were also native to the feminine mind, because mind has no sex. Beyond this, Evans shows that women can be as fully engaged in and fulfilled by what we call today "the life of the mind" as a man. Hence she makes her heroines into what critics have scoffingly labeled walking encyclopedias.

Evans was born in Georgia, the oldest of eight children. Although her parents were well off in her early childhood, by the time she was ten her father had declared bankruptcy and moved his family to Texas in a covered wagon. He had little success there or in Mobile, Alabama, where he resettled in 1849. It was *Beulah,* in 1859, that restored prosperity to her whole family. The Civil War caused the author, a fervent partisan of the Confederacy, to break her engagement with a New York journalist whom she had met on a business trip. She did not marry until 1868 when she was thirty-three years old and a famous author. Her husband, Colonel Lorenzo Madison Wilson, was twenty-seven years older than she, a wealthy neighbor, a widower with grown children. Taking over the management of his large estate, cultivating one of the most famous gardens in Mobile, and supervising the Wilson children still at home, Evans slackened in productivity. At intervals, however, she published; her last novel appeared, astonishingly, as late as 1902. Thus, though her canon is small, her career spans almost fifty years.

Evans' first novel, *Inez, A Tale of the Alamo* (1855), begins as a conventional woman's fiction but changes into a melodramatic attack on Catholicism. The story opens in a boarding school where two adolescent cousins, Florence Hamilton and Mary, who is also Mr. Hamilton's ward, are receiving a fashionable education and where Florence is secretly in love with one of the tutors. The two girls, one erratic and troubled, the other calm and Christian, present a conventional contrast of heroines. Hamilton fails in business and decides to go to Texas; he offers Mary the chance to go to another aunt, but she insists on making her life with those who had taken her in when she became an orphan. The story now moves to San Antonio, which, despite the overlay of Jesuitical melodrama, is very well depicted in its physical details and local routine. One regrets, since fictional depictions of early Texas are so rare, that Evans did not put greater stress on local realism in *Inez*.

In San Antonio, however, her concern becomes the attraction that Florence, the unstable cousin, feels for Catholicism, and the efforts of a vicious priest to gain control of the spiritual life and worldly goods of the entire Hamilton family, which includes the two girls, the father, and a weak-minded aunt who is quickly converted. A conflict develops between Mary and the priest as good and bad angels fighting for Florence's soul. The story is complicated by the introduction of a third character, Inez, a beautiful Mexican girl who is also an object of the priest's desire for power. The melodrama peaks in a fifteen-page debate between Mary and Florence on the doctrine of intercession and other points of Catholic versus Protestant theology. Texts are cited, books taken down from the shelves, authorities exchanged. Only Evans would have made such a scholarly dispute the climax of an exciting novel; only she found such excitement in pure ideas; only she believed so passionately that women could feel with their minds as well as their hearts.

After this episode, Florence reverts to her original protestantism, and the priest prepares to take drastic measures; but the war for Texas independence intervenes, and the story again changes its focus. Mr. Hamilton dies, having been kicked by a horse, and the rest of the family flees Texas with a larger group of Americans. Mary, whose health has been failing all along, dies en route; Mary's sweetheart (a minor character) thereupon returns to Texas where he dies at the Battle of San Jacinto, Inez (who has secretly loved him) along with him. Only Florence, saved for protestantism and her tutor, is left alive.

Beulah (1859) is an ambitious and interesting work with many points in common with *St. Elmo*. The book has been interpreted by its few critics as a study of religious doubt, and it is quite true that Beulah is one of the few heroines of woman's fiction who suffers a genuine crisis of faith. Of course many heroines lack a perfect faith at the outset of their stories, or find their previously secure faith tested by hardship and tribulation. But Beulah's situation is somewhat different. A bitter childhood has led her early to the position of accepting nothing on trust, of subjecting everything to the scrutiny of her mind and the determination of will. She carries this position so far as to insist on forging her own religious faith, and thus questioning the tenets of accepted religious belief. For many of the tried heroines of woman's fiction, the religious question is whether they *can* believe; for Beulah, it is whether she ought to.

However, even though the religious question is important, it is clearly subordinated to the larger pattern of conventional woman's fiction. Beulah is twelve years old when the story opens, a poorhouse orphan and self-appointed guardian there of her younger sister Lillie and Lillie's friend Claudia. Life in the poorhouse is terrible because of the constant humiliation and reminders of dependency (the matron is very kind, but has little power, power being vested in the board of governors), but matters get much worse when the elegant Mrs. Grayson adopts Lillie and Claudia while refusing to take Beulah because she is ugly. Beulah is sent instead to a Mrs. Martin's house as nurse and babysitter for the youngest child. She carries out her job with exemplary ability, yet festers inwardly with bitterness, defiance, and hate. Mrs. Grayson refuses to let her see Lillie who soon dies of scarlet fever. Alienated more than ever, Beulah responds by developing a masochistic delight in berating herself for her ugliness and stupidity, and in doing her job to the point of exhaustion. She is saved from a self-willed death out of pure spite and anger only by the intervention of a fascinating older man, Dr. Hartwell.

Attracted by her stubbornness and by latent ability that he senses in her, this eccentric, wealthy, and widowed man, himself stern, angry, and alienated, offers to let Beulah live with him so that she can become educated and support herself, as an adult, in a dignified fashion. A brief, bitter rivalry with Hartwell's sister culminates in that lady's expulsion and Beulah grows up in Hartwell's home as though she were his daughter. He is a wealthy, sophisticated man; his house is richly appointed, and although the relationship between the two swings uneasily between conflict and harmony, Beulah on the whole is very well pleased with her new situation.

When she comes of age she prepared to carry out her original plan of becoming a teacher and supporting herself. Hartwell is attractive but tryannical and Beulah is anxious to get away from him all the more because she loves him. And she is tired of dependency. For all his intelligence and psychological acuity, Hartwell cannot really credit such a motive in a woman and is dumbfounded when Beulah positively rejects his offer of formal adoption. To Hartwell and other characters in the novel her gesture appears pig-headed and foolish. Moral scruples should not deter a woman from taking advantage of an offer of lifelong support.

Beulah on her part feels that Hartwell has violated the terms of their original understanding and was wrong to make the offer. She feels that his icy snubbing of her after she leaves his house is profoundly unjust. She persists in her plans, realizing that his coldness is intended to make her feel guilty and return to him. Hurt but resolute, she gets a room and a job.

In this segment of the book Beulah's life is contrasted to that of two friends: Cornelia Graham, a wealthy invalid whose idle life has no meaning and who lacks the religious faith to accept her approaching death, and Clara Martin, a conventional girl who longs for a life of womanly dependency but who is forced by circumstances to work for her living. Naturally enough, Clara also espouses a conventional religious faith. Beulah and Cornelia have many discussions about the meaning of a woman's life and the basis of religion, and largely in reaction to Cornelia's situation, Beulah decides that just as one must work, so one must also believe. Yet among all her acquaintances she finds no true believer except Clara, whose simple faith is inadequate to the more complex woman's needs. While she expends her physical energies at work, Beulah devotes her mental energies in the evenings to a search, through world literature, for the basis of a rational faith.

Beulah also finds little to satisfy her in her friends' examples of the possibilities of woman's life. But here she has her own faith fully developed. Cornelia's immersion in ballroom politics before her illness has created contempt for her own sex. Clara (who secretly loves Dr. Hartwell) thinks women need to be taken care of and tells Beulah how foolish she was to go out on her own. Beulah's response, and the rhetoric in which it is expressed, typifies the character and the author:

You are less a woman than I thought you, if you would be willing to live on the bounty of others when a little activity would enable you to support yourself. . . . I don't believe one word of all this languishing nonsense. As to my being nothing more nor less than a sickly geranium, I know better. If you have concluded that you belong to that dependent family of plants, I pity you sincerely, and beg that you will not put me in any such category. Duty may be a cold shadow to you, but it is a vast volcanic agency, constantly impelling me to action. What was my will given to me for, if to remain passive and suffer others to minister to its needs? Don't talk to me about woman's clinging, dependent nature. You are opening your lips to repeat that senseless simile of oaks and vines; I don't want to hear it; there are no creeping tendencies about me. . . . I can stand up. . . . I feel humbled when I hear a woman bemoaning the weakness of her sex, instead of showing that she has a soul and mind of her own, inferior to none.

This daring rhetoric is given to the heroine, not that she may later realize its folly, but that she may later make it good. Of course she overworks herself; of course she is lonely. "She was very lonely, but not unhappy," Evans writes, and her distinction is crucial.

After a few years, in which Beulah carries out her plan and also performs such acts as nursing the sick during a yellow-fever epidemic, Hartwell reappears and makes an offer even more tempting than his last one. He asks Beulah to marry him. Now in fact Beulah loves Hartwell as a lover, and that is one reason why she had resisted his offer of adoption. But still she will not marry him. He makes it clear that to marry him will be to recant her former position on woman's independence and to submit entirely to his will. Beulah cannot agree to this, and feels that her love for such a man must represent an impulse toward self-surrender that is dangerous and unworthy. Her refusal sends Hartwell off on four years of wandering in the Orient, during which time Cornelia dies, Clara makes a happy marriage, and Beulah buys herself a little house and settles in with the matron from the poorhouse as companion. Like so many other heroines of woman's fiction, she begins to supplement her teaching income by writing, and soon finds herself a famous author. During these years her religious doubts dissolve in the recognition that there can be no intellectual ground for faith but that this is a limit of the intellect and not of faith. Hartwell's return finds each of them finally ready for the other. For both of them marriage will be a compromise, as it must be; but Hartwell is prepared to compromise at last, and Beulah no longer equates compromise with defeat.

Macaria, or The Altars of Sacrifice, was published in Richmond in 1864. Copies were smuggled through the blockade and it was reissued in the North. It is incidentally a strong defense of the southern cause as necessary resistance to tyranny (the Civil War is compared to the Revolution, with the Confederates as patriots) and it expresses complete faith in the eventual triumph of the South. However, the war functions in the novel's structure as the culmination of the life education of its two heroines, Electra Gray and Irene Huntingdon. At the opening of the novel these two young women are widely separated in social class and potential; at the end, they are making plans together for a life of usefulness and independence. The pattern is reminiscent of *The Children of Light.*

Electra, a poor orphan, lives with her aunt and cousin Russell Aubrey, whom she secretly and hopelessly loves. The Aubreys are poor and disgraced because the father had killed a man in a brawl, been sentenced to hang, and killed himself. Russell is determined to regain the world's respect. Electra too is ambitious; she wishes to become an artist. She is "a dreamer, richly gifted.

. . . Hers was a passionate nature; fierce blood beat in her veins, and would not always be bound by icy fetters. There was no serene plateau of feeling where she could repose; she enjoyed keenly, rapturously, and suffered acutely, fearfully." When the aunt dies, and Electra realizes that Russell has no more than cousinly feelings for her, she rejects the opportunity to live with a second aunt and goes instead to New York under the patronage of an older man, an artist named Chilton. She becomes his pupil and in effect his ward. Passionately in love with her, Chilton tries to get her to marry him, but Electra, while agreeing to remain with him for his lifetime (he is in poor health), will not bind herself as his wife. She accepts a rather anomalous relationship as truer to her feelings than the more conventional relation which to her would be hypocritical and constricting. Wilson does not suggest that Electra becomes Chilton's mistress, but she does not deny it either. After Chilton's death Electra goes alone to Paris and continues to develop as an artist. Work and loneliness seem to be her destiny.

Irene, daughter of the town's richest citizen, is a contrasting temperament. Her "intellect was of the masculine order, acute and logical, rather deficient in the imaginative faculties, but keenly analytical. . . . [She] evinced a calm, equable temperament, uniformly generous and unselfish, but most thoroughly firm, nay, obstinate, in any matter involving principle, or conflicting with her notions of propriety." Neither this balanced personality nor her economic and social advantages makes her any better adjusted to life than Electra, for "from early childhood Irene had experienced a sensation of loneliness." Her father's irascible, exacting, and inconsistent temper and his wish completely to dominate her life and determine her values make life continuously unpleasant for her. In her childhood, Mr. Huntingdon had promised her to her cousin Hugh, a handsome, manly, but shallow and weak person. Without much fuss, but firmly, Irene makes it clear that she will never marry Hugh; and neither four years of exile to a New York boarding school, nor two subsequent years of living with the constant coldness and disapproval of her father, changes her decision. Ignoring her father's bad behavior, Irene must act as his hostess in a social routine that seems empty and useless to her. Secretly she loves Russell Aubrey, who is making his way up in the world; but Aubrey is her father's special aversion, and though she will not marry against her own wishes, neither will she marry against her father's. Hence she is alienated and solitary, her life wasted.

Without Electra's talent, Irene turns her energies and skills to service. She becomes especially interested in schools and orphanages and even goes so far—very far for a woman in fiction—as to intercede with legislators for comprehensive laws establishing schools and asylums. When the Civil War begins, she calls Russell to her (she has never permitted him to get even an inkling of her feelings, though his love for her is evident) and tells him, on the eve of his departure for battle, that she loves him. This is the only direct self-gratification that her life permits. Like Beulah and other Evans characters, Irene has a tendency to overdo her duty; when everything else is closed, zealous performance of duty becomes a means of venting suppressed energies. In the atmosphere of inhibition and frustration within which the aspirations of the women in *Macaria* are buried, this revelatory scene is charged with erotic energy as much as if Irene had called Aubrey to her bed. And the same is true of Russell's death scene, when he calls for her so that he may die in her arms.

Irene's father also dies in battle, and Electra patriotically returns to the South, running the blockade and carrying secret messages carefully pasted under her watercolors. The end of the novel, which predicts a successful outcome to the South's campaign, finds the two women united and making plans for the future. Irene is going to open a school of design for women, and Electra is to be the head teacher. "Our Revolution has beggered thousands [of women] and deprived many of their natural providers; numbers of women in the Confederacy will be thrown entirely on their own resources for maintenance. All cannot be mantua-makers, milliners, or school-teachers; and in order to open for them new avenues of support, I have determined to establish . . . a School of Design for Women." Such rivalry as they may have felt in love is extinguished in the stronger bond of their common lot as single women—a lot now expanded to include the whole feminine sisterhood.

Electra, though happy to be useful and independent, still repines at their loneliness. Irene responds that "it is very true that single women have trials for which a thoughtless, happy world has little sympathy. But lonely lives are not necessarily joyless; they should be, of all others, the most useful." The underlying situation of woman's fiction is only exacerbated and intensified by the war: that is, the situation of a world in which women cannot count on men for comfort, guidance, or support. At the same time, in one respect the war makes an improvement, because if the world has always been one in which women have to make their way alone, it is now no longer a world in which tyrannical and preemptive men are around to obstruct them. The wartime context provides the opportunity to make some long standing arguments about women more forcefully: their need to be independent, their need to find companionship with each other, their need to associate for mutual improvement, their need to expand the range of professional opportunities and achievements.

But Evans is unwilling to abandon the idea that their power center is the home, and she strongly argues against the vote. Her depiction in some sections of the book of electioneering and voting practices (both Mr. Huntingdon and Russell Aubrey are politicians) shows an atmosphere of violence, corruption, brawling, and drunkenness that suggests why for her and many other women at this time the idea of the vote was unacceptable. In effect, she says, the atmosphere was so terrible on an election day that no woman dared to step outside her door. How would woman retain her own particular effectiveness if she were to enter this arena? The suffragists said that women would purify the arena (has time proved them right?), but others felt that

women would be either corrupted or destroyed in such an
atmosphere.

St. Elmo is in many ways a reprise of Beulah, with the poor
heroine adopted into wealth and assailed by temptations to turn
aside from her planned path of independence. Beulah's adoption
by Dr. Hartwell had something of the deus ex machina in it, and
the domiciling of Edna Earl with the Murrays seems even more
contrived. The characterization of Dr. Hartwell had a strong
component of fantasy in it, and that of St. Elmo Murray is still less
believable. Those critics who assume, as does the entry for Augusta
Evans in Notable American Women, that "the predominantly
feminine novel reading audience was undoubtedly fascinated by
the Byronic hero, reclaimed from sin by the heroine's cautious
affection and silent prayer" have, I believe, doubly missed the
point. They overlook the fact that Edna does not save St. Elmo
but in fact refuses to do so, resisting the greatest temptation that
can be put in the path of a romantic, enthusiastic, and pious girl,
especially if she is in love with the scoundrel. They also overlook
the probability that women read books like St. Elmo and Jane
Eyre and Wuthering Heights and Gone With the Wind not for
the heroes but for the heroines. The most exciting thing about the
heroes of these novels is the intensity of their love for the heroine.
This love is a measure of her power, for in a world where women
are traditionally assumed to be the playthings of men nothing can
be more satisfying than to see the tables turned. And when the
man who becomes a slave of love is himself a trifler with women,
the heroine's power is shown to be all the greater. The Byronic
hero thus is particularly appealing when he becomes a victim
precisely because he has victimized so many others. The heroine
must be mighty indeed to ensnare so invulnerable a creature, and
all the more so because she catches him in spite of herself—it has
not been part of her intention, since she is no trifler.

We must remember, however, that the Byronic hero is by no
means normative in woman's fiction. The man whose life is un-
blemished by acts of brutality or exploitation, who comes not as a

conqueror or manipulator but as a friend and guide, is the one
who catches the imagination of most of the women novelists.
Byronic figures when they appear are usually immediately rejected
by the heroine, and marriages to the Byronic type when they take
place are invariably shown to be mistakes. St. Elmo himself is
vindicated to the virtue-loving reader not so much he becomes a
minister at the end, although this is what persuades Edna that she
may marry him, but because his Byronism is the reaction of a
generous and sensitive nature to heartless betrayal by his best
friend and his fiancée. Edna responds, when she hears his sad
story, that to react to cruel treatment with cynical venegefulness
is the way of weakness, not of strength. When St. Elmo himself
learns to see his Byronism as a sick response to a terrible event, he
can begin to mend himself. Edna helps him to reperceive himself,
less by her analysis of his character than by her refusal of his
proposal. She will not do for him what every person must do for
himself. "Give yourself to me! Give your pure, sinless life to
purify mine!" he pleads. "I can never be your wife," she answers.
"I have no confidence in you. . . . I am no viceregent of an
outraged and insulted God! I have no faith in any man whose
conscience another keeps." The effect of this scene is com-
pounded by the fact that Edna loves St. Elmo and knows it. Her
one act rejects two powerful feminine temptations: to marry and
to save the man she loves.

This apotheosis of a heroine is also a composite of heroines who
have gone before her. Brought up in the Tennessee mountains by
her devout grandfather, the first twelve years of Edna's life are
passed in an atmosphere of natural grandeur, love, and religious
piety, and these purely beneficent forces have given her character
its firmness and its values. She is also beautiful, and hence in her
earliest circumstances there are none of the embittering, alienating influences that sour the lives and tempers of so many heroines
of woman's fiction. When her grandfather dies she determines to
go to the city and get some factory work. There is a train wreck
and Edna, injured, is taken in by Mrs. Murray, a proud, kind,

and somewhat remote woman who is a rich widow with an only
son. After a while Mrs. Murray decides to keep Edna with her
and sponsor her education, so that she may rise above a factory
girl's life. Mrs. Murray puts Edna under the guidance of a
learned, elderly pastor for her education and the girl makes
incredible progress.

Mrs. Murray's son, St. Elmo, a restless wanderer, returns soon
after Edna joins the household. He is impressed by Edna's
courage, honesty, and intelligence. She is disgusted by his egomania, his rudeness, his cynicism, and his unthinking tyrannizing
over others. As a test of her character (that he considers himself
entitled to make such tests is sign of his arrogance) he gives her
the key to an ornate strongbox in his room, bidding her not to
open it while he is away. She does not open it, of course, and this
act—which St. Elmo had considered beyond the moral strength
of a woman—begins to return him to his senses. Evans makes it
clear that, as far as she is concerned, in his wrath and bitterness
St. Elmo is indeed partly deranged.

When he next returns Edna is seventeen, her education completed. She is getting ready to go out in the world as a teacher,
but is beset with temptations to abandon that plan. First, a young
man of the neighborhood, considered by all to be a fine catch,
proposes to her. Then, Mrs. Murray, who over the years has come
to love Edna and depend on her, asks to adopt her. Finally, St.
Elmo himself proposes. Each offer is more difficult to refuse than
the last, but Edna resists them all. She has been secretly writing
essays and sending them to the New York magazines, she is beginning to get a reputation, she has an offer of governessing in
New York, and she is going to go.

In New York her reputation, her opportunities, and her conquests continue to mount. She lives in the Andrews home less as a
servant than as a respected guest, though she does not neglect her
duties to Felix (twelve, and a cripple) and Hattie (ten). She
writes for the city's leading journal and becomes involved with its
editor, Mr. Manning, who proposes to her. The visiting English-

man of the season also proposes but Edna, with the ferocious energy that characterizes an Evans heroine, keeps working. She writes two successful didactic novels, one hypothesizing a unified scheme of world mythology, the other expounding a philosophy of womanhood. In the second book she takes a staunch anti-suffragist line, insisting that the moral progress of the nation depends on woman's retaining the elevated place that she holds in men's imaginations. If she loses that place, the one thing that guides men toward the right will be lost. Hence, paradoxically, it is absolutely essential that women not get the vote, for their numbers at the polls are of no account compared to their potential to sway the hearts and minds of men in their traditional sphere.

This virtually apocalyptic vision of the disaster that will follow if woman does not keep her place makes its argument not to shut her away from the world, but to insure that she stays where she does the world's work best. The idea that woman must also be personally gratified by the work she is doing is, in Evans' view (for she identifies herself with Edna's position), weakness. The lesson of life is to learn not to do what you like, but to learn to like what you must do. Is it not odd that Edna, who has resolutely rejected the conventional destiny of woman, should advocate the conventional so strongly? Or that the author, who holds Edna up as the apotheosis of womanhood, should use her as a mouthpiece for such views? It has been observed above that, precisely because her heroines were stretching limits, Evans had to identify a position beyond the limits. Moreover, she was a political conservative, opposed to universal male suffrage and an advocate of government by the propertied. Insofar as the suffragist movement was identified with general political liberalism, it would fall under her blanket disapproval. Too, like many other women of the time, the specific issue of the franchise seemed to her a distraction from more important woman's issues like education, career opportunities, and the general improvement of male attitudes toward women and women's attitudes toward themselves. Again, voting meant something different to Evans from what it means to us—

it meant venturing out into a street running with blood and whiskey to cast a ballot at a polling place thronged with buyers and sellers of votes.

Finally, however, it is possible that she feared a situation in which women had all they asked for. Her heroines required antagonism and conflict; they took a positive delight in impediment, because then they could overcome it. If the obstacles were removed, what would be left for a heroine to do? A world in which everything was easy would be a world entirely unresponsive to the needs and energies of a Beulah or an Edna Earl. Thus eventually Augusta Evans began to argue not that women must conquer the world, but that the world must stay as it is so that something remained to be conquered.

In *Vashti, or Until Death Us Do Part* (1869), the last of Evans' novels to fall within the period of this study, she has reached this point. All the women in *Vashti* are frustrated and held back, and the author decrees that this must be the way things are. The titular heroine has been duped into marriage with a man she adores but who marries her only for money; when she discovers his motives, some hours after her marriage (but before its consummation), she settles part of her wealth on him and separates from him permanently. Because she believes marriage to be a sacrament, she will neither sue for divorce nor permit her husband to sue. She lives in a state of hypercharged emotionality, bemoaning her lot and yet clinging to it against all temptations to lighten it. Given the nature of the plotting, it seems fair to assume that the choking of her sexual desires is part of her agony, but also part of the reason she clings to her martyrdom—to do otherwise would be to accept her own sexuality as a legitimate need.

Down the road from Vashti lives a young girl named Salome, ward of Miss Gray and passionately in love with Miss Gray's brother, an upright and censorious Christian physician named Ulpian. Although Ulpian is never remiss in pointing out to Salome her many shortcomings—she is selfish, spoiled, and

rude—he tutors her only from Christian duty. He does not love
her and articulates an ideal of feminine modesty and decorum
that Salome can never hope to approach. The young girl has a
beautiful singing voice and, perceiving that Ulpian will never
love her, determines to make a career as an opera singer. Miss
Gray and Ulpian agree that opera, with its public display and
inevitable exposure to loose and worldly people, is not an accept-
able career for a virtuous woman. But Salome defies them, and
one day she disappears. When, some years later, Ulpian goes to
Paris to find her, he discovers that on the eve of her debut she
had been stricken with an illness that destroyed her voice and that
she has since lived obscurely and virtuously as a lace-maker. In
this plotting, Evans suggests that a defiance that she would
earlier have endorsed (for Salome's determination is like Beulah's
and Edna's) now earns her disapproval. Salome is to have neither
a husband nor a career, while Vashti is to have the semblance of
a woman's life without the substance.

But Evans is not holding out this grim view of life for women
only. Despite his elevated ideas of the feminine character, Ulpian
falls deeply in love with Vashti (he thinks she is a widow), who
in her histrionic self-absorption is very far from his ideal. When
he finds out that Vashti is a married woman he immediately
leaves the country, returning to press his suit when Vashti's
husband dies. But Vashti herself has fed so long on grief that she
cannot survive her emancipation. So Ulpian like Vashti and
Salome is bereft of love and gratification in his life; it would be
lovely if he could return Salome's feelings for him, but one has no
choice of whom one loves. "Patience is the only practical religion,"
advises the author, and her advice holds for both sexes.

In Evans' earlier novels there had been a justification of characters who defied conventions in the pursuit of duty, because it
was duty. In *Vashti,* however, defiance of convention is equated
with assertion of the impulse to gratify the self and hence is forbidden. The world of *Vashti* is one where pleasure and duty, or
pleasure and reality, are inevitably at odds with each other.

Since self-expressive behavior even in pursuit of duty has a pleasurable component, self-expression is no longer permitted. The heroines expend their energies in the intensity with which they dramatize their frustrations; thus the tension that produced Evans' earlier driven heroines has become unbalanced and her women are driven back upon themselves.

What it was that caused this change in her writing we cannot say, but in a sense we may take it as symptomatic of the end of a genre that had dominated American writing—in terms of the quantity of novels published and sold—for some forty years. In the same year that Evans published *St. Elmo,* Martha Finley published the first Elsie Dinsmore book, where little Elsie, resisting her father's command to sing for his guests on Sunday, falls off the piano stool and gashes her forehead, taking the strategy of self-abuse for the purposes of manipulating others further than it had been taken before, and more crudely. In 1868, Louisa May Alcott published the first part of *Little Women.* These two publishing events marked, in a different way from the appearance of *Rutledge,* the decline of woman's fiction as we have studied it, because they represent the transformation of woman's fiction into girl's fiction. The story of feminine heroism now becomes a didactic instrument for little girls; as an adult genre, woman's fiction becomes the gothic romance. Both of these trends imply the disruption of the creative tensions that had produced the woman's fiction of the fifties, either because the tensions were dissipated in the freer atmosphere of the last third of the century, or because new opportunities for women had the opposite effect of exacerbating them beyond a point that this particular fictional mode could control.

Ultimately we cannot do more than guess at the causes of this change. Adult woman's experience in America may have become too heterogeneous and complex to be reasonably represented by the formula of feminine heroism. A new generation of women writers may naturally enough have wished to do something different from the successful patterns established in the 1850s. Readers may have become bored, especially those who had grown up on the genre. Possibilities for woman may have seemed far to eclipse the relatively limited number of options set out in woman's fiction. The home may have come to seem increasingly less tenable as a social unit, let alone a feminine power base. Rapid social change may have engendered tensions that called for escapist literature rather than moral earnestness. Immigration and the rise of enormous fortunes, industrial civilization, and cities fragmented into ethnic groups, may have made it ever more difficult to maintain the rural or suburban and middle-class values of woman's fiction.

The new, massive doubts about traditional Christianity must certainly have undermined the evangelical certainty of woman's fiction: witness the immense success of that curious transmogrification of the woman's fiction into a novel of heaven in Elizabeth Stuart Phelps's (the daughter's) *The Gates Ajar* in 1869. Hardly a novel at all, this enormously popular story is a long meditation on the nature of Heaven, in which it is asserted that Heaven certainly exists and looks exactly like earth without earth's sufferings, death, poverty, and disease. If grand pianos give us pleasure, then there are grand pianos in Heaven, for Heaven is made for pleasure. Critics have noted that this book was an attempt to save the idea of heaven for a troubled constituency. It was just as much an attempt to save the domestic, rural, middle-class earth by locating its platonic ideal in heaven. This fading earth was the earth woman was supposed to rule by her influence; if it was lost, so was she.

In many ways *Little Women* is the most technically accomplished work to rise from the genre of woman's fiction, and yet it is a children's book rather than a woman's book. From the perplexities, complexities, and absurdities of *St. Elmo* in 1867 to the clarity and control of *Little Women* the following year is an enormous leap in artistry; the difference lies not merely in the inherent talents of the two authors, but also in the fact that Alcott has compromised with the genre, simplified it, in order to direct her message at children. When one of the March sisters exclaims that there is nothing in the world so beautiful as families and is talking about the family in which she lives, she expresses the domestic ideal as though it were a reality. But all woman's fiction had shown the real family to be a source of suffering, conflict, and frustration for the heroine—as indeed it was in fact for Louisa May Alcott. Her own family, with well-meaning but self-absorbed and unwittingly tyrannical Bronson Alcott at its head, with Mrs. Alcott unable to withstand him, and with all the Alcott daughters psychologically scarred, looked much more like a family in woman's fiction than did her own fictional March family.

I have already proposed that the flowering of this fiction created the ground from which, after the Civil War, a group of women who were literary artists developed along with an audience to appreciate them. Some of the veteran authors like Mary Jane Holmes and E. D. E. N. Southworth continued to employ the woman's formula into the 1870s and 1880s, but the new generation of serious writers looked for new forms. To judge by the best sellers of the post-war decades, the feminine audience had become appreciative of a more androgynous literature. Works like *Ben Hur* and *In His Steps* are of poorer literary quality than much woman's fiction, but depict a community of men and women and imply general religious and social interests common to both sexes.

The literature directed toward adult women after the Civil War, as well as the writings of many of the new women artists, are in many ways less socially progressive and optimistic than earlier woman's fiction; however they may be an esthetic advance. The earlier woman's writer eschewed an artistic mission, but avowed a social and moral purpose that energized her writings. The first generation of women artists had to struggle, like the men, with feelings of irrelevance.

It is easy to fault the earlier group of writers on artistic grounds and to criticize their social vision, however progressive it seemed at the time, and to some degree both fault lines run together.

Almost all the women wrote well, but they could have written much better and none of them were interested in formal innovation or in language as a power in itself. They stuck very close to formula, indeed they depended on it. Though their sharp ears and eyes enabled them to master realistic description and dialogue, and their novels contain invaluable social history, the constraints of stereotype kept them all from creating full, believable, multifaceted, unpredictable characters. In this respect, though I have spoken censoriously of Louisa May Alcott above, she stands out above all the rest for creating not one, but several authentically human women characters. We may agree that woman's fiction dealt with many disagreeable aspects of real life, and still fault it for its many evasions. We observe that woman's fiction urged women on to independence and strength of mind, but also hymned the perfections of its heroines to a point that might well have encouraged self-complacency and a morbid narcissism instead. The authors' hope that home, rightly structured, could prove a bastion against, even a counterforce to, a commercial, greedy, acquisitive society, seems naive now. But that lesson had to be administered by history and did not clearly emerge until the Gilded Age had done its work.

Some of our obvious reservations about this fiction may in time come to seem as dated as the fiction itself seems now. When we think of what these novelists might have demanded from women in comparison to what they actually asked for, they seem very conservative; but perhaps some of our thrashings about to redefine women in the latter part of the twentieth century will look equally dated some time hence. When we look at the context from which woman's fiction emerged, and recognize its role in the struggle against time-honored but destructive images of women as permanent children, toys, sexual animals, mindless drudges, or painted shells, then we may see it, in my view, properly. It was important in the great nineteenth-century campaign to make women think better of themselves—a campaign whose object is still not fully achieved—to perceive themselves, in their own language, as beings with an "immortal destiny."

A Note on Popularity

In speaking of the contemporary popularity of many of the authors discussed in this study, I have accepted the assessments of biographers and scholars who have specialized in the history of popular fiction. However, it must be noted that in the present state of research into popular literature such assessments are necessarily provisional. Many statements about sales and reputation are offered in the scholarship without adequate documentation; it would appear that most numerical estimates are in fact educated guesses or impressionistic conclusions based on a variety of sources of differing specificity and reliability. The problem is further complicated by the lack of a consistent measurement of popularity, and a failure fully to weight and define the various factors that are being considered. The claim of "most popular" has been advanced for Susan Warner, for E. D. E. N. Southworth, for Mary Jane Holmes, and for Augusta Evans; but even if the exact numbers of readers were known for all of them— something that is presently far from the case—it would still be necessary to make a judgment about how to assess popularity. Is the criterion to be sales of a single best-selling book? If so, within what time span? Is it to be aggregate sales of all books? If so, again, over what time span? How are we to assess the readership for the works' serializations? What role in judging popularity are we to allow to reviews and excerpts in the press? If a novel was dramatized, is the theater audience to be added to the total? At present, scholarship lacks a clear understanding of what it means, in quantitative and qualitative terms, by the term "popular," and it also lacks conclusive evidence of numbers on which to make precise assertions in many cases. Reputations and sales studies exist for many major American authors, but not for those whose popularity is nevertheless unquestioningly accepted and asserted.

Chronological Bibliography

[An asterisk identifies texts quoted in other than the first edition.]

1822 Sedgwick, Catharine Maria. A New-England Tale; or, Sketches of New-England Character and Manners. [anon.] New York: E. Bliss & E. White.

1824 Sedgwick. Redwood: A Tale. [anon.] New York: E. Bliss & E. White.

Smith, Margaret Bayard. A Winter in Washington; or, Memoirs of the Seymour Family. [anon.] New York: E. Bliss & E. White.

1827 Hale, Sarah Josepha. Northwood: A Tale of New England. Boston: Bowles & Dearborn.

1828 Smith. What is Gentility? A Moral Tale. [anon.] City of Washington: Pishey Thompson.

1830 Sedgwick. Clarence; or, A Tale of Our Own Times. [anon.] Philadelphia: Carey & Lea. *New York: George P. Putnam, 1849.

1834 Gilman, Caroline. Recollections of a [New England] Housekeeper. By Mrs. Clarissa Packard [pseud.]. New York: Harper & Brothers.

1837 Lee, Hannah Farnham Sawyer. Three Experiments of Living. [anon.] Boston: William S. Damrell.

Lee. Elinor Fulton. [anon.] Boston: Whipple and Damrell.

1838 Embury, Emma Catherine. Constance Latimer; or, The Blind Girl. New York: Harper & Brothers.

Follen, Eliza Lee Cabot. Sketches of Married Life. Boston: Hilliard, Grey and Co. *Boston: Hilliard, Gray and Co., 1839.

Gilman. Recollections of a Southern Matron. New York: Harper & Brothers.

1839 Hale. The Lecturess; or, Woman's Sphere. [anon.] Boston: Whipple and Damrell.

1840 Gilman. Love's Progress. [anon.] New York: Harper & Brothers.

1843 McIntosh, Maria Jane. Woman an Enigma; or, Life and Its Re-

vealings. [anon.] New York: Harper & Brothers. *London: The
Novel Newspaper, no. 326, 1843.

1844   Graves, Mrs. A. J.   Girlhood and Womanhood; or, Sketches of My
       Schoolmates. Boston: T. H. Carter & Co., and Benjamin B.
       Mussey.
       Tuthill, Louisa Caroline.   The Belle, The Blue, and The Bigot;
       or, Three Fields for Woman's Influence. [anon.] Providence:
       Samuel C. Blodget.

1845   Hale.   Keeping House and Housekeeping: A Story of Domestic
       Life. New York: Harper & Brothers.

1846   Cooper, Susan Fenimore.   Elinor Wyllys; or, The Young Folk at
       Longbridge. A Tale, by Amabel Penfeather [pseud.]. Philadel-
       phia: Carey and Hart.
       Hale.   "Boarding Out": A Tale of Domestic Life. [anon.] New
       York: Harper & Brothers.
       McIntosh.   Two Lives; or, To Seem and To Be. New York: D.
       Appleton & Co.
       Tuthill.   My Wife. Boston: William Crosby and H. P. Nichols.

1848   Leslie, Eliza.   Amelia; or, A Young Lady's Vicissitudes. Philadel-
       phia: Carey and Hart.
       McIntosh.   Charms and Counter-charms. New York: D. Appleton
       & Co.
       Phelps, Almira Hart.   Ida Norman; or, Trials and Their Uses.
       Baltimore: Cushing & Brother. *N. Y.: Sheldon, Lampart &
       Blakeman, 1855.

1849   Nichols, Mary Sargeant.   Agnes Morris; or, The Heroine of Domes-
       tic Life. [anon.] New York: Harper & Brothers.
       Nichols.   The Two Loves; or, Eros and Anteros. [anon.] New York:
       Stringer and Townsend.
       Southworth, Emma Dorothy Eliza Nevitte.   Retribution; or, The
       Vale of Shadows. A Tale of Passion. New York: Harper &
       Brothers. *Philadelphia: T. B. Peterson, c. 1856.

1850   Briggs, Emily Edson.   Ellen Parry; or, Trials of the Heart. By
       Olivia [pseud.]. New York: D. Appleton & Co.
       Dupuy, Eliza Ann.   The Conspirator. New York: D. Appleton & Co.
       Haven, Alice Emily Bradley Neal.   The Gossips of Rivertown:
       With Sketches in Prose and Verse. By Alice B. Neal. Philadel-
       phia: Hazard and Mitchell.
       Hentz, Caroline Lee Whiting.   Linda; or, The Young Pilot of the
       Belle Creole. A Tale of Southern Life. Philadelphia: A. Hart.
       *Philadelphia: T. B. Peterson, c. 1856.

1851   Chesebro', Caroline.   Dream-Land by Daylight: A Panorama of
       Romance. New York: Redfield.
       Hentz.   Rena; or, The Snow Bird. Philadelphia: A. Hart. *Phila-
       delphia: T. B. Peterson, c. 1851.
       Phelps, Elizabeth Stuart.   The Sunny Side; or, The Country Min-

ister's Wife. By H. Trusta [pseud.]. Boston: John P. Jewett and Co.

Southworth. The Mother-in-Law; or, The Isle of Rays. New York: D. Appleton & Company. *Philadelphia: T. B. Peterson, c. 1860.

Southworth. Shannondale. New York: D. Appleton & Co.

Warner, Susan. The Wide, Wide World. By Elizabeth Wetherell [pseud.]. New York: George P. Putnam. *London: J. Nisbet, 1852.

1852 Chesebro'. Isa: A Pilgrimage. New York: Redfield.

Cary, Alice. Hagar: A Story of To-Day. New York: Redfield.

Hentz. Eoline; or, Magnolia Vale. Philadelphia: A. Hart. *Philadelphia: T. B. Peterson, c. 1852.

Phelps. A Peep at "Number Five;" or, A Chapter in the Life of a City Pastor. By H. Trusta [pseud.]. Boston: Phillips, Sampson and Company. *Boston: Phillips, Sampson and Company, 1855.

Phelps. The Angel over the Right Shoulder; or, The Beginning of a New Year. Boston: John P. Jewett and Co.

Southworth. The Discarded Daughter; or, The Children of the Isle. Philadelphia: A. Hart.

Warner, Anna. Dollars and Cents. By Amy Lothrop [pseud.]. New York: George P. Putnam.

Warner, S. Queechy. By Elizabeth Wetherell [pseud.]. New York: George P. Putnam. *Philadelphia: J. B. Lippincott, 1902.

1853 Chesebro'. The Children of Light: A Theme for the Time. New York: Redfield.

Hentz. Helen and Arthur; or, Miss Thusa's Spinning-Wheel. Philadelphia: A. Hart. *Philadelphia: T. B. Peterson, c. 1853.

McIntosh. The Lofty and the Lowly; or, Good in All and None All-Good. New York: D. Appleton & Co.

Robinson, Therese Albertine Louisa. The Exiles. By Talvi [pseud.]. New York: George P. Putnam.

Southworth. The Curse of Clifton: A Tale of Expiation and Redemption. Philadelphia: A. Hart. *The Mountain Girl's Love. Philadelphia: T. B. Peterson, c. 1868.

Victor, Metta Victoria Fuller. The Senator's Son; or, The Maine Law A Last Refuge. Cleveland: Tooker and Gatchel.

1854 Cummins, Maria Susanna. The Lamplighter. [anon.] Boston: John P. Jewett & Company. *New York: The Odyssey Press, 1968.

Dorr, Julia Caroline Ripley. Farmingdale. By Caroline Thomas [pseud.]. New York: D. Appleton & Co. *The Mother's Rule. New York: D. W. Evans & Co., 1860.

Hayden, Sarah Marshall. Early Engagements, and Florence (A Sequel). By Mary Frazaer [pseud.]. Cincinnati: Moore, Anderson, Wilstach, & Keys.

Hentz. The Planter's Northern Bride. Philadelphia: A. Hart.

Holmes, Mary Jane. Tempest and Sunshine; or, Life in Kentucky.

New York: D. Appleton & Company. *New York: The Odyssey Press, 1968.

Hornblower, Jane Elizabeth Roscoe. Vara; or, The Child of Adoption. [anon.] New York: Robert Carter & Brothers.

Pike, Mary Hayden Green. Ida May: A Story of Things Actual and Possible. By Mary Langdon [pseud.]. Boston: Phillips, Sampson and Company.

Smith, Elizabeth Oakes Prince. Bertha and Lily; or, The Parsonage of Beech Glen. A Romance. New York: J. C. Derby.

Smith. The Newsboy. [anon.] New York: J. C. Derby.

Southworth. The Lost Heiress. Philadelphia: T. B. Peterson.

Stephens, Ann Sophia. Fashion and Famine. New York: Bunce & Brother.

Terhune, Mary Virginia Hawes. Alone. By Marion Harland [pseud.]. Richmond: A Morris. *New York: G. W. Dillingham, 1898.

Victor. Fashionable Dissipation. Philadelphia: See, Peters & Co.

1855 Baker, Harriette Newell Woods. Cora and the Doctor; or, Revelations of a Physician's Wife. [anon.] Boston: John P. Jewett and Co.

Chesebro'. Getting Along: A Book of Illustrations. [anon.] New York: James C. Derby.

Hayden, Caroline A. Carrie Emerson; or, Life at Cliftonville. Boston: James French and Company.

Hentz. Robert Graham. Philadelphia: Parry & McMillan.

Holmes. The English Orphans; or, A Home in the New World. New York: D. Appleton & Co.

Moore, Mrs. H. J. Anna Clayton; or, The Mother's Trial. A Tale of Real Life. [anon.] Boston: James French and Co.

Nichols. Mary Lyndon; or, Revelations of a Life. An Autobiography. [anon.] New York: Stringer and Townsend.

Parton, Sara Payson Willis. Ruth Hall: A Domestic Tale of the Present Time. By Fanny Fern [pseud.]. New York: Mason Brothers.

Southworth. India: The Pearl of Pearl River. Philadelphia: T. B. Peterson.

Southworth. The Missing Bride; or, Miriam the Avenger. Philadelphia: T. B. Peterson. *Philadelphia: T. B. Peterson, c. 1874.

Stephens, A. The Old Homestead. New York: Bunce & Brother.

Stephens, Harriet Marion Ward. Hagar the Martyr; or, Passion and Reality. Boston, W. P. Fetridge & Co.

Terhune. The Hidden Path. By Marion Harland [pseud.]. New York: J. C. Derby. *New York: Sheldon & Co., 1864.

Warner, A. My Brother's Keeper. New York: D. Appleton & Co.

Wilson, Augusta Jane Evans. Inez: A Tale of the Alamo. [anon.] New York: Harper & Brothers.

1856   Baker.   The First and the Second Marriages; or, the Courtesies of
           Wedded Life. By Mrs. Madeline Leslie [pseud.]. Boston: C. Stone
           & Co.
       Cary.   Married, not Mated; or, How They Lived at Woodside and
           Throckmorton Hall. New York: Derby & Jackson.
       Chesebro'.   Victoria; or, The World Overcome. New York: Derby
           & Jackson.
       Chesebro'.   Philly and Kit; or, Life and Raiment. New York:
           Redfield.
       Dorr.   Lanmere. New York: Mason Brothers.
       Hentz.   Ernest Linwood. Boston: John P. Jewett and Co.
       Holmes.   'Lena Rivers. New York and Auburn: Miller, Orton &
           Milligan.
       Hornblower.   Nellie of Truro. [anon.] New York: Robert Carter
           & Brothers.
       McIntosh.   Violet; or, The Cross and the Crown. Boston: John P.
           Jewett and Co.
       Moulton, Louise Chandler.   Juno Clifford: A Tale. By a Lady.
           [anon.] New York: D. Appleton & Co.
       Parton.   Rose Clark. By Fanny Fern [pseud.]. New York: Mason
           Brothers.
       Pike.   Caste: A Story of Republican Equality. By Sydney A.
           Story, Jr. [pseud.]. Boston: Phillips, Sampson and Company.
       Preston, Margaret Junkin.   Silverwood; A Book of Memories.
           [anon.] New York: Derby & Jackson.
       Ritchie, Anna Cora Mowatt.   Mimic Life; or, Before and behind
           the Curtain. A Series of Narratives. Boston: Ticknor and Fields.
       Tuthill.   Reality; or, The Millionaire's Daughter. New York: C.
           Scribner.
       Warner, S.   The Hills of the Shatemuc. [anon.] New York: D.
           Appleton and Co.
1857   Baker.   The Household Angel in Disguise. By Mrs. Madeline Les-
           lie [pseud.]. Boston: Shepard, Clark and Co.
       Cummins.   Mabel Vaughan. [anon.] Boston: John P. Jewett and
           Company.
       Denison, Mary Andrews.   Gracie Amber. New York: Sheldon,
           Blakeman & Co.
       Dupuy.   The Planter's Daughter: A Tale of Louisiana. New York:
           W. P. Fetridge & Co.
       Holmes.   Meadow-Brook. New York: Miller, Orton & Co. *New
           York: Carleton, 1870.
       Moore.   The Golden Legacy: A Story of Life's Phases. By a Lady.
           [anon.] New York: D. Appleton and Co.
       Ritchie.   Twin Roses: A Narrative. Boston: Ticknor and Fields.
       Sedgwick.   Married or Single? [anon.] New York: Harper &
           Brothers.

Southworth. Vivia; or, The Secret of Power. Philadelphia: T. B. Peterson.

Stephens, A. The Heiress of Greenhurst: An Autobiography. New York: Edward Stephens.

Terhune. Moss-Side. By Marion Harland [pseud.]. New York: Derby & Jackson.

1858 Denison. Old Hepsy. New York: A. B. Burdick.

Haven. The Coopers; or, Getting Under Way. New York: D. Appleton and Co.

Pike. Agnes. [anon.] Boston: Phillips, Sampson & Co.

Rose, Henrietta. Nora Wilmot: A Tale of Temperance and Woman's Rights. Columbus, Ind.: Osgood & Pearce.

Stephens, A. Mary Derwent. Philadelphia: T. B. Peterson and Brothers.

Townsend, Virginia Frances. While It Was Morning. New York: Derby & Jackson.

1859 Denison. Opposite the Jail. [anon.] Boston: Henry Hoyt.

Holmes. Dora Deane; or, The East India Uncle. New York: C. M. Saxton.

Wilson (Evans). Beulah. New York: Derby & Jackson. *New York: Carleton, 1865.

1860 Cummins. El Fureidîs. [anon.] Boston: Ticknor and Fields.

Harris, Miriam Coles. Rutledge. [anon.] New York: Derby & Jackson.

Moore. Wild Nell, The White Mountain Girl. New York: Sheldon & Co.

Warner, A., and S. Warner. Say and Seal. By Susan Wetherell and Amy Lothrop [pseud.]. Philadelphia: T. B. Lippincott & Co.

1863 Chesebro'. Peter Carradine; or, The Martindale Pastoral. New York: Sheldon & Co.

Holmes. Marian Grey; or, The Heiress of Redstone Hall. New York: Carleton.

McIntosh. Two Pictures; or, What We Think of Ourselves, and What The World Thinks of Us. New York: D. Appleton & Co.

1864 Cummins. Haunted Hearts. [anon.] Boston: J. E. Tilton and Co.

Denison. The Mill Agent. Boston: Graves and Young.

Terhune. Husbands and Homes. By Marion Harland [pseud.]. New York: Sheldon & Co.

Wilson (Evans). Macaria; or, Altars of Sacrifice. Richmond: West & Johnson. *New York: G. W. Dillingham, 1896.

1867 Wilson (Evans). St. Elmo. New York: Carleton.

1869 Baker. Juliette; or, Now and Forever. By Mrs. Madeline Leslie [pseud.]. Boston: Lee and Shepard.

Wilson (Evans). Vashti; or, "Until Death Us Do Part." New York: Carleton.

Bibliographical Note
on Secondary Material

Basic reference tools for this study were Lyle Wright's bibliographical volumes, *American Fiction, 1774–1850* and *American Fiction, 1881–1875,* published at San Marino by the Huntington Library, in revised editions, in 1969 and 1965 respectively: the Union Catalog of pre-1953 imprints; the Library of Congress Catalog; Frank Luther Mott's *History of American Magazines,* Volume I, 1741–1850 (New York: D. Appleton, 1930), and Volume II, 1851–1865 (Cambridge, Mass.: Harvard University Press, 1938); and Albert Johannsen's three-volume study, *The House of Beadle and Adams* (Norman: University of Oklahoma Press, 1950).

General literary studies that treat this fiction include Herbert Ross Brown, *The Sentimental Novel in America* (Durham, N.C.: Duke University Press, 1942); F. L. Pattee, *The Feminine Fifties* (New York: D. Appleton, 1942); Frank Luther Mott, *Golden Multitudes* (New York: Macmillan, 1947); James D. Hart, *The Popular Book* (Berkeley: University of California Press, 1951); Alexander Cowie, *The Rise of the American Novel* (New York: American Book Co., 1951); Helen Waite Papashvily, *All the Happy Endings* (New York: Harpers, 1956); Carl Bode, *Anatomy of American Popular Culture* (Berkeley and Los Angeles: University of California Press, 1959); Leslie Fiedler, *Love and Death in the American Novel* (New York: Criterion Books, 1960); Russel Blaine Nye, *Society and Cul-*

ture in America, 1830–1860 (New York: Harper & Row, 1974). The best of these is Brown, but he has no interest in women's issues, does not analyze individual authors or novels, and quotes out of context. Except for Papashvily, the other works treat woman's fiction in a much larger context and are necessarily superficial, presenting the genre as though it were all written by a single woman, or generalizing from one or two novels by an author to her entire canon. All of these critics, except for Brown, assume a tone of jovial contempt for the genre, if not of downright hostility. Pattee explains his title by identifying these "feminine" adjectives for the decade: fervid, fevered, furious, fatuous, fertile, feeling, florid, furbelowed, fighting, funny. Papashvily characterizes all the novelists as people with a grudge against men, and their composite novel as "a witches' broth, a lethal draught brewed by women and used by women to destroy their common enemy, man." Fiedler sees all major American fiction as an attempt by embattled he-men to rescue the novel from "the genteel, sentimental, quasi-literate, female audience (female in sensibility whatever the nominal sex of the readers who composed it) and a product which satisfied it." The patronizing continues in such recent articles as: Henry Nash Smith, "The Scribbling Women and the Cosmic Success Story," *Critical Inquiry,* 1(1974), 47–70; John T. Frederick, "Hawthorne's 'Scribbling Women,'" *NEQ,* 48(1975), 231–240; Dee Garrison, "Immoral Fiction in the Late Victorian Library," *AQ,* 28(1976), 41–55. Of a different type is Susan Geary's study of these novels as publisher's artifacts, "The Domestic Novel as a Commercial Commodity: Making a Best Seller in the 1850s," *PBSA,* 70 (1976), 365–395.

Recent work on the history of women has begun to provide a context for my study that did not exist when I began it. Much scholarship is in progress, and significant contributions have appeared since this book was accepted for publication. Among these I would cite especially the following: *Dimity Convictions,* by Barbara Welter (Athens: Ohio University Press, 1976); *Perish the Thought; Intellectual Women in Romantic America 1830–1860,* by Susan P. Conrad (New York: Oxford University Press, 1976); *The Bonds of Womanhood: "Woman's Sphere" in New England 1780–1835,* by Nancy F. Cott (New Haven: Yale University Press, 1977); and *The Feminization of American Culture,* by Ann Douglas

(New York: Knopf, 1977). *Dimity Convictions* collects several influential articles, some of which are cited below. Susan Conrad's intellectual women do not overlap, except for Elizabeth Oakes Smith, with the popular novelists; indeed it is Conrad's contention that the "scribblers," as she calls them, were deliberately anti-intellectual. Nancy Cott discusses the early growth of the cult of domesticity in a sympathetic manner.

One might easily write a chapter on the Douglas study, which has been quickly and widely accepted as a major contribution to American intellectual history. It is less about women than its title might suggest, since its true focus is Puritan doctrine as it declined in the nineteenth century. Douglas sees women as partners with a demoralized clergy in the sentimentalization (a word she uses synonymously with feminization) and degradation of the old style Calvinist world view, and takes them severely to task. She treats several of the northern writers who appear in my book, and from a much less sympathetic viewpoint than mine. Given her vantage point, Douglas' harshness is logical; but I do not share her definition of sentimental, or her unqualified admiration for early Puritanism as a "culture."

The beginnings of scholarship on these women and their times did exist when I began my investigations, and I owe much to many pioneering critics and scholars. Ann Douglas (who also published as Ann Douglas Wood) was among the first in the field with several important articles on the women writers that viewed them as canny professionals spouting orthodoxy as a means of concealing or distracting attention from their own radical departure from role. Her articles include "The Fashionable Diseases: Women's Complaints and Their Treatment in Nineteenth-Century America," in *Clio's Consciousness Raised,* ed. Mary Hartman and Lois W. Banner (New York: Harper & Row, 1974), pp. 1–22; " 'The Scribbling Women' and Fanny Fern: Why Women Wrote," *AQ,* 23 (1971), 3–24; "Mrs. Sigourney and the Sensibility of the Inner Space," *NEQ,* 45 (1972), 163–181; "The Literature of Impoverishment: The Women Local Colorists in America, 1865–1914," *Women's Studies,* 1(1972), 3–45; "Heaven Our Home: Consolation Literature in the Northern United States, 1830–1880," *AQ,* 26(1974), 496–515. A different view is found in the dissertation by Mary

Ryan, "American Society and the Cult of Domesticity, 1830–1860," University of California at Santa Barbara, 1971. Ryan argues that the novels are meant to be orthodox espousals of the cult but are unconsciously rebellious. Both of these approaches imply a split between the message intended and the actual convictions of the authors and differ in this respect from my own view. Although I do not doubt that these women had as many conflicts, conscious or unconscious, as human beings generally do, I do not find their fiction beset by contradictions, defenses, or duplicities. As I have argued, this was not a profoundly radical fiction by any means, neither on the surface or in its depths; but such progressive ideas as it had are clearly there and constituted its major intention.

The volume *Clio's Consciousness Raised* (op. cit.) collects many pioneering essays. Besides the Wood piece already cited these include: Carroll Smith-Rosenberg, "Puberty to Menopause: The Cycle of Femininity in Nineteenth-Century America," pp. 23–37; Regina Morantz, "The Lady and Her Physician," pp. 38–53; Linda Gordon, "Voluntary Motherhood: The Beginnings of Feminist Birth Control Ideas in the United States," pp. 54–71; Daniel Scott Smith, "Family Limitation, Sexual Control, and Domestic Feminism in Victorian America," pp. 119–136; Barbara Welter, "The Feminization of American Religion: 1800–1860," pp. 137–157. The collection *Liberating Women's History,* ed. Berenice A. Carroll (Urbana: University of Illinois Press, 1976) also contains pertinent essays: "Education and Ideology in Nineteenth-Century America: The Response of Educational Institutions to the Changing Role of Women" by Adele Simmons, pp. 115–126; "Sex and Class in Colonial and Nineteenth-Century America" by Ann D. Gordon and Mari Jo Buhle, pp. 278–300.

Two book-length studies are G. J. Barker-Benfield, *The Horrors of the Half-Known Life* (New York: Harper & Row, 1976), about the influence of men's gynecological attitudes toward women on their more general perceptions of the sex; and Kathryn Kish Sklar, *Catharine Beecher: A Study in American Domesticity* (New Haven: Yale University Press, 1973), a biography that touches on many woman-focused reform movements. The two standard histories of the woman's rights movements are of basic importance: Eleanor Flexner, *Century of Struggle* (Cambridge, Mass.: Harvard University Press, 1959; rev. 1975), and William L. O'Neill, *Everyone Was Brave* (Chicago: Quadrangle Books, 1969). I omit mention of several recent studies of images of women in American fiction that deal exclusively with male authors.

Other articles of importance are: Barbara Welter, "The Cult of True Womanhood, 1820–1860," *AQ* 18 (1966), 151–174 (a pioneering but simplistic approach that is now outdated but was immensely stimulating when it appeared); Gerda Lerner, "The Lady and the Mill Girl: Changes in the Status of Women in the Age of Jackson," *Midcontinent American Studies Journal,* 10 (1969), 5–15 (This argues that woman's position deteriorated in the early nineteenth century in comparison to the late eighteenth century; a group of scholars, influenced perhaps by Eva Fige's *Patriarchal Attitudes,* sees the nineteenth century as a low point for women, but ultimately, I believe, the facts will not support this interpretation); Glenda Gates Riley, "The Subtle Subversion: Changes in the Traditionalist Image of the American Woman," *Historian,* 32 (1969–70), 210–227 (on Sarah J. Hale and the *Lady's Book*); Kirk Jeffrey, "The Family as Utopian Retreat from the City: The Nineteenth-Century Contribution," in *The Family, Communes, and Utopian Societies,* ed. Sallie TeSelle (New York: Harper & Row, 1972); Gail Parker's introduction to *The Oven Birds* (Doubleday: Anchor Books, 1972), pp. 1–76 (mostly about the writers after 1870 but with some material on the earlier group); Carroll Smith-Rosenberg, "The Hysterical Woman: Sex Roles and Role Conflict in Nineteenth-Century America," *Social Research,* 39 (1972), 651–678; Carroll Smith-Rosenberg and Charles Rosenberg, "The Female Animal: Medical and Biological Views of Woman in Nineteenth-Century America," *Journal of American History,* 60 (1973), 332–356; Johnny Faragher and Christine Stansell, "Women and Their Families on the Overland Trail, 1842–1867," *Feminist Studies,* 2 (1975), 150–166 (a study based on women's letters and diaries of how they felt about pioneering); Kirk Jeffrey, "Marriage, Career, and Feminine Ideology in the Nineteenth Century: Reconstructing the Marital Experience of Lydia Maria Child, 1828–1874," *Feminist Studies,* 2 (1975), 113–130; Carroll Smith-Rosenberg, "The Female World of Love and Ritual:

Relations Between Women in Nineteenth-Century America," *Signs*, 1 (1975), 1–30.

In general, the earliest scholarship after the resurgence of the woman's movement tended to stress woman's oppression in the nineteenth century and even to argue that her position had deteriorated in comparison to the previous century. Since 1971 scholarship has stressed the general and widespread restlessness and agitation for improvement of woman's lot and has assumed a clear improvement over the past centuries, however oppressed woman might have been in comparison to an ideal of freedom and parity with men. I share this latter position. Welter's four-pronged definition of "true womanhood"—piety, purity, submissiveness, and domesticity—is not useful as a model. In woman's fiction, for example, purity was so taken for granted that it was ignored, while a range of self-assertive and aggressive behavior, including the undomestic, was seen as consistent with "true womanhood." Too much contemporary scholarship fails to distinguish between earlier and later parts of the nineteenth century; indeed there is an increasing trend toward treating the century as a single block, even though the situation was clearly different for women of 1820 and of 1870. The emphasis on medical history is most illuminating and yet has one unfortunate side-effect, that of locking woman's history into a history of attitudes toward her anatomy. Woman's fiction shows authors attempting to escape the view that anatomy is destiny by ignoring biological sex altogether, and the general movement to transcend sexuality and hence to ignore some aspects of female anatomy as a motif in early feminine emancipation must be brought into focus. Overviews of recent research in literature and history may be found in review essays by Elaine Showalter and Barbara Sicherman in *Signs*, 1 (1975), 435–460 and 461–486 respectively. Another useful overview is Daniel Walker Howe, "American Victorianism as a Culture," *AQ*, 27 (1975), 507–532.

Among a great deal of nineteenth-century material I have found the following seven works particularly helpful: Lydia Maria Child, *The Mother's Book* (Boston: Carter, Hendee, and Babcock, 1831); Mrs. A. J. Graves, *Woman in America, Being an Examination into the Moral and Intellectual Condition of American Female Society*

(New York: Harper & Brothers, 1844); Edward D. Mansfield, *Legal Rights, Liabilities, and Duties of Women* (Salem: J. P. Jewett, 1845); Maria J. McIntosh, *Woman in America: Her Work and Her Reward* (New York: D. Appleton, 1850); Elizabeth Oakes Smith, *Woman and Her Needs* (New York: Fowles and Wells, 1851; rpt. Arno Press); Edward Henry Dixon, *Woman, and Her Diseases* (New York: Ramney, 1855); Harriot Keziah Hunt, *Glances and Glimpses* (Boston: J. P. Jewett, 1856) [autobiography of one of the first woman physicians].

Brief biographies of many of the women considered in my book may be found in *Notable American Women*, 3 vols. (Cambridge, Mass.: Harvard University Press, 1971). Among those not treated there, the *Dictionary of American Biography* has entries for Caroline Chesebro', Julia Dorr, Emma Embury, Eliza Follen, Miriam Harris, Hannah F. S. Lee, Therese Robinson, and Virginia Townsend. The *National Cyclopedia of American Biography* has an entry for Harriette Newell Baker; *Appleton's Cyclopedia of American Biography* has one for Harriet Marion Stephens. I have not located biographical entries for Mrs. A. J. Graves, Caroline Hayden, Sarah Marshall Hayden, Jane Elizabeth Roscoe Hornblower, Mrs. H. J. Moore, and Henrietta Rose. Sarah J. Hale's lengthy *Woman's Record* of 1853 is an additional source (among its 2,500 entries relatively few are American literary women, however). I have relied heavily on John Hart, *Female Prose Writers of America* (Philadelphia: E. H. Butler, 1852; revised and expanded edition 1854), for biographical details and quotations from reviews that are collected nowhere else.

Additional useful published material, biographical and critical, on individual writers, includes the following:

Alice Cary: Mary Clemmer Ames, *A Memorial of Alice and Phoebe Cary* (New York: Hurd & Houghton, 1874).

Lydia Maria Child: Kirk Jeffrey, "Reconstructing the Marital Experience of Lydia Maria Child," op. cit.

Augusta Jane Evans: William P. Fidler, *Augusta Evans Wilson, 1835–1909: A Biography* (University, Ala.: University of Alabama Press, 1951).

Sarah J. Hale: Ruth E. Finley, *The Lady of Godey's* (Philadelphia: Lippincott, 1931); Glenda Gates Jackson, "The Subtle Subversion," op. cit.

Caroline Lee Hentz: Rhoda C. Ellison, "Mrs. Hentz and the Green-Eyed Monster," *AQ,* 22 (1950), 345–50; Ellison, introduction to Arno Press reprint of *The Planter's Northern Bride.*

Elizabeth Stuart Phelps: Elizabeth Stuart Phelps (posth.), *The Last Leaf from Sunny Side, with a Memorial by Austin Phelps* (Boston: Phillips, Sampson & Co., 1853).

Anna Cora Mowatt Ritchie: Eric R. Barnes, *The Lady of Fashion* (New York: Scribners, 1954).

Catharine Maria Sedgwick: Mary E. Dewey, ed., *Life and Letters of Catharine Maria Sedgwick* (New York: Harper, 1871); Sister Mary Michael Welsh, *Catharine Maria Sedgwick: Her Position in the Literature and Thought of Her Time up to 1860* (Washington, D.C.: Catholic University of America, 1937); Edward Halsey Foster, *Catharine Maria Sedgwick* (New York: Twayne, 1974).

Elizabeth Oakes Smith: Mary Alice Wyman, ed., *Selections from the Autobiography of Elizabeth Oakes Smith* (Lewiston, Me.: Lewiston Journal Co., 1924); Susan P. Conrad, *Perish the Thought,* op. cit.; Watts, Emily Stipes, *The Poetry of American Women from 1632 to 1945* (Austin: University of Texas Press), pp. 97–105, 187–190.

E. D. E. N. Southworth: Regis Louise Boyle, *Mrs. E. D. E. N. Southworth, Novelist* (Washington, D.C.: Catholic University of America, 1931).

Ann Sophia Stephens: Madeline B. Stern, "The Author of the First Beadle Dime Novel: Ann S. Stephens," in *We the Women* (New York: Schulte Publishing Co., 1963), pp. 29–54.

Mary Virginia Terhune: Mary Virginia Terhune, *Marion Harland's Autobiography* (New York: Harper & Row, 1910).

Susan and Anna Warner: Anna Warner, *Susan Warner* (New York and London: G. P. Putnam's Sons, 1909).

Sara Payson Willis (Parton): Ann Douglas. "Why Women Wrote," op. cit.

Index

WOMAN'S FICTION

Designed by Elizabeth L. Anderson.
Composed by York Composition Company, Inc.,
in 11 point Intertype Baskerville, 2 points leaded,
with display lines in Deepdene.
Printed letterpress from type by York Composition Company
on Warren's Number 66 text, 50 pound basis.
Bound by John H. Dekker & Sons, Inc.
in Joanna book cloth
and stamped in All Purpose foil.